GW00786394

Tackling Computer Projects

A step-by-step guide to better projects

PM Heathcote
B.Sc.(Hons), M.Sc.

Pat Heathcote is a Senior Lecturer in Computing at Suffolk College, Ipswich, where she has taught since 1982 on A Level Computing, BTEC and Accountancy courses, as well as a range of other computing courses. Prior to coming to Suffolk College she was for many years a programmer at McGill University in Montreal, Canada, and also held posts as a Systems Analyst with a large hospital, and subsequently with a firm of computer consultants. She is an Assistant Examiner for Advanced Level Computing with the Associated Examining Board.

DP Publications Limited
Aldine Place
London, W12 8AW
1992

Acknowledgements

I would like to thank Ruth Holman for reading the draft manuscript with great care and making numerous suggestions for improvement which have been incorporated into the final version. Her considerable experience of writing project guidelines and moderating projects for the Associated Examining Board has made her contribution invaluable. I would also like to thank my A Level computing classes of 1992 for providing the inspiration for this book, Joan Elsey of the Ipswich Gilbert and Sullivan Society for patiently answering all my questions, Ed Morgan for advice on layout, my husband for proof reading the manuscript and my daughter Flora for helping me to put it all together.

A CIP catalogue record for this book is available from the British Library

ISBN 1 858050 02 2
Copyright PM Heathcote © 1992

First Edition 1992

Printed in Great Britain by
The Guernsey Press Co Ltd
Vale, Guernsey

Foreword

Pat Heathcote's considerable experience with Computing students on both A Level and BTEC courses has undoubtedly provided her with the insight to recognise difficulties faced by students and the expertise with which to address those problems. Her thoroughness in dealing with the minutiae of examination requirements has produced a book which will prove invaluable to students of all abilities, as well as to their lecturers.

The sample projects offered are typical of those submitted by students, and clearly identify many of the pitfalls to be avoided while also encouraging good practice. The new emphasis on the quality of the user interface reflects today's expectations of software sophistication, setting a major landmark for all Computing projects. Equally, user involvement at every possible stage throughout development sets the scene for projects of real worth, and equips the student with a tool whose value will reach far beyond the confines of examination success.

The inclusion of a package-based project should stimulate many more students to explore this relatively uncharted territory. The great variety of suitable packages available makes this an exciting voyage of discovery, often providing computerised solutions which closely parallel professional software.

Students wishing to gain high grades for projects submitted either for BTEC NDCS or for A Level Computing would do well to pay close attention to all the advice given in this book.

Ruth J Holman
Lecturer in Computing, Filton College, Bristol
Assistant Examiner, AEB
Project Moderator, AEB

Sept '92

Preface

Aim

The aim of this book is to provide students with a comprehensive and practical guide on how to tackle a computing project for an Advanced Level or BTEC National computing course, using either a programming language or a software package. It will also be useful to students doing a project for a GCSE computing course or a Higher National computing course, since the principles remain the same at any level.

Need

Practical computer projects frequently comprise up to 30% of the final mark on an Advanced Level computing course, and are a mandatory part of many BTEC courses. Students very often find it difficult to think of a suitable idea for a computer project, and having come up with an idea, find the analysis and design stages extremely difficult to get started on. This is very understandable because in the relatively short programming assignments set in the first year of a two year course, the students are normally given a program specification and are not required to do much in the way of analysis and design. Their experience of using packages may also be quite limited, making it difficult to evaluate different methods of solution.

The student therefore needs to be given at this point:

- plenty of ideas for possible projects to spur his/her imagination, with some advice on what constitutes a suitable project

- a complete specimen project of each type (programming and package implementation), together with advice on how each stage (analysis, design, etc) is tackled.

Approach

This book is suitable for students either on a taught course or studying independently, as it can be used with no additional help required from a lecturer. Answers to all questions are given in the text.

Part 1 of the book follows through all the steps involved in writing a computer project, from the initial idea right through to the final documentation, with two specimen projects being used to illustrate the various stages of development and implementation. The student is constantly referred to these two specimen projects in Parts 2 and 3 as they work through the text. Quick answer questions within each chapter encourage the students to think about the material covered and to develop the skills needed for their own projects.

Parts 2 and 3 contain the two complete specimen projects, with margin comments to draw the reader's attention to important points. The first project is implemented in Pascal and the accompanying listing is used to illustrate many useful techniques in Turbo Pascal such as pop-up windows and the use of function keys (all explained in the text) which Pascal students may find useful in their own projects. The second example illustrates how to tackle a project using a software package instead of a suite of programs. Borland's Paradox database (Version 3.5) has been used for this purpose but the actual package used is not of any significance here as the emphasis is on how to analyse, design, test and document the system.

Lecturers' supplement

A disk which contains both source and executable code for the Pascal project, and the Paradox application (which requires Paradox 3.5 software to run) is available free to lecturers who adopt this book as a class text.

Contents

PART 1

How to approach each stage of a project

Part 1 takes you through all the stages involved in choosing and completing a successful computer project, using two specimen projects as examples of programming and package-based implementations.

Table of Contents

How to approach each stage of a project

Chapter 1 - Choosing a Project

Objectives

By the end of this chapter you should

- *understand what constitutes a suitable project*

- *understand the constraints on the choice of hardware and software*

- *know how to go about choosing your own project*

- *know how to work out a schedule to meet the project deadline*

- *have looked at summaries of several past projects of different types*

Requirements for a computer project

Generally, when a project forms part of a computing course, you will be expected to produce a **complete, well-documented system**. You have to demonstrate that you can solve an information processing problem using the most appropriate means available.

You are more likely to develop a successful project if you can find a real user with a real problem to be solved. Otherwise the project turns into a textbook exercise with invented problems and unrealistic solutions.

Choice of hardware and software

If you are developing a project for a real user, you may be asked to produce software that will run on the equipment they already own, for example a PC or Apple Macintosh. This may be impossible if you do not have access to the same hardware or software at your college, school, home or office. If this is an exam project rather than something you are doing for payment, you would be well advised to use the hardware and software that you have easy access to, even if the system is never actually implemented for the user. Most users understand the constraints that you are working under and will still be happy to explain their current system and what the requirements of a new system would be. There is always the possibility that you could convert it at a later date if they really want it!

You may not have much choice of hardware, and this book assumes that you will have access only to a microcomputer or terminal with a standard keyboard input and a printer of some kind.

There may be a wide range of software to choose from. If you want to write a complete database application, software such as dBase III+ or dBase IV may be a good option. A computer aided design system may be easier to program in 'C'. If you are thinking of computerising the accounts of a small business, a specialised accounting package may be your best choice. But ultimately, you will have to choose from the software that you or your college or school have, even if the project could be done better or faster another way.

The choice of project

Choosing a project is the first hurdle. It needs to be sufficiently meaty to enable you to gain the maximum possible marks, but not so ambitious that you cannot get it finished in the time available. About 20% of the marks may be awarded for 'Analysis of requirements', which will include finding out how the current system works and what the inputs and outputs are, as well as what the user would like the new system to do. Obviously, it is going to be much easier to get these marks if you have a real user with a real problem to be solved, or a real application which would benefit from computerisation.

By contrast, if for example you choose to create a new computer game, it may be difficult to fulfil criteria such as the following, taken from the AEB A-Level Computing marking scheme:

> 'Demanding, open-ended problem with real constraints imposed by the situation'

> 'Extensive and perceptive investigation and consideration of user needs'

> 'Very good, clear statement of realistic system objectives'

> 'Project performs according to stated objectives'

The difficulty lies in the fact that you may have to make up your own rules as you go along, as there really are no specific objectives to be fulfilled. This makes it almost impossible for the examiner to award top marks for the Analysis, Design, and Implementation of the project.

Choosing your own project

The most important things to remember when you choose your project are:

- choose something that interests you - after all, you are going to spend the next several months on it. If you are a member of a football club or cricket club, or have a part-time job in a restaurant, shoe shop or sports centre, for example, observe or ask how things are done at present. Organisations such as clubs or societies involve administrative functions which could often benefit from some form of computerisation.

- many ideas which at first seem lacking in scope can be turned into very good projects with a little imagination. Careful work on the user interface, file design and output goes a long way. But be realistic - is it really worth using a computer to keep records of fifteen people in the badminton club who each pay an annual subscription of £5.00?

- whatever your strengths and weaknesses in computing, as soon as you start work on your project you will probably realise you don't know how to tackle part of it. Perhaps you don't know enough about file design, or you would like to use the function keys in a program but don't know how. You may find some of the answers in this book, but very likely you will have to do extra research on your own. Try the library first, and if that has nothing, splash out and buy a good book on Pascal, or DBase, or whatever package you intend to use. A list of recommended books can be found at the end of each chapter.

- if the thought of 'data processing' and updating files bores you, consider other areas of your syllabus such as compiler writing, expert systems, simulation, graphics or process control. Again, you will have to do your own research and this will probably mean both time and money, but it could be worth it.

Drawing up a schedule or timetable

Obviously your schedule will depend on the length of time you have available to complete the project. On a two year A level course, you should probably start thinking of ideas in the summer term of your first year, and start on the analysis in the holidays or immediately you return in September. Spend time doing careful design work for the whole project before you start programming in the second half of the term.

Testing the system and writing up the documentation can take as long as writing the programs, so be sure to leave enough time for this before the deadline. Once you have done the initial design work you can draw up a detailed schedule of programs to be designed, coded and tested.

A sample schedule

task	start date	finish date (estimated)
Analysis	Sep 5	Sep 30
Design	Oct 1	Oct 31
Programming	Nov 1	Jan 30
System testing	Feb 1	Feb 28
Documentation	Mar 1	Mar 30
Hand in:		Apr 7

and for each program module:

module		design	code	test
name	description	(Estimated completion dates)		
M1_MainMenu	Main menu	Nov 1	Nov 3	Nov 3
M121_AddPatron	Add module	Nov 5	etc	
etc				

A similar schedule of tasks to be performed can be drawn up if you are using a software package.

Ideas for computer projects

Projects can be put roughly into 'categories', and a number of project summaries from various categories are given below.

Database and file based projects

Many good projects involve file handling of some sort. Nearly all these projects will involve keeping information on a master file or database file and updating it. This in itself is not enough to form a project - ask yourself what the POINT of the system is. There is no point putting data INTO a system if you don't get anything OUT of it, so concentrate on what the output will be. Generally speaking a reasonably substantial project will involve more than one file - perhaps a file of transactions as well as a master file, or two master files linked in some way. It may well involve considerably more than two files, with different file organisations.

1. **Newsagent's Database**

   Summary: The main objectives of this system are:

   - to make delivery orders easier to implement

   - to allow paper price changes to be made quickly and easily

   - to allow data retrieval for a specific customer

   - to print a daily sheet for each paperboy specifying which papers are to be delivered to each customer

   - to make paper orders to suppliers more accurate by calculating exactly the number of papers needed

   - to make a billing system that is both itemised and clear.

   Comment: This is an ambitious project which could be made more manageable by omitting the billing side, while making provision for this to be programmed at a later date. The newsagent's requirements need careful analysis; for example, how are customers' holidays recorded, when no papers are required? The current method of recording data needs to be looked at and suitable report formats agreed with the prospective user. This is a good project for someone with experience as a paperboy or who has worked in a newsagent's shop.

2. **Dressmaking Service Job Control**

   Summary: The project is designed to assist in the smooth running of a dress-making and clothes alteration business. Personal details on all customers (name, address, measurements, past orders etc) are to be kept on a computerised file, and another file of 'jobs in progress' is also stored, giving details of date received, costs, hours worked and so on for costing purposes. When the job is completed an invoice is printed and the job details moved to the 'History file', linked to the correct customer.

   Comment: This project can involve some complex data structures and file handling, using for example a linked list to hold the file of past jobs linked to customer. The low volume of data may make it hard to justify the use of a computer but the system could be looked upon as a prototype for a much larger operation.

Statistical analyses

Some projects involve collecting data in order to perform some sort of analysis, perhaps for the purpose of providing management information. This sort of project will also involve keeping data on one or more files.

3. **WildRide Theme Park Management Program**

    Summary: The aim of this system is to aid the management of the amusement park by supplying information about the popularity of the park at various times of year, and the relative popularity of each of the free and paying attractions.

    Comment: Very careful attention needs to be paid here to both the input and the output; input would take place in small booths situated at the park entrance and at each individual attraction, and would need to be quick and easy. Reports would need to summarise the input data in a useful way and perform some kind of analysis of the data. Is it enough to record the number of people using the facilities on a certain date? Perhaps, for example, weather needs to be recorded as well!

4. **Theatre Audience Analysis**

    Summary: A local theatre wishes to find out how best to increase the size of its audiences, and plans to distribute questionnaires to members of the audience to ascertain such facts as where they heard about the production, whether they saw any posters or advertisments, how far they have travelled to the performance, and so on. The results will be analysed to discover the most effective way of advertising.

    Comment: At Advanced level, the project needs to be broader in scope than a straighforward analysis of data from a questionnaire. It could incorporate a simple text editor to enable the questions and multiple choice answers to be entered, stored on a file and edited. The program performing the analysis could then be general enough to handle any number of questions, each having any number of possible answers, and reproduce these on the report.

Computer aided learning packages

5. **Learning package for young children**

    Summary: This project is designed to help young children to learn various different skills by the use of different fun games. The package incorporates a simple multiplication test, where the child enters the table he or she wishes to be tested on, and is then asked a series of ten questions, being told the right answer if the given answer is wrong. A second option in the program is designed as a spelling aid. This section consists of three stories with words left out, and the child has to choose the correctly spelt word for each space from a list of alternatives.

    Comment: This is a project which, if done for A Level or equivalent, can all too easily fall into the lowest category of being an 'undemanding problem of insufficient scope, with little or no investigation of user needs'. It will need to do more than display 10 random multiplication questions and check the student answer, making an appropriate response. In the spelling section, are the three stories always the same ones? The children would very quickly tire of such a program! It can be improved by, say, holding a large number of stories on a random file and generating a random number to select which story to display. But overall this is a project to be avoided unless you have something very original up your sleeve.

6. **Circuit Design and Test Software**

Summary: This suite of programs allows the user to create simple circuits using basic electrical components, and then have them checked by the computer to see if all the components and connections are correct. The circuits can then be printed out. The system is designed to help tenth and eleventh year students to learn how to design circuits and have them tested by computer simulation before using actual electrical components.

Comment: This is an interesting project requiring some knowledge of graphics programming. It was originally implemented in BASIC using a BBC B computer. The program used a 16 x 9 'grid' and the user could position the cursor in any square of the grid and enter a predefined symbol from a list appearing at the bottom of the screen, using a single keystroke. The circuit testing is extremely complex and a simpler problem is to test whether each component is connected to something on each side (i.e. no gaps in the circuit).

7. **Typing tutor for child with impaired vision**

Summary: This project is designed to help children with severely impaired vision to learn keyboard skills.

Comment: If the project is done by a student who has personal knowledge of a child with impaired vision and can therefore perform a real analysis of user needs, this can be developed into an interesting and useful project.

Expert systems

8. **An Expert System Shell**

Summary: An expert system is designed to make the task of passing on your expert knowledge to other people as easy as possible. The first step is to set up the 'knowledge base', consisting of the possible outcomes and the questions which need to be asked to determine which outcome is the correct one. For example, your knowledge base could consist of British birds, and the questions would be 'Does it have a red breast?', 'Does it have a yellow beak?', and so on. The expert system **shell** is the software that allows the expert to enter and store the knowledge, and the non-expert to get an answer to his query by replying to questions posed by the computer until it is able to make a decision. The objectives of this project, then, are to:

- have facilities for creating, editing and storing a knowledge base
- be able to make decisions at least as accurately as a human expert
- be able to make a decision even though it has not been given all the information
- explain its decision to the user

Comment: This is a really interesting project for someone interested in Expert Systems. You would need to look at other Expert System shells such as Crystal or EASIE, do some research into how expert systems work, and then devise your own algorithm. This one used a system of allowing the user to give a 'weight' to each answer so that the outcome with the highest 'score' was selected.

Computer aided design

9.   Computer aided design package

Summary: The aim of the project is to create software which enables a user to enter drawings constructed from various geometrical shapes (lines, circles, rectangles, etc), and to move, size and rotate them.

Comment: This is a very complex project involving an understanding of the mathematics involved in rotating an object. It is best implemented using a 'GUI' (graphical user interface) using a mouse and symbols for line, circle, box, and so on.

Unsuitable topics

The system must involve a user inputting data of some kind, and obtaining output.   The production of a document about some aspect of computing is therefore **not** suitable. For example:

- a project which consists of a comparative study of two wordprocessors
- the production of a magazine using a desktop publishing system
- a general description of how to use a particular spreadsheet or database package

Specimen projects described in this book

Two specimen projects are used to illustrate all the stages involved in developing and documenting a project. The first of these is used to illustrate the analysis and design stages in detail, and is implemented using a Pascal program. This program is also used to demonstrate many useful techniques in Pascal, and because of this is considerably longer than would be expected for an A level project.

The second project has been kept as simple as possible, while still being well up to the required standard for a top grade, and is implemented using a database package. More and more students are choosing to implement their projects using various packages rather than writing a program, and this example provides guidance on what is expected in the design, implementation and final report.

In Parts 2 and 3, the projects are both shown in a form suitable for handing in to an examiner. Neither project is without its faults; but it is sometimes more useful to see weaknesses exposed than to be presented with the ultimate perfect solution! Where possible, margin comments draw your attention to both good and not-so-good points, and you may find other aspects which you feel you can improve upon in your own project.

In several places, the AEB project guidelines have been quoted as an example of what examiners expect from student projects. However, BTEC students and A-Level students studying for exams with other Examining Boards will find these guidelines are equally valid and relevant to their own projects. Naturally, you should study carefully the particular set of guidelines you have been given in addition to any advice in this book.

Summary

This chapter has covered:

- *how to choose and schedule your project*

Further reading

All examining boards produce guidelines for students writing computer projects, and may offer for sale specimen projects done by past students. For example, the AEB has a package of four sample projects with marks and comments available from their publications department, currently priced at £1.50 each.

Chapter 2 - Analysis

Objectives

By the end of this chapter you will have considered the following points in the analysis of a system:

1. output — what will be the output from the new system? Is hard copy required? How often? Is there some output from the current system or a similar system that you can look at?

2. input — what format does the input take? What input documents are currently used, and what are the data requirements?

3. objectives — exactly what is the new system designed to achieve?

4. processes — what is done, where, when and how? How are the objectives going to be fulfilled in the new system?

5. data — how much is there? Will the master file contain 50, 500 or 5000 records? How often does it change, or new records have to be added or deleted? Do these changes come in batches of several at a time, or in ones and twos?

6. exceptions — How are exceptions and errors handled?

7. security — Is security an issue? Should there be limited access to some or all parts of the new system?

8. problems — what are the drawbacks or problems with the current way of doing things?

9. constraints — are there any constraints on hardware, software, cost, time and so on?

10. suggested solutions — does the user have a particular solution in mind?

The investigation

Once you have decided on your project topic, you must make a full investigation of the user's needs (the user may be a person you know, or know of, or you may have a **potential** user in mind if, for example, you are writing a text editor or an expert system shell). Be aware, though, that examination boards usually stress the need to actually find a **real** user and obtain **real user feedback**. Having a 'potential' user may reduce the project to one of a distinctly hypothetical nature, not able to satisfy any user at all - and scoring only modest marks.

The exercise of designing a questionnaire, or preparing a list of questions and holding interviews, should be regarded as an important part of the project; it is in practice quite impossible to guess what a real user would want from, say, a club membership system or sports hall booking system. A project based on a real user's problem will win hands down every time over one which tries to guess an imaginary user's requirements.

The analysis is concerned with finding out about the **current** system (if there is one), and what the **requirements** are for the new system.

We will now look at how these issues are tackled in the first of the two specimen projects, introduced below.

SPECIMEN PROJECT 1 - Gilbert and Sullivan Society Patrons List

INTRODUCTION

The local Gilbert and Sullivan Society is a thriving amateur Operatic Society with about 75 members and a number of patrons. The patrons are supporters of the Society - perhaps ex-members, or people interested in Gilbert and Sullivan operas - who make an annual donation of a minimum of £5.00 (but often considerably more) towards the Society's costs, the main expense being about £12,000 for an annual production at the local theatre.

The patrons do not take part in rehearsals, shows or concerts: they are more akin to a "fan club" of a pop group, although they would probably rather be described as Patrons of the Arts!

In return for their support, all patrons are sent information about the Society's activities and receive a Priority Booking form giving them the first choice of seats for the Autumn production. Also, their names appear in the programme as Patrons.

The Society maintains a list of the Patrons in alphabetical order of surname, and keeps a record of what each patron has donated each year.

REQUIREMENTS

Further consultation with a committee member of the Society leads you to understand that the Patrons Secretary, who has been in office for a number of years, is finding the job simply too time-consuming and a new Secretary has been appointed to take over in a few months time. She has a computer at home and would like a computerised system which would hopefully ease the workload. The requirements are as follows:

- A database of patrons is to be maintained in alphabetical order with the facility to add, change and delete records easily.

- When a Patron makes a donation, this is to be recorded, and a record is to be kept of previous donations.

- Various printed reports such as:

  - A list of patrons' names in alphabetical order for insertion into the programme for the Society's annual production of a Gilbert and Sullivan opera.

  - The donation made by each patron in the previous financial year, running from April 1 to March 31. This report should include a total of all donations at the bottom of the report as the total figure is required for the annual statement of accounts.

  - A list of names and addresses, printed 'three up' on address label stationery.

Comments on this project

This is a fairly stereotypical project, involving at least one file which will need updating from time to time. A fairly modest but perfectly acceptable project could consist of:

- one file of, say, members, using an appropriate file organisation

- a well designed hierarchical menu system allowing the user to choose from several available options

- modules to add, change or delete members from the file

- a module to print or display the complete contents of the file

- a couple of useful reports; for example mailing labels and a list of members satisfying some specified criterion.

For a really good mark, however, you will in general need at least two files which relate to each other in some way; perhaps a file of transactions or subscriptions from which data is posted to the master file. The specimen project has enough scope to score top marks if it is done well; a lot will depend on the analysis and design, and indeed this is true of any project.

You may at first think that the requirements are already so clearly defined that there does not seem to be much analysis left to be done. If so, you are mistaken!

Preparing for an interview

The first step in a project will usually be to plan an interview with the user, or perhaps design a questionnaire to be filled in. If you are going to interview the user, make sure you have a list of questions prepared, and a notebook handy to write down the user's answers. Alternatively, you might consider taping the interview and writing it up later.

The involvement of a real user right from the start is a vital ingredient of a good project. You must show evidence of investigative competence in order to earn top marks in the analysis section, so your questionnaire or list of questions should be included in your report as well as a transcript or summary of the interview.

You will find that preparing questions in advance of an interview focusses your attention on what information is needed, and the interview is less likely to end up as a vague chat about possibilities which still leaves a lot of unanswered questions.

If you have used a questionnaire, samples of responses can be put into an Appendix, and a summary in the analysis section of your report.

Quick Answer Questions

Suppose that you have decided to take on the task of computerising the patrons list.

1.   Assume that you have the opportunity to interview the person who currently handles the patrons list. What questions will you ask her?

2.   What documents could you ask to look at?

(answers on the next page)

QAQ Answers

1. You should go through the list of points given at the start of the chapter to make sure they are covered. Some information, such as for example the objectives of a new system, may have to be deduced, without asking a direct question. Here is a possible list:

    a. How many patrons are there? *(establish the volume of data)*

    b. What is the turnover of patrons; how many leave each year, and how many new ones join? *(how often does the data change?)*

    c. What information do you keep on each patron? *(what data is stored?)*

    d. How do you store this information at the moment? *(how is the data stored?)*

    e. What items do you mail out to the patrons each year? Do they receive a reminder to send their subscription (donation)? *(establish the output)*

    f. Are the address labels already computerised, for example using a wordprocessor? Are there some occasions when you want to send correspondence to some patrons but not others? *(processes)*

    g. How are donations currently recorded? What do you do with the cheques or cash? *(processes)*

    h. If a patron fails to pay a subscription, what do you do about it? *(how are exceptions handled?)*

    i. It has been mentioned that the new Patrons Secretary intends to operate this system on her computer at home. What type of computer is it? Does she have a printer? *(constraints on hardware?)*

    j. What software does she have available? *(constraints on software?)*

    k. Do you have a particular package in mind for this project, or is it up to me to decide that? *(does the user have any suggested solutions?)*

    l. When would be a good time to put a new system into operation? *(constraints on time?)*

    m. Are there any problems with the current system that you hope will be overcome with the new system? *(establish what problems there are)*

2. Ask to see, for example:

    *   a sample of how the data on a patron is currently kept *(data)*

    *   a theatre programme with patrons' names in it *(output)*

    *   items mailed to patrons which require mailing labels *(output)*

    *   the document which records subscriptions *(input)*

Of course, the Patrons Secretary may not be able to show you all these. The record of subscriptions, for example, may be confidential, in which case you'll have to make do with a description.

The interview

It would be unrealistic to think that the interview is going to be a straightforward matter of going through the questions and writing down the answers. In all probability you won't have to ask all the questions because the Patrons Secretary will volunteer a lot of information which you hadn't even thought of asking.

Here are the results of the interview. (Joan is the Patrons Secretary, Mrs Joan Emsworth).

You: *(after polite preliminaries)* Approximately how many patrons does the Society have?

Joan: There are about 100 patrons. Four or five drop out every year and about the same number join, but it's been pretty stable over the past few years. Most people stay as patrons for years, we've got some who've been patrons since the fifties!

You: *(crossing off question 2)* What information do you keep on the patrons?

Joan: Name and address, obviously. Then I keep how they want their name in the programme - for instance some like 'Mr R Chandler', or they might want 'Mary and Bob Chandler' , or they might want to remain anonymous. At the bottom of the list in the programme we put 'Also those wishing to remain anonymous'.

You: Oh, right, I hadn't thought of that. Do you keep any other information?

Joan: I note the year, like '92', down on the card as soon as they have paid the subscription, so I know who has paid.

You: You say 'card' - do you keep a card index file, with a card for each patron?

Joan: Yes, that's right.

You: Don't you note the amount of the donation on the card?

Joan: No, I have a separate book for that. You see when I get a cheque, I write it down in a cash book, which has duplicate pages. Usually I get most of the cheques in March and April, because the reminder goes out late February. Then I just note down on the patron's card that I have had the subscription for this year. When I see the Treasurer, I tear out the duplicate page from my cash book and give it to her with all the cheques I have received. It's a very simple system and it works very well.

You: *(beginning to wonder why you're messing about with a system that already works so well, but ploughing on)* What do you do if someone doesn't pay their subscription?

Joan: Well, I keep them going for another couple of years. It used to be longer but that's all I do now.

You: When you say you keep them going, you mean you continue to send them stuff and hope they'll pay up next year?

Joan: Yes, that's right. If they don't pay in 1992, I send them a priority booking form and so on for 1992 anyway, and then in 1993 I'll send them another reminder in February. If I don't hear from them they don't get mailed any more.

You: How many times do you mail each patron every year?

Joan: As I say, in February they get a short newsletter, the concert brochure and a reminder to pay their subscription. In April I send them all a notice of the Annual General Meeting, though it seems a waste of postage as we never get more than about two or three turning up. Then I send Priority Booking forms out in June, for the show in November. The other thing is a newsletter which goes out in December or January.

You: Are the envelopes addressed by hand at the moment?

Joan: No, someone else does those on their wordprocessor. She took that on two or three years ago. I have to remember to tell her when someone is no longer a patron, or sometimes I hear that they have died.

You: Yes, I suppose if some of them have been patrons since the fifties, they must be quite elderly. Do you think it would be possible for me to see a specimen card from your card file, and the letters you send out to patrons? And I'd like to see a copy of last year's theatre programme too if possible.

Joan: Yes, I'll find those for you.

You: Well, I think that's about it. Oh, I nearly forgot. Do you know what kind of computer the new Patron's Secretary has?

Joan: I'm afraid I haven't the faintest idea! I'll ask her if you like.

You: Yes, thank you. Shall I write down exactly what I need to know, and then she could write down the answers?

Joan: That's a good idea. I'm afraid I don't know anything about computers.

You: Thank you very much, you've been most helpful. Can I come back to you if I think of anything else?

Joan: Yes, of course. Good luck!

In Appendix A (pages 2 - 44 and 2 - 45) you will find copies of all the documents that Joan produced for you.

Quick Answer Questions

1.   Draw up a list of questions about the hardware and software owned by the new Patrons Secretary, to give to Joan.

2.   What do you think the problems are with the existing system?

3.   Is security an issue in this system?

(answers on the next page)

QAQ Answers

1. Ask

    *   what type of computer she has

    *   whether it has a hard disk

    *   what size of floppy disk drive

    *   what type of printer she has

    *   what software packages she has available - you might, for example, decide to use a database package.

2. There are several problems:

    *   the system is very time consuming, with data having to be entered both on the patron's card and in the cash book

    *   errors could occur if the patrons secretary forgot to note down on the patron's card that the subscription had been paid

    *   without going through every card in the file manually, it would be difficult to determine which patrons had not paid a subscription

    *   as someone else does the mailing labels, both sets of names and addresses have to be kept up to date.

3. It is always worth giving careful thought to security, even if, as in this project, the system will be operated by only one person. You might consider, for example, having two 'access levels' so that the file can only be initialised, or data altered, if the correct password is typed in, while data can be 'viewed' by anybody. Showing that you have given thought to security is likely to earn you marks in the project.

Problems with the existing system

Make sure you have really understood what the problems are in the current system, when you get to work on your own project. Ask the user what he or she thinks are the problems, if appropriate. The Analysis section of the project report needs to include a paragraph or two on this subject. The problems discussed in this sample project are fairly typical; duplication of data entry and difficulty in extracting information from manual files are common reasons for introducing computers into an organisation.

Identifying the output

The initial request made to you specified various reports.

1. List of patrons' names for the programme

The purpose seems clear enough; it is a list for inclusion in the programme. But is the suggested output really what is required? Will it have to be typed out again by the person who typesets the programme? Or is last year's programme just edited each year, in which case would it be more useful to have a list of **changes** to the patrons list? An alternative would be to have the list output as a text file on disk, from where it could be imported directly into a desktop publishing system such as PageMaker. You will have to go back to the Patron's Secretary for answers to these questions.

We can see from the list of patrons in the 'Mikado' programme (Appendix A, page 2 - 44) that the names are not in the format of 'Hawes, M.' which may well be the key field of the patron's record. Hawes may want to be listed as 'Mike and Jane Hawes'. The output is, however, sequenced on surname and initials.

Also, provision has to be made for 'those wishing to remain anonymous'.

2. Donation (ie subscription) made by each patron in the past financial year

It would probably be a good idea to keep a separate file of all payments made during one year (just as currently, payments are recorded in a separate Cash Book.) Then, if you have made a wrong entry, or entered something twice, or not at all, it will be easy to trace and correct. The payments can then be posted from the 'subscriptions' file to the master 'patrons' file.

(This keeps the transaction data separate from the master file data, and gives you the two files needed for a substantial project. If you wanted to be less ambitious, you could limit the project to just the patrons file and still gain a good mark.)

In passing, it is worth noting that having the subscriptions on a separate transaction file provides what is known as an 'audit trail'; in other words, by examining the contents of the transaction file it is possible to see exactly how a balance has been arrived at. Otherwise, if the treasurer's records show for example that £750 worth of subscriptions have been paid in, but the computer report produced from the patron's file shows total subscriptions of £800, it is much more difficult to trace the error.

3. Mailing labels

You will have to get hold of some label stationery so that you can work out the exact spacing of the names and addresses on the page.

Quick answer questions

1. Can you think of any other reports or screen displays which might be included in this system?

2. What facts need to be ascertained for each suggested output?

Answer to QAQ

1. No other output has been suggested. However, there does need to be some way of identifying, in about June when the priority booking forms are sent out, those patrons who have not paid a subscription this year or the previous year. A list of such people could be printed out.

    It will very often happen that as the project progresses, either you or the user will think of other things which should or could be included. Make a note of them and if you don't have time to implement them, include them in the appraisal at the end of the project, as ideas for future enhancements.

2. For each suggested output:

    *   exactly what data is required on the report or record being produced?

    *   what is the format of each data item - for example, how many decimal places are needed on numeric items? In what format will dates be printed?

    *   are totals required at all?

    *   what form of output is required; hard copy, a screen display, output to a file, or more than one of these, perhaps with the user choosing one or more options at run time?

    *   is the report required in any particular sequence?

Identifying the data requirements

Once you have established exactly what **output** is needed, it should be quite easy to determine what data will have to be entered in order to produce the required reports.

In this system, for example, after the initial data entry when the entire patrons list is transferred from a card file to a computer file, there will be quite low volumes of data entry. From time to time the patrons' details will have to be amended (e.g. change of address, additions to and deletions from the list). Also, subscriptions will need to be recorded.

One must try and retain a sense of reality here and realise that the Patrons Secretary is not going to run to her computer every time a patron's cheque lands on the doormat. It will be far easier to continue recording the payments in the cash book, and enter, say, a page or two at a time whenever convenient. Luckily, the manual procedure is already in place. Further consideration of the input can be left until the Design phase.

Quick answer question

What general points need to be considered when identifying the data requirements of a system?

(Answers on next page)

Answers to QAQ

The kinds of questions you need to ask are:

- does the input match the output; in other words, is the data input sufficient to generate all the desired information? Conversely, is data being input for which there is no apparent purpose?

- what is the volume of input? Are there peak periods?

- what is the format of the data collection documents?

- who will be doing the input; will it be an expert who enters large volumes of data without looking at the screen, or an amateur who needs prompts and on-screen help when necessary?

- have the **manual** procedures (eg form-filling, batching, filing) to support the system been specified?

In the specimen project, occasional amendments to the patrons file will be entered by the patrons secretary, probably from a letter giving her a new address or a new patron. Subscriptions can be entered from the existing cash book. She may very well need some on-screen help and friendly-looking screens, but there is no need here to specify or design special forms for data collection.

If in your project, special forms are being used for data collection, you should include a sample in the analysis section of your report, or refer the reader to the sample shown in an Appendix. Similarly, if you have to design a form, include the new form in the Design section.

Ascertaining the objectives

The objectives of the proposed new system need to be formally identified and stated. Turn to page 2 - 6 (paragraphs 3.1 and 3.2) to see how they have been written down.

General objectives for a system

The objectives for your own project will be different from those for this project.

They may be, for example:

- to provide management information of some kind
- to provide a better service to customers, members of a club, or anyone else affected by the new system
- to save time and effort for the person who is currently performing the task manually
- to perform some task better or more accurately than has previously been possible
- to cut costs or save money in some way
- to give enjoyment or entertainment to the user

These general objectives need to be stated in more specific terms for each individual project.

There are other objectives which are often given by students, but which are somewhat dubious. For example:

- *to create a user friendly system*

Ugh! This is a most overworked phrase. Granted, any system wants to be as easy to use as possible, but it is really not an end in itself. When stated as the first objective, it usually means that the student has not actually thought about what the real objectives are.

- *to enable me to learn more about object-oriented programming (or whatever)*

This needs to be a beneficial spin-off rather than the primary purpose of the project. If there isn't a real purpose, perhaps you should think of another project! The objectives will relate to the desired **output** of the system.

Analysis of the system is not something you can do in three quarters of an hour. You must try to think yourself into the position of the 'user' and understand all the complexities of their task, if you are going to produce something really usable at the end of it all. You will probably keep coming back to your interview notes throughout the project, as problems crop up in the design and development stages. It is very important to keep notes of the preliminary investigation or interview which you can refer to, and which you can include in your final report.

Drawing a data flow diagram

A data flow diagram is often a good way of summarising the sources and destinations of data, and the processing that takes place. A data flow diagram for the specimen project is shown in Part 2 on page 2 - 8.

Writing up the analysis

A possible framework for writing up the analysis is given below:

1. **Introduction**

    1.1   Background

    1.2   Initial user information

2. **Investigation**

    2.1   The current system (include interview questions and notes if appropriate)

    2.2   Problems with the current system

3. **Requirements of new system**

    3.1   General objectives

    3.2....3.n   (List specific requirements)

4. **Constraints**

    4.1   Hardware

    4.2   Software

    4.3   Cost

    4.4   Time

5. **Limitations of the new system**

    5.1   Areas which will not be included in computerisation

    5.2   Areas considered for future computerisation

6. **Recommendations**

7. **Data flow diagram** (could be included at 2.1 above)

Of course, not every analysis will fit the model precisely! It is merely intended as a starting point from which you may diverge.

Pause: *Decide whether these headings are appropriate for the analysis of the specimen project. You can look at the write-up in Part 2, pages 2 - 4 to 2 - 8.*

Action: *Write up the analysis for your own project.*

Summary

*This chapter has covered the **analysis** of a system, which is concerned with how the **current** system works, and what the **requirements** of a new system would be. It involves:*

- *interviewing the user*

- *establishing the objectives of the new system*

- *identifying the input, output, data characteristics and processing methods used*

- *finding out how errors and exceptions are handled*

- *finding out what the constraints are if a new system is to be installed*

- *writing up the analysis.*

Further reading

1. *Practical Systems Design* by Daniels and Yeates (£12.95)

2. *Computing - An Active-Learning Approach (Section 5)* by P.M.Heathcote (DPP 1991 £9.95)

Chapter 3 - Design

Objectives

By the end of this chapter you will have covered the following points in the design of a system:

1. Consideration of possible solutions
2. Proposed solution
3. Output
4. Analysis of data requirements
5. Data validation
6. Input
7. User interface design
8. File design and access methods
9. Data structure design and data organisation
10. Relationship between files
11. File and general system security
12. Charts showing overall systems design
13. Program specification(s)
14. Design of test strategy

Take time over design

The Design stage is a crucial part of any project, since a poor design will almost certainly mean that the project will not be successfully implemented. Programming should not start until the design is completed. Someone once made the point that the design stage is often rushed in order to allow time at the end of the project to correct the mistakes that were caused by rushing the design stage...

Consideration of possible solutions

You need to consider carefully how the objectives will be best achieved. Should you use a package, or write a suite of programs? What programming language would be most suitable? Is that language available for you to use, or are you constrained by the software which you or the end user have access to? Are there any constraints on hardware? Are you sure that a computerised solution is really the best one, or would it be preferable to improve the manual methods? (If so, think of another project!)

The most important person to consider is the end user - in the case of the first specimen project, the new Patrons Secretary. If she has a BBC micro only running BASIC, then your choices are pretty limited. Even so, you should at least discuss how this system could be implemented using a database, for example.

Assume for the moment that she conveniently has the same type of microcomputer that you have available for development, and that she also has the same database and wordprocessing software, or could run the progam if it was written in BASIC or was given to her as an executable file in Pascal or some other language. In other words, any hardware and software constraints are determined by what you have installed at your school or college - for example, you may have only one particular database package available to use.

Pause: *Think of two or three ways in which this system **could** be implemented, and what the advantages and disadvantages are of each approach.*

Action: *Write down a similar discussion for your own project, and then justify your proposed solution.*

Proposed solution

Your proposed solution, describing the software and hardware you intend to use, should be stated and justified. You may be able to justify your choice on the grounds of what facilities a particular language or package has which will make your job easier, or the end product better in some way, or on cost grounds, or because your chosen language is the only one available in which you have sufficient expertise to undertake a programming task.

The trend in the past few years is for more and more students to choose to use a software package for their projects rather than writing a suite of programs. As the facilities offered by the various packages are generally quite easy to learn to use, and packages are becoming both cheaper and more powerful, this approach makes a good deal of sense and you should give it serious consideration. The implementation will probably be very much quicker, allowing you more time for thorough testing and documentation, both important aspects of a project.

For the Gilbert and Sullivan Patrons List, however, you will see from the report in Part 2 that a suite of Pascal programs is to be written. These will be compiled and the object code stored on a floppy disk from which the system can be run or installed on to the hard disc of the PC used by the new secretary.

Output

Referring back to the analysis, the following output is to be produced:

1.   List of patrons as they appear in the programme

2.   The same list but output to a text file for importing into PageMaker, the desktop publishing system used to produce the programme

3.   List of current year subscriptions

4.   Mailing labels for all patrons

5.   A list of patrons giving subscriptions paid for the past three years. This will enable the Patrons Secretary to identify patrons who have fallen by the wayside and are no longer paying a subscription. These patrons could be highlighted by printing, say, 5 asterisks next to their names.

6.   There should be a facility for printing out all the data on the patrons file. If there is no hard copy backup,

the secretary is totally reliant on the computer. One can just imagine the scenario:

Joan: *(Telephone rings)* Hello, Joan here.

Paul: *(He's the Chairman of the Society)* Hello, Joan. I wonder if you could let me have Gordon Matthews address, he's been a Patron for years so I expect you have it somewhere.

Joan: *(Heart sinks).* Well, Paul, to tell you the truth I could have told you that in a flash before the system was computerised, but as it happens all the information is on the computer now and it's gone in for repair.

Paul: What on earth did you want to get involved with computers for?

Analysis of data requirements

This initially involves writing down all the data items that are to be used in the system, and the format of each data item; for example is the item a real number, integer, string or boolean variable? How many characters are to be allowed for a string field such as a person's name? Will it have separate fields for surname and initials, or one field with initial following surname, or perhaps preceding it? Will there need to be a field for 'title' (Mr, Mrs etc)? If mailing labels are involved these are important considerations.

You should also **justify** the inclusion or omission of data items. For example, should 'Date of becoming patron' be included, even though it is not required on any report? You must make a decision and explain your reasoning in the project report.

Quick answer question

Make a list of all the data items that will be needed for the Patrons list. You should relate this list to the desired **output**.

Answers to QAQ

The basic information that needs to be kept for each patron is:

Name (surname followed by initials, so that you can sort the list on this field)
Address
Date that they became a patron (not used at present but is currently held and is of interest to the Society)

To get the list of patrons' names for the programme, you need:

Name in the format that it is to appear
Whether the patron wishes to remain anonymous (Y/N *or* ANON in name field?)

To get the donation made by the patron in the past financial year, you will need to record the payment as it is made. You also have to keep a record of the previous two year's subscriptions so that the report mentioned in (5) above can be produced.

Subscription (current)
Subscription (last year)
Subscription (2 years ago)

You must consider carefully the data needed for the mailing labels. Obviously, name and address are required. You should consider whether you need just one field for the name followed by initials, or 3 fields; surname, initials and title (Mr, Mrs etc). If your project includes personalised letters, you will need all three fields, so that you can start the letter in the format 'Dear <title> <Surname>'. It is also desirable to address envelopes to, say, 'Mr F.Smith' rather than to 'Smith F'.

We will cut corners a little in the specimen project and just use one field for name and initials. This can be mentioned in the appraisal.

Probably three lines of address and one for the postcode is plenty. When you get round to deciding the lengths of these fields, be sure and get hold of some label stationery. At three up, you won't get more than 25 or so characters printed across each label on a standard printer with an 80 character width, so you have:

> Address line 1
> Address line 2
> Address line 3
> Postcode

You may not have decided yet how patrons are going to be deleted from the file. They may be physically deleted, or 'flagged' as deleted by setting a special field in the record to 'True', for example, in which case that extra field will need to be specified. For now, postpone a decision.

Data validation

Any item of data that will be input by the user will be prone to error. As far as possible, you want to make sure that the program will not 'crash' (terminate unexpectedly) whatever the user enters.

In addition, various checks can be made to specific fields such as range checks, checks for particular characters (e.g. Y or N), checks that a particular record exists and so on. You have to try and anticipate all the errors that users might make and prevent them from making them, or give them a chance to correct the error before the computer accepts the data.

Data validation is an important aspect of your project, and will earn you extra marks if it is carefully planned and explained. In your report, discuss the reasons for the validations you have chosen. If, for example, the key field on your master file is numeric, consider including a check digit validation, and explain the reason for use, the suitability for the data item, and the technical method used.

You can now start building up a table, filling in the format of each data field and any validation checks that need to be carried out on input data.

Field description	Field name	Format	Dec places	Validation check
Name (surname + initials)	P_Name	string[25]		convert to caps
Name for programme	P_NameInProg	string[30]		convert to caps if "anon"
Address Line 1	P_Address1	string[25]		
Address Line 2	P_Address2	string[25]		
Address Line 3	P_Address3	string[25]		
Postcode	P_Postcode	string[8]		
Year of becoming a patron	P_YearJoined	integer		>= 1950 and <= current year
Subscription (current)	P_SubCurrent	real	2	>= 5.00 and <50.00
Subscription (last year)	P_SubLastYear	real	2	(not input)
Subscription (2 years ago)	P_Sub2YrsAgo	real	2	(not input)

Checklist of facts to record about each data item

> 1. a plain language description
> 2. computer abbreviation (field name)
> 3. identity of the record(s) containing the data element
> 4. the format e.g.
>   alphanumeric
>   decimal, binary, etc
>   integer, real, or logical (boolean)
>   number of decimal places
> 5. range(s) of values that are valid
> 6. any special feature of the data element, eg key field, check digit validation

Input

In this section, you can identify what data entry will be required.

There are two different types of input for the Patrons List project:

- **maintenance** transactions: additions, changes and deletions to the patrons file
- **update** transactions: payment of subscriptions. When a patron pays a subscription, the date and the amount will be recorded on a file of subscriptions. From there it will be posted to the patrons file.

Update transactions

Although it would be quite possible to enter subscriptions straight onto the patrons file, it would be preferable to use a separate file for holding subscriptions, and to post subscriptions automatically to the patrons file. We will then have a record of each subscription in the order in which they were entered, which could make it easier to trace any errors which arise.

We can add some more fields to our data list:

Field description	Field name	Format	Validation check
Amount of subscription	S_Sub	Real	>=5.00 and <50.00
Date of subscription	S_Date	string[8]	normal date validation

S stands for Subscription File. The date field has provisionally been put down as string[8], so it will be entered as, for example, 10-03-93. There doesn't seem any obvious reason why this would not be quite acceptable. Of course, you couldn't sort the file on date order if the date is in that format, but in this system there is no need to sort the transactions; they need to be in the order in which they were entered.

The screens for the maintenance of the patrons file and the entry of subscriptions can now be laid out using screen layout charts. (A blank screen layout form which you may photocopy for your own use is given at the end of this book.)

The user interface

Data entry screens

When you design your screen layouts, you should pay particular attention to the design of each screen. Users will be easily put off by unattractive screens such as the one below:

```
ENTER PATRONS NAME;
Bloggs J
Enter Date Joined;
Jan 1991
error: please re-enter
1991
ADRESS (line 1)
14 Ferndown Ave
ADRESS (line 2)
etc
```

Quick answer question

What is wrong with the above input screen? (You should be able to find quite a lot!)

(answers below)

Answers to QAQ

It looks thoroughly amateurish! For example, you could pick out the following faults:

> There is no heading to the input screen.
>
> The fields are all squashed up in the left hand corner, which is not pleasing to the eye.
>
> The user's input is not on the same line as the prompt.
>
> The use of semi-colons is wrong; a colon would be preferable.
>
> There is no consistency in the use of capitals in the prompts.
>
> The word 'address' is misspelt twice.
>
> There is no indication of how long the name and address fields might be.
>
> There is no guidance given to the user as to how the date should be entered, even after they get it wrong.

You can probably find even more to criticise. Remember that marks will be awarded for the quality of the user interface so it is worth taking trouble over.

Guidelines for screen design

There are many good books written on the subject of screen design, but a few commonsense rules will go a long way.

- be sensible in your use of colour. Dark blue text on a black background is almost illegible, yellow on green is merely unpleasant.

- do not overdo blinking, reverse video, and so on. It becomes tiring and irritating to the user.

- use both uppercase and lowercase. All-uppercase sentences are harder to read, and less attractive.

- be consistent in your terminology: for example on menu screens, use Q for 'Quit' on every menu, not E for 'Exit' on some, and '5. Return to main menu' on another, or even 'Q. Return to main menu'. It should be 'Q. Quit to main menu'.

- Don't use obscure error messages such as 'Error X551'. Use plain English.

- Help the user wherever possible. For example, the instruction 'Enter date' with no clue as to the correct format leaves the user floundering. Give an on-screen example of the required format.

- Use shading to show the maximum length of each field.

You might also consider the use of pop-up windows, or using the bottom two lines of the screen for help messages.

Pause: *Have a look at the specimen screen layout chart for the addition of a new patron, given below.*

Action: *Draw up screen layout charts for each data entry screen in your own project using a similar screen layout form. (You can photocopy the blank form at the end of this book.)*

Screen Layout

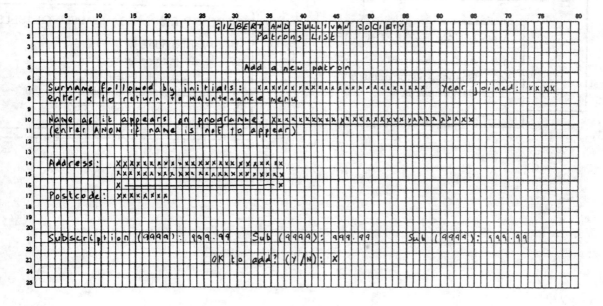

Menu structures

Most projects will probably start by displaying a menu of options from which the user may choose, and some of these choices may lead to submenus. Use the following guidelines when designing your menus:

1. Each menu should be given a title which uniquely identifies it, such as 'Main Menu', 'Maintenance of Patrons file' and so on. You may also have a title at the top of each screen which identifies the project; eg 'Gilbert & Sullivan Patrons List'.

2. The heading on each submenu should display the choice that was made on the previous menu, so that the user always has a clear idea of what option is currently operative. For example, if the user selects 'Maintenance of Patrons file' from the main menu, the next menu should be headed 'Maintenance of Patrons file'.

3. The last option on each menu should take the user back to the previous level of menu. A standard 'Q. Quit to ....' is useful here.

4. You can use different colours for different levels of menu. This helps to orient the user.

When you have decided on your menu structure, you should draw up an outline chart showing movement between menus, and include this in your project report. An example is given below.

Chart showing movement between menus

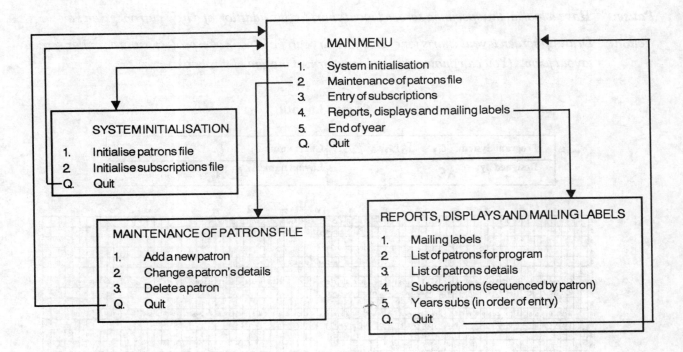

Report formats

For each report in the system, a report layout sheet needs to be drawn up showing exactly where on the page each item appears. The report layout sheet will show the title, subtitle and column headings, the format of each data item (such as the number of decimal places), groups, totals and so on. A sample report layout sheet is given below, and there is a blank form at the end of the book.

You will only get 80 characters across the page if you are using normal print on a dot-matrix printer, for example. If you use condensed print, about 130 characters can be printed across the page. Designing a report form is often a matter of trial and error so use a pencil and have an eraser handy!

Report Layout

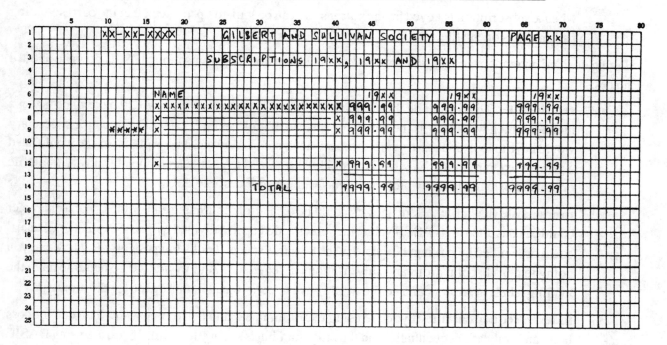

User access levels

You need to consider whether all the users should be given access to all parts of the system. In many applications, the first thing a user has to do on starting up is to enter a password which will determine how much, if any, of the data he or she will be able to see or change.

In your project, you could include a discussion of user access levels as one of the topics under the overall heading 'user interface', or you may choose to consider it under a separate heading 'Security'. This topic is considered further in the next chapter.

File design and access methods

A decision now has to be made as to what file organisation to use for the Patrons File and the Subs File. There is a measure of conflict here between what is easy to **program**, and what is easy to **use** when the system is complete. Ideally, you should design a system that is easy to use and acquire the programming skills to put it into effect, if you don't already possess them. Time will be much better spent finding out how to create and maintain a file of a suitable organisation, than in finding out how to make the computer draw pretty graphics and play a tune when the user signs on!

Patrons file

There are several reasons why random access would be better than sequential access for the patrons file:

- it will be possible to go directly to a particular record to change it or view it

- a number of additions, changes and deletions to the file can be made directly from keyboard input, without having to have them sorted in any way

- patrons subscriptions can be put on the transaction file in any order and they will not have to be sorted before being posted to the patrons file

- when a subscription is keyed in, the patrons file can be looked up to check that the corresponding patron exists on the file.

Having decided on random access, you now have to decide on the file organisation. It boils down to about 4 choices:

- **relative file.** This would be the simplest to program, but each patron would have to be given a number which would act as the key field. Instead of looking up Spencer D, the patrons secretary would have to look up Patron number 46, or whatever number he had been given, so she would need a printed list to refer to. This would probably be quite acceptable and indeed is a very good file organisation to use in many projects. It may well be your best choice.

- **random file (hash file).** Here, the key could be the Patron's surname and initials. Each character could be converted to its ASCII value, the values added up and divided by say 150 or 200. 'Clashes' could be handled by putting the record in the next free space. Tricky but possible. But how are you going to get a list of patrons and subscriptions in sequence? And woudn't it be better to have the mailing labels in sequence? The file would have to be sorted. Put this on ice for the moment.

- **indexed sequential file.** If you are using COBOL, this could be your answer. You can process both randomly and sequentially, and the programming is straightforward. If you are using BASIC or Pascal, it is much more complex because you have to create and maintain your own index.

- **binary tree.** Maybe you haven't written any programs dealing with a binary tree. Don't let that put you off - the algorithms are fully explained in Chapter 5. This is a good choice of file organisation here; the file can be processed sequentially or randomly and keyed on surname and initials. It is a rather unusual choice but it will demonstrate the possibilities of a different file organisation, and is the method chosen for the specimen project.

Choosing a binary tree data structure will involve more complex programming than would be necessary for a relative file. You need to consider the options very carefully for your own project, and justify your final choice in the report.

Subscriptions file

There's no need for anything complex here - the transactions are entered and posted in any order, stored and printed in the same order that they are put on the file. This is a serial file, with each new transaction being added to the end of the existing file.

Data structure design and data organisation

A binary tree is a type of data structure; it has been covered in the paragraph above. We have arrived at the idea of two files quite easily here since there is obviously a master file, and we made the decision earlier to put subscriptions onto a separate transaction file. However, it will not always be so straightforward, and this aspect of the design is covered more thoroughly in the next chapter using a second specimen project as an illustration.

Relationship between files

Again, this topic is covered in the next chapter. For the Gilbert and Sullivan project, we have already decided to use a master file and a transaction file, with name as the key field in both files. This is a typical example of a one-to-many relationship between files; that is, one master file may potentially have many transactions. (Generally speaking in this particular system each patron will only pay one subscription, but with this file relationship it will make no difference if they make several payments.)

File and general system security

A fuller discussion of this topic has been left to the next chapter.

In a project such as the Gilbert and Sullivan project, security may not seem to be a particularly important issue, but nevertheless it is probably a good idea on any system to prevent unauthorised access. Who is to say whether the Patrons Secretary's visiting nephew may not decide to add 'Mickey Mouse' and 'Princess Di' to the files on a wet Sunday afternoon? You should also be aware that examiners are placing increasing emphasis on this aspect of a project, and you would be well advised to include at least a discussion of security and for top marks, some implementation of passwords and user access levels.

Backup of individual files also needs to be thought about.

Quick answer question

What facilities for backing up the master and transaction files could you make in this system?

QAQ Answer

It could be an option on a menu, or you can include instructions in your user manual on how to use the operating system commands to make backups. The important thing is to show you have thought about how it should best be done.

You also need to think about the security of the whole system: even if the data is not confidential, what will happen if the hard disk fails? You must ensure that there is a procedure for recovery after such an event, and explain what it is.

Charts showing overall systems design

This refers to systems flow charts or other types of system chart, **not** program flow charts.

System outline chart

You may find it useful to use a **systems chart** at this stage. This is a summary of the **input, processes, files** and **output** in the system, laid out as shown below:

INPUT	PROCESSES
surname & initials	update patrons file
name for programme	record subs
address	post subs
etc	etc

FILES	
patrons	
subs	OUTPUT
	list of patrons for programme
	mailing labels
	etc

Systems flow chart

Systems flow charts for the specimen project are shown on pages 2 - 15 and 2 - 16.

Pause: *Decide which type of chart is most appropriate for your own project.*

Action: *Draw up the chart(s) for your own project.*

Program specification(s)

The design section is concerned with overall systems design, not with the detailed design of each program. Therefore it is not necessary to include detailed structure diagrams or pseudocode; instead, work out the main functions that the system will perform, and draw a single page hierarchy chart showing how the modules relate to each other. (See page 2 - 18.)

You can add descriptive footnotes for the larger modules, or you may find it useful to draw up a list of modules from your hierarchy chart, giving the name and purpose of each module, for inclusion in the project report. The list of modules can be copied to your work schedule (see page 1 - 4).

Design of test strategy and test data

It may seem strange to start thinking about testing before you have even started coding, but in fact it is an essential task if everything is going to work correctly once it is installed. You may have to write some programs specifically for test purposes; for example, a program which displays the contents of a file before and after updating, so that you can check that the update has been performed correctly. You must also take into account that your test file may be only 10 or 20 records, whereas the real file may have several thousand records. Will the system still work?

You will not be expected to enter more than a maximum of 50 records of test data. Examiners do not want you to waste your limited time typing in hundreds of data records for test purposes.

The overall test strategy and the test data, then, belongs in the design section of your report. For the sake of convenience the discussion of how to design a test plan and test data has been put in Chapter 6.

Summary

*This chapter has emphasised the importance of careful **design** of a system, involving:*

- *deciding what software to use*

- *looking closely at the desired **output** in order to determine the **input** and **processes** required to produce it*

- *giving careful attention to the user interface*

- *choosing and justifying appropriate file structures and data structures*

- *planning, in outline, how each part of the system will work using diagrammatic techniques such as system charts, charts showing movement between menus, systems flow charts, structure or hierarchy charts or other appropriate methods.*

- *designing a test strategy and test data.*

Further reading

1. *Human-Computer Interface Design Guidelines* by C.M.Brown (Ablex Publishing Corp., £25.95)

2. *Dbase III + Programmers Reference Guide* (Sybex, £24.95)

3. *Dbase IV Student Edition (includes 120 record version plus tutorial text)* (Adison Wesley £36.95)

Chapter 4 - Using a Package

Objectives

This chapter discusses the use of packages in general, and introduces a second specimen project which is implemented using a database package. Particular attention is paid to:

- file design
- data structure and data organisation
- relationship between files
- file security
- using the special features of the chosen package

Pros and cons of using a package

When you have chosen your project topic, one of the important decisions you may have to make is whether to use a package or a program. Particularly with a database type of project, the use of a package may well offer substantial advantages over writing a suite of programs, not least in the time saved in implementing your design. This will enable you to spend more time on testing and documentation.

You may be put off this approach because you have not had a great deal of time to look at packages, and are not quite sure of what could be achieved using, say, SuperCalc or Paradox, whereas you have spent a great deal of time learning to program and at least you know what is involved in writing a suite of programs. There may be very little documentation available for the package within your school or college, and if it has recently been installed, the staff may not have had much time to get to grips with it either. No wonder many students stick to Pascal or BASIC!

In spite of all the difficulties, you should give serious consideration to using a package. You may have to spend several hours going through a tutorial to get to know its capabilities, and inexpensive guides to all the well-known packages are available from good bookshops. The time saved in implementing your design should more than make up for the time spent in learning the intricacies of the software.

Many projects may use a combination of programming and package. DBase is an obvious example, where you may use either the programming language or the 'front end' provided by the package. Paradox 3.5 has a 'Personal Programmer' which enables you to quickly build a customised system. Most spreadsheets have a macro language to enable you to write programs.

The second specimen project has been implemented in Borland's Paradox 3.5, making use of the Paradox Personal Programmer. Learning the software from scratch and implementing the design took only a small fraction of the time that would be required to write a Pascal program do the same task!

SPECIMEN PROJECT 2 - SHORT COURSE DATABASE

INTRODUCTION

The Computing Section of XXX College runs a programme of one- and two-day courses on various packages, operating systems, and so on for clients from local government departments, businesses and industries. Commercial rates of about £120 per day are charged for each person on a course, although some courses are given specifically for one organisation in which case a block fee is charged. No more than ten people are taken on a course, and any course which has more than 6 people attending will be double-staffed for at least part of the time.

Profits from running these courses are put into a special budget which pays for additional hardware and software, better facilities such as equipment for projecting a screen image via an overhead projector, carpets, comfortable chairs and so on.

REQUIREMENTS

A database of some kind is required to provide information to management on the number of these courses being run, course costs and profits, and so on. A breakdown of the number of hours worked by each member of staff is also required.

Comments on this project

This is a fairly standard type of database project for which some kind of package would probably be ideal. A lot more information needs to be obtained, probably by means of an interview, to determine exactly what output is required and how the data is to be collected.

Pause: *Turn to Part 3 and read pages 3 - 4 to 3- 12, covering the Analysis section and part of the Design section of the report before proceeding to the discussion of data structure design and file design.*

Data structure design

The data that needs to be held for this system is:

course code
course title
course date
duration of course in hours
name of each member of staff teaching on a course
hours of teaching or preparation by each member of staff
fee charged per person
number of people on course
total receipts
total costs + costs breakdown
(Profit can be calculated and displayed but does not need to be stored)

A decision now has to be made as to how to organise this data. The first possibility is to just have one file, with course number as the key field. Because there is more than one member of staff teaching on a single course, we would have to have several fields such as:

name of staff 1, hours for staff 1
name of staff 2, hours for staff 2
name of staff 3, hours for staff 3
etc

This is problematical for several reasons.

1. We do not actually know the maximum number of staff that could be involved on a single course

2. A lot of space will be wasted on the database if we allow for say 4 or 5 staff members, when often only two will be involved

3. It will be difficult to obtain a report on the hours worked by one particular member of staff, since he or she could be recorded as 'staff 1' on one occasion, 'staff 2' on another occasion and so on.

The problems arise because of the **many-to-many** relationship between courses and staff; one course has many staff, and one staff teaches on many courses. We need to find another way of organising the data which does not involve this particular relationship.

This is where **normalisation** of the database comes in. To get a database into **first normal form,** all repeating groups have to be removed. This implies that we should have a separate record not only for each course but also for each member of staff teaching on the course. For example, the database could have records as shown below:

course no.	course title	course date	duration	staff name	staff hours	fee charged	etc
XED081	Intro to MSDOS	27/09/92	6	Turner J	6	£120	
XED081	Intro to MSDOS	27/09/92	6	Biddle M	6	£120	
XED081	Intro to MSDOS	27/09/92	3	Horsfall A	3	£120	
XED072	Advanced LOTUS	30/09/92	12	Biddle M	12	£280	
XED072	Advanced LOTUS	30/09/92	12	Lawson B	8	£280	
XED072	Advanced LOTUS	30/09/92	12	Stokes E	4	£280	

This solves the problems mentioned above but introduces another one; data duplication! Not only is it very wasteful of space and time-consuming to enter the data, we risk inconsistencies creeping in if for example we realise the cost of the LOTUS course was reduced to £260, but fail to make the change in all three records. It also becomes much more complex to answer simple questions such as 'How many courses have been run?' since we no longer have just one record per course.

Notice that each record is now no longer uniquely defined by the course number; the primary key (ie the field or fields which uniquely define a particular record) now consists of the course code and the staff name.

The database needs to be put into **second normal form**, which means that no column in the table which is not part of the primary key depends on only a portion of the primary key. For example, the course title depends on the course number but not on the staff name, so it should not be in this table.

To put the table into second normal form, write down a list of the subsets of the primary key (and the list will include the whole primary key) and place each of the other columns with the appropriate primary key.

(STAFFHRS table):- <u>course code, staff name</u>, staff hours   *(key fields underlined)*

(COURSES table):- <u>course code</u>, course title, course date, duration, fee charged .... total costs

(STAFF table):- <u>staff name</u> no fields depend only on staff name.

Notice that after the table has been put into second normal form, each table contains only records with unique primary keys; that is, no two records in any table have identical keys. The key may of course consist of more than one field, as in the case of the first table where the key is course code plus staff name.

Relationship between files

We therefore end up with three files or tables in the database. The course code is the field that is common to the first two tables, and we will be able to combine the contents of the two tables for reports using this link. Each record in the COURSES table will have a unique course code, but many records in the STAFFHRS table will refer to one course. This **one-to-many** relationship is satisfactory here.

The third table at present contains only staff names. Two points spring to mind:

- it would probably be useful to hold more details on each staff member, such as Department, work and home phone numbers and possibly address. The user needs to be asked about this.

- using the name as the key field is not really satisfactory since even if, with a relatively small number of staff involved, names are unlikely to be duplicated, a name such as Polevchensky or even Young (Yonge?) could easily be misspelt on the file. It would then either have to be left as it was when the mistake was discovered, or every record on the file involving the member of staff would have to be individually corrected - a major task!

The relationship between the three files is defined using a diagrammatic technique on page 3 - 17.

Quick answer question

If we did decide to assign a unique id to each member of staff, what changes would be made to the database?

QAQ Answer

We would need to replace 'staff name' with 'staff id' in the first table, and have a third table with columns 'staff id' and 'staff name', as well as any other fields the user decides are necessary.

Pause: *Be sure you fully understand how to normalise data in a database. This feature is crucial for top grade projects of this nature.*

Action: *Consider whether, and if so how, this applies to your own project. How many files will you need? How will they be related?*

File security

The ability to keep files secure, and possibly to prevent some users from seeing certain fields on a database, or changing the data in particular fields or all fields, is of great importance to users in very many systems. While it may be difficult to exclude the really determined hacker, even elementary precautions can protect data from casual snoopers or accidental erasure by inexperienced users.

File security is a new area on many syllabuses that is being strongly encouraged in project work. Many packages make it simple to implement password protection, write-protection for selected files, user access rights and so on. For example, Paradox allows you to specify a master password and optionally, auxiliary passwords which grant other users access without them needing to know the master password. You can assign as many auxiliary passwords as you like to a single table, or you can assign the same auxiliary password to several tables so that authorised users need only remember a single password.

In this system, we will have a master password which will allow the owner free access to all parts of the system, and an auxiliary password which will allow holders to read the contents of files but not make any changes. Reasons for security measures need to be discussed in the Design documentation.

One of the marking criteria for a top mark in the design section (taken from the AEB project guidelines) is

'very good consideration/design of file and general system security'.

You are strongly recommended to implement some form of file protection wherever appropriate, whichever Examination Board you are studying with.

Using the special features of the chosen package

If you have chosen to use a package, you should spend time exploring its capabilities, and where possible make use of them. This could involve, for example:

- designing an introductory screen
- designing customised menus
- designing data entry screens
- incorporating custom-made help screens
- validating user input
- using calculation facilities for some fields if appropriate
- using sorting facilities
- designing specially formatted report forms
- using passwords and security features
- using macros or programming capabilities

Generally speaking, the more sophisticated your use of the package facilities, the better the mark you are likely to get for implementation. In the systems maintenance section of your report you must describe the main features of your chosen package, and also the actual steps you had to take in using the package to achieve each of the major processes in your system. This is the package equivalent to program module descriptions and pseudocode, and provides the evidence of the work you have done in tailoring the package to the user's needs.

For a good grade, customisation of the package is essential. It is not sufficient to simply use the built-in facilities of a database or spreadsheet package, for example, to input and edit data and make queries or print standard format reports.

The second project in Part 2 shows typical documentation for a system that makes use of a software package.

Summary

This chapter has discussed the use of a software package in developing a project. File design and normalisation have been covered in more detail, and the importance of paying adequate attention to file and system security has been emphasised. A second specimen project was introduced in order to demonstrate the use of a software package in building a system.

Further reading

1. *DBase for Business Students* by J.Muir (DPP 1992, £4.95)

2. *MS Works* by D.Weale (DPP 1992, £4.95)

3. *Spreadsheets for Business Students* by C.West (DPP 1991, £4.95)

4. *Mastering Paradox 3.5* by Alan Simpson (Sybex, £25.50)

A specimen project (Property Development System) showing how the marking scheme is applied when a package is used is obtainable from the AEB.

Chapter 5 - Pascal techniques

Objectives

This chapter is largely aimed at students who will be implementing their projects in Turbo Pascal. It covers:

- defining standards for procedure names, variable names, indentation and comments
- setting up a file with more than one record type
- sending output to a text file
- printing reports
- writing a program as a series of modules
- using subroutines with parameters for frequently used sections of code
- making use of string handling routines
- programming function keys
- implementing pop-up windows
- checking for the presence of a file on disk
- using graphics
- binary tree routines
- debugging your program

Implementing a project in Pascal

The first specimen project (Gilbert and Sullivan Society Patrons List) has been implemented in Pascal, and a complete listing is included in Appendix F. Please do not be alarmed by its length; you will not be expected to produce anything of this complexity. Many excellent Pascal projects will typically be less than half as long.

The specimen program has been written as a teaching vehicle and as such incorporates many different techniques, some of which you may find useful in your own project. It must be emphasised that it could just as well have been implemented using a relative file instead of a binary tree, and not using graphics screens, pop-up windows, function keys and all the other bells and whistles, and still score very good marks.

Bear in mind that only a small proportion of the marks (e.g. 15% for AEB) is allocated to the technical solution, that is, the coding or use of a package. Therefore, do not spend a disproportionate amount of time on complex coding and leave yourself insufficient time for thorough testing and documentation. Concentrate on producing a well-structured and easy-to-understand program from a carefully thought out design; the important thing is to write a program that works!

Programming standards

Before you sit down at the keyboard and begin whacking in code, it will pay you to spend a little time thinking about such things as indentation, comments, and the naming conventions you will use for your variables and procedure names. An enormous amount of time will be saved in the long run because your program will be very much easier to follow through and debug, and you won't have to be continually looking through pages of code to see what you called a particular variable. Here are a few suggestions:

1. **Establish a 'hierarchy' for module names**

    Draw a structure diagram for the whole program on a large sheet of paper. (You should have done this already in the Design stage). Preface each module on the top level with a letter and a number (e.g. O1_OpeningScreen, M1_MainMenu). On the next level, M1_MainMenu may call M11_SysInitMenu, M12_MaintenanceMenu, and so on. This way, if you are looking at a routine called M121_AddPatron, you know it was called from the routine prefaced M12, which in turn was called from M1.

    Some routines (such as one which asks the user to press any key to continue) may be called from many different modules, so this convention can't be used. Routines can often, however, be grouped into types and given a letter which signifies which group they belong to and where the code is physically located in the program. Thus all the A_ routines come before all the B_ routines, and so on. Note that an M121_ routine has to be placed above an M12_ routine, though, because it is called by it.

    The diagram below illustrates this.

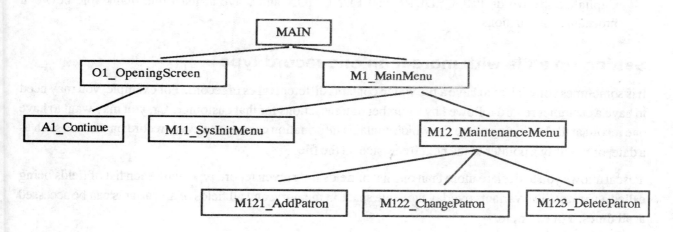

A hierachy chart

2. **Use a prefix to identify the file to which a variable belongs.**

    All the fields in PatronsRec, for example, can be prefixed with a P_. Then you can see at a glance whether you are dealing with a variable which is a field of a particular record on a given file.

3. **Don't use underscores in the middle of variable names.**

    It is much better to use capital letters to separate the words in a variable name, such as CurrentYear, rather than use current_year. Not only are the names just as easy if not easier to read, you avoid the problem of continually forgetting whether you have or have not used an underscore in that particular name.

4. **Use indenting after each while, repeat, begin etc but indent only 2 or 3 characters.**

    It is absolutely essential to use indentation to show where loops and If statements begin and end. However, two or three characters is plenty of indent; more than that and you start running off the right hand side of the page.

5. **Never write an 'end' without a comment to say what is ending.**

    For example:

    ```
    end; {with}
    ```
    or
    ```
    end; {M12_MaintenanceMenu}
    ```

    This will save you hours of debugging time. Don't put the comments in afterwards; put them in as a matter of habit as soon as you write the word **end**.

6. **Use comments after every procedure heading to state its purpose.**

    Again, put these comments in as soon as you have written the procedure heading; not months later. Don't forget to put your name, and the date you started the program, as well as its purpose, immediately under the **program** heading. Some procedure names may be clear enough to forego the comment.

7. **Separate your procedures and functions visually.**

    Capitalise the words PROCEDURE and FUNCTION and leave at least one blank line between procedures or functions.

Setting up a file with more than one record type

It is sometimes convenient to have a file which contains different types of record. For example, you may need to have a customer record followed by a number of transactions for that customer. Or, you may want to have one record at the beginning of the file which contains information common to every record on the file, such as a date, or possibly a pointer to the next free space on the file.

Pascal allows you to declare more than one list of fields for a given record type, with each list of fields being called a *variant*. The variants overlay the same space in memory, and all fields of all variants can be accessed at all times. For example:

```
type PatronType = record
    case ControlRec : Boolean of
      True:   ( CurrentYear  : integer;
                NextFree     : integer);
      False:  ( Surname      : string[20];
                Address1     : string[25];
                ....
                ....
                Subscription : real;)
    end; {record type declaration}
```

If the variable ControlRec is set to True when you read the record, values will be read into variables CurrentYear and NextFree. Otherwise you will be reading a normal data record.

Sending output to a text file

If you want to write information to a text file so that it can later be imported into a desktop publishing package, edited using a word processor or simply printed out later, you do not need to declare a typed file. Simply declare a variable of type **text** in your list of variable decarations.

eg

```
var
    MyTextFile   : text;
    StudentName  : string;
    StudentMark  : integer;
```

A student's name and mark can then be written to the file with the statement

```
writeln(MyTextFile,StudentName,StudentMark);
```

This is the technique that has been used in the module D6_NamesToFile, which sends the names of patrons as they are to appear in the theatre programme to a text file for importing into PageMaker.

Printing reports

When printing a report, rather than displaying information on the screen, there are certain points to remember:

- every page in the report should have a page number and usually the current date as well

- the report title and column headings should appear at the top of every page

- you must keep a linecount, that is, a variable which is incremented every time you print a line. When it reaches a certain value, say 50, throw to a new page by writing the character #12 (Form feed). If you set the linecount to 50 initially and test it before you print a line, you will automatically start by throwing to a new page and printing the headings. Then set the linecount back to zero and increment the page count. (see module M145_YearsSubs).

Writing a program as a series of modules

If you are writing a reasonably substantial project, you will probably find that you have at least a dozen or two modules on your structure chart. (If you have thus far ignored all advice to draw a structure chart, now is the time to go and do it!) A very good way of tackling the code is to write the 'shell' first and then code each module as you come to it. Thus you start by coding something similar to the following:

```
PROGRAM GSPatron;
{ written by ....}                        (put in comments as you go)
                                          (now code the main program)

PROCEDURE A1_Continue;
begin
end; {A1_Continue}

PROCEDURE M11_SysInitMenu;
{displays system initialisation menu}
begin
end; {M11_SysInitMenu}

PROCEDURE M121_AddPatron;
begin
end; {M121_AddPatron}

PROCEDURE M122_ChangePatron;
begin
end; {M122_ChangePatron}

PROCEDURE M123_DeletePatron;
begin
end; {M123_DeletePatron}

PROCEDURE M12_MaintenanceMenu;
begin
end; {MaintenanceMenu}

PROCEDURE M1_MainMenu;
begin
end; {M1_MainMenu}

PROCEDURE  O1_OpeningScreen;              (then insert these lines..)
begin
end; {O1_OpeningScreen}

{*************** Main Program *************}    (start coding here)
begin
  O1_OpeningScreen;
  M1_MainMenu
end.
```

If you do this you will find it very much easier to ensure that all the modules are physically located in the correct order, and you will be able to test each module as you write it without having 'undefined procedure' errors cropping up all the time. The compiler will not mind if your procedures don't acually do anything, so long as they are there!

You can now start by coding the menus and sub-menus, referring to your hierarchy chart.

Using subroutines and passing parameters

A subroutine is simply a general term for a procedure or function. Of course, you will already be using procedures if your program is written in a modular way, but even modular programs often contain chunks of unnecessarily repetitive code. Also, many students shy away from passing parameters to their procedures because they are not quite sure how to do so.

In fact, it really couldn't be simpler. For example, suppose you find that over and over again you need to display a phrase or sentence at a chosen location on the screen.

eg Display 'Main Menu' at screen coordinates (36,5).

This can be done with the statements

```
GoToXY (36,5);
write ('Main Menu');
```

What is needed is a procedure which will go to a particular location on the screen and display a given piece of text. Call the procedure A6_WriteXY. The **parameters** that need to be passed are the x and y coordinates, and the text to display. The procedure can then be called with the statement

```
A6_WriteXY (36,5,'Main Menu');
```

The procedure heading lists the parameters in the same order as they are given in the calling statement, stating what type of variable each one is. Note that the parameters must all be of predefined types; e.g. **string80** must be declared with a **type** statement in the block which contains this procedure.

eg   `PROCEDURE A6_WriteXY(x,y:integer; DisplayText:string80);`

You can look up the complete procedure in the listing given in Appendix F.

Pause: *Look up the subroutines A1_Continue, A7_GSTitle and A8_GetOneChar. Notice that the variable 'choice' in A8_GetOneChar is preceded by 'var'. This is because it will be changed within the procedure, and the new value passed back to the module which called it.*

Action: *Identify tasks in your own project that will be performed more than once, and code them as separate procedures or functions.*

Remember also to use local variables in your procedures wherever possible. You should keep the number of global variables to a minimum so that new procedures can be added without having to make any changes to the main program.

Functions

A **function** is a type of subroutine similar to a procedure but called and written in a slightly different way. It always returns a single value in the actual function name, so that the function type (real, integer etc) has to be specified. For example, A8_GetOneChar could be rewritten as a function called OneChar, with the following function header:

```
FUNCTION OneChar(x,y,integer;char1,char2:char):char;
begin
  repeat
    GoToXY(x,y);
    OneChar:=ReadKey;
    write (OneChar);
    OneChar := UpCase (OneChar); {UpCase is a standard Turbo Pascal function}
  until OneChar in [char1,char2]; { which converts a character to uppercase}
end; {OneChar}
```

The function would be called with a statement such as:- `Reply := OneChar (28,10,'Y','N');`

String handling routines

The Turbo Pascal data type **string** is a very useful data structure. It consists of one byte holding the length of the string, followed by a number of bytes each holding one character, up to a maximum length of 255. Thus string[80] contains 81 bytes; one length byte followed by 80 character bytes. There are several useful built-in functions for manipulating strings, which you can look up in a Pascal manual if you need them. They include:

concat   combines several strings into one string (you can alternatively use the + symbol)

copy   extracts a substring from a larger string

delete   removes characters from a string

insert   inserts a substring into another string

length   returns the number of characters currently held in a string variable

pos   tells you where in a string a character is

val   converts a string to an integer or real value if possible

Validating input using the Val function

Val is such a useful function it merits further discussion. As you probably know, a Pascal program will crash if you use a read or readln statement to read an integer or real variable and the user enters an invalid character such as an alphabetic character. The way round this is to read the input into a string variable and use the **val** routine to convert it to a number. If the input contains an invalid character, the variable **code** will be non-zero. (You must declare **code** as an integer variable - it can have any name you choose, of course).

```
eg   repeat
       gotoxy(65,6);
       readln(BatchTotalStr);
       A4_StripBlanks(BatchTotalStr);
       val(BatchTotalStr,BatchTotal,code);
     until code = 0;
```

One problem which you may encounter is that if the user enters any blank spaces after the number, the string is regarded by **val** as invalid, and **code** will return a non-zero value, even though the number looks perfectly all right on the screen. In order to avoid this happening, a procedure A4_StripBlanks removes any trailing blanks from the input. The code for this can be seen in the listing in Appendix F.

Reading into a string and padding with blanks

If you are reading input of variable length such as names and addresses from the screen, it is often useful to store the fields as fixed length fields so that when you subsequently use them in a printed report, they all line up correctly. The Pascal function **eoln** returns the value TRUE when <Enter> is pressed, and FALSE otherwise. You can accept characters one by one into a string variable TextString and pad out to **slength** with blanks as follows:

```
for counter:= 1 to slength do
   if eoln then TextString[counter] := ' '
    else read(TextString[counter]);
{endfor}
readln;
```

Because this procedure is needed so frequently in the specimen project, with strings of differing lengths being input, a procedure A3_ReadField has been used. TextString is defined as a string variable; however, the true desired length of the string (slength) is passed as a parameter, and byte 0 of the string is set equal to this length with the statement TextString[0] := chr(slength). So far as Pascal is concerned, this is then the length of the string.

Pause: *Take time to examine the procedures A3_ReadField, A4_StripBlanks, and A5_UpCaseStr. The latter procedure converts a whole string to uppercase; useful to free the user from having to use uppercase on a name which is being used as a key field, for example.*

Action: *Write some small programs to test out these procedures, or consider whether you need to use these techniques in your own project.*

Programming function keys

If you want to let the user use 'special' keys such as the function keys F1 to F10, Esc, cursor keys and so on, you will have to accept input character by character using the **readkey** function, which reads a character from the keyboard without echoing it on the screen. If the result is #0, then a special key has been pressed and you must call **readkey** again to capture the second part of the key code.

The following table lists some of the keys on the keyboard and the codes they return.

Key	1st code	2nd code
F1 - F10	0	59 - 68
Esc		27
Backspace		8
Tab		9
Enter		13

An extra complication arises because if the user presses backspace, expecting it to function in the normal way, it will not, unless you force it to do so. You have to write the backspace character, then a space, then another backspace, and remember to delete the character already entered from the input string; unless, of course, you are already at the beginning of the input string! Sounds complicated, and it is. A2_ReadString is a function which just checks for the function key F1 being pressed, and you can modify or extend this routine to suit your own purposes.

Pop-up windows

The Turbo Pascal **Window** command is useful for displaying a 'window' on screen to hold, for example, a menu or an error message. The problem with it is that it wipes out the portion of the screen underneath, so that you cannot make the text that was underneath the window reappear. It is therefore not powerful enough to create true pop-up windows.

To do this, you need to save the contents of the screen before you open the window and then restore the screen when you close it. In order to understand exactly how to do this, you will have to consult a Pascal manual (see reference at the end of this chapter). However, if you just want a workable routine to use in your own project, try looking at B1_WindowDisplay and its associated subroutines (all prefixed with B_). A brief explanation of these routines is given below.

> **B4_SetUpWindows** {this calls **B2_VidSeg** which locates the video display memory for either a colour or monochrome screen. It then opens up to *maxwin* logical screens}

> **B5_OpenWindow** {This opens a window of the desired size, using coordinates for top left and bottom right passed as parameters to B11_WindowDisplay. It then uses **B3_FastBox** to draw a double box around the window}

> Next, an appropriate routine is called depending on which particular window display is wanted. These are

> > **B11_WindowNumber1** {displays help message for entering date in correct format, called from M13_EntrySubs}

> > **B12_WindowNumber2** {displays a warning message if the date on the subs file does not match the current year entered by user, called from M124_OpenSubsFile}

> > **B13_WindowNumber3** {displays a help screen to enter current year in correct format, called from O1_GetCurrentYear}

> **B6_CloseWindow** {closes the window and restores the screen 'underneath'}

Checking for the presence of a file on disk

As far as humanly possible, you want to ensure that your program will not crash, even if the user forgets to put the data disk in the drive, or uses a different computer which uses drive b: instead of a:, or loads the wrong disk in the drive. All these eventualities can be catered for by turning off the automatic error-checking associated with all input-output operations, and doing the checking within the program. This automatic checking can be turned off and on using the {$I-} and {$I+} compiler directives. When I/O checking is off, an I/O error does not cause the program to halt. To check the result of an I/O operation, you must instead call the standard function IOResult. This returns a code depending on the result of the I/O operation, with 0 being returned if the operation is successful. You should remember to turn automatic error checking back on after successfully opening a file.

Turn to M111_InitialisePatronsFile to see this technique being used.

Using graphics

Turbo Pascal has a powerful graphics capability which you may wish to use, even if only to create a fancy opening screen. Remember to include the 'uses graph' clause at the top of the program, and you will have to know where the graphics driver is on your system. All the routines you need are included in a directory named 'bgi' and you may find it convenient to copy the contents of this directory onto your floppy disk (in a directory called 'bgi') for use during program development. The code needed to initialise the graphics driver is given in O1_OpeningScreen.

In graphics mode you are working in pixels, not screen coordinates. In CGA's low resolution mode, for example, the screen has 320 by 200 pixels, while a VGA screen has 640 by 480 pixels. If you want to draw something in the lower righthand corner of the screen, therefore, you need to know how many pixels your particular screen has. Turbo Pascal provides the answer with two GRAPH unit functions called GetMaxX and GetMaxY, which return the maximum x and y coordinates of the screen.

A number of routines are available for outputting text in various fonts and styles. You need to look in the Turbo Pascal manual to see what is available, or try running the routine O1_OpeningScreen to get an idea of what you can do.

A word of caution; do not expend too much time and energy on wonderful opening screens when you should be concentrating on getting the project to work satisfactorily. This is the 'icing on the cake' that can be quickly done when everything else is finished, and **not** a way to postpone the problem of getting a file update module to work!

Binary tree data structure

The master file in the specimen project is organised as a binary tree, and the modules to create and maintain this file are explained below.

1.   File Initialisation (M111_InitialisePatronsFile)

The first record on the file (record 0) is used as a control record to point to the next free space on the tree. Initialisation, therefore, sets the pointer to 1 (record 1 being the first empty data record) and writes 100 empty records to the file. (This number will be dynamically increased as required as more patrons are added.)

2.   Adding a new patron (M121_AddPatron)

This module first accepts the name of the patron, and looks it up on the file using a tree search (C2_FindPatron). If the name is not found, the record is written to the next free space on the file (obtained from the control record), pointers are adjusted accordingly, and the control record updated and rewritten. Each patrons record includes a left pointer and a right pointer as shown below.

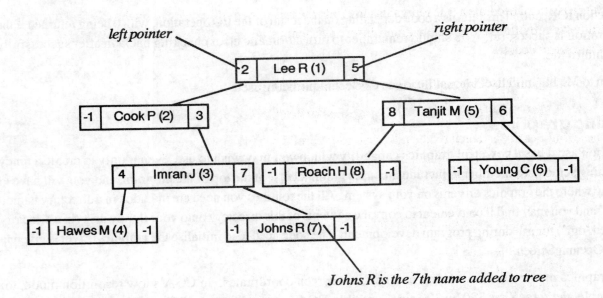

Johns R is the 7th name added to tree

Thus, for example, to find Johns R, records 1 (Lee), 2 (Cook), 3 (Imran) and 7(Johns) are read, following the appropriate pointers.

The basic algorithm for C2_FindPatron is given below. The pointer to the root is set each time the patrons file is opened; it will be -1 if the control record shows the next free record on the file is 1 (ie no records on file) or 1 if the next free record has any other value. (see the last two lines of M125_OpenPatronsFile)

```
p := PointerToRoot
if p = -1 then Present := false        {because the tree is empty}
else
  Present := True                      {until proved otherwise}
  read record(p)                       {read the root}
  while record(p).name <> required name and Present = True
    if record(p).left = -1 and record(p).right = -1
    then Present := False              {end of tree branch}
    else                              {keep searching}
      if record(p).name > required name
      then p:= record(p).left
      else  p:= record(p).right

    if p = -1 then Present := False    {we're at a leaf, nowhere to go}
    else read record(p)

  endwhile
```

3.   Changing a patron (M122_ChangePatron)

A similar procedure to Add is followed, with the patron being looked up and details displayed if present so that the user can make required changes.

4.   Deleting a patron (M123_DeletePatron)

The patrons record is not physically removed from the file, since this would mean many pointers would have to be reset. A 'delete flag' is set to 'Y' if the patron is deleted, and the record left in place. Since so few patrons are deleted each year (4 or 5) this method is quite satisfactory. If the number of deletions warranted it, it would be quite easy to incorporate a 'file reorganisation' into the end-of-year routine, reading the existing file serially, omitting records flagged as deleted, and inserting them into a new file using a procedure similar to the AddPatrons procedure.

5.   Printing and displaying information in sequence of patron's name

(M141_Mailing_Labels, M142_PatronsForProg, M143_PatronsDetails, M144_SubsByPatron)

All these routines depend on the 'tree traversal' routine, and two variations are used, both essentially the same algorithm, with D8_ScreenTraverse being used to display information on screen, and D8_PrintTraverse calling an appropriate module depending on which printout is required. The recursive tree traversal algorithm is shown below:

```
procedure Traverse (p:integer);
if  p<> -1 then
  read record(p)
  Traverse (record(p).left)
  read record(p)
  call required print routine to print a line
  Traverse (record(p).right)
endif
```

The procedure is called with the statement Traverse (PointerToRoot).

Adding records to the end of a serial file

The file (Subs.dat) is basically a serial file, with records being added to the end of it in no particular sequence. This is achieved using the random access verb 'Seek' provided in Turbo Pascal to get to any desired position in the file. Initially, the file can be set up with one empty subs record. When the file is subsequently opened, the file pointer is set using

```
SubsFilePtr := FileSize(SubsFile) -1;
```

FileSize is a library function in Turbo Pascal returning a pointer to the end of the file.

A record can then be written to the end of the file with the statements

```
seek (SubsFile,SubsFilePtr);

write(SubsFile,SubsRec);
```

Additional records can be written without using 'seek'; the pointer is automatically incremented after each 'write' statement.

Debugging your program

First of all, some general tips:

- always save your program before you run it. Then, if it causes the machine to hang up and you have to reboot, at least you haven't lost your latest changes. In Turbo Pascal, all you have to do to save is press F2.

- do not be tempted to make too many changes at once. Make a change, save it and test it before you put in the next change. This requires patience but it is a case of 'more haste, less speed'.

- it is usually much easier to debug from a printed listing than from the screen, because you can see more of the program laid out in front of you. It also allows you to really look at the code instead of guessing at the problem and making random changes in the hope that they will make the problem go away.

and one common source of error:

- many puzzling errors such as 'END expected' are often caused because somewhere in the program you have used the wrong type of parenthesis to close a comment. Check all your comments. Of course you may really have a missing end statement, but if you have followed good advice and commented every End statement this should be easy to find.

Using Turbo Pascal's editing and debugging tools

Turbo Pascal has some very useful editing and debugging tools and it will save you hours of effort if you learn to use them properly. Being able to quickly move around your program, go straight to a particular procedure in a long listing, search for and replace all occurrences of particular variable or procedure names, move blocks of code around and perform many more such functions are invaluable aids in program development.

For debugging, depending on the version you are using, choose the Debug, Watches (version 6.0) or Break/watch (version 5.5) menu, and Add Watch to examine the value of a variable as the program executes. You can step through the program one instruction at a time by pressing the function key F7, or position the cursor at a particular point and press F4 to execute up to that point, and then step through from that point using F7. You will find you will quickly be able to see exactly why your program is not performing as expected when you can follow each line as it is executed and watch the values of relevant variables change.

Do try to beg, borrow or buy a manual and learn to use these features and many more for quick and easy editing and debugging. A quick reference to 'hot keys' and editing keys used in Turbo Pascal 6.0 is given in Appendix I at the end of this text.

Quick Answer Questions

1. How do you get straight to the top or bottom of your program on screen?

2. How do you quickly locate a routine, say M141_MailingLabels?

3. How do you delete a line?

4. How do you mark and move a block of code?

QAQ Answers

1.   Use Ctrl-PgUp and Ctrl-PgDn.

2.   In version 6.0, go to the top of the listing with Ctrl-PgUp, and then use the Search menu FIND option. Enter the name of the procedure you wish to find.

3.   Ctrl-Y deletes a line.

4.   In version 6.0, put the cursor at the start of the block you wish to move. Then keep one finger on the shift key and press the down arrow (or right arrow) until the block is highlighted. Press Shift-Delete to Cut, and then move the cursor to where you want to insert the block. Press Shift-Insert.

      You can remove the highlight by pressing Ctrl K and then H.

These questions are only designed to point out that there are many, many useful editing and debugging facilities available and you should spend time at the beginning of your project getting to know them well.

Summary

This chapter has covered:

- *some general points to aid in the development of a program or suite of programs*

- *various techniques for the Turbo Pascal programmer, including useful string handling routines, function keys, pop-up windows, compiler directives and graphics*

- *tips on editing and debugging in Turbo Pascal*

Further reading

1.   *Turbo Pascal 6 - The Complete Reference* by Stephen O'Brien (Borland Osborne / McGraw Hill 1991, £23.95)

2.   *Pascal Programming* by B.J.Holmes (DPP 1990, £10.95)

Chapter 6 - Testing

Objectives

By the end of this chapter you will have learned

- the objectives of testing
- the difference between 'black box' and 'white box' testing
- the steps involved in software testing
- how to draw up a test plan
- how to present the results of testing

Testing objectives

Your project will have to include a section on testing: what strategy you adopted, the test data, the test plan, how it was carried out and what the results were. But what is the **purpose** of testing? It may seem obvious that it is to prove that the system works correctly.

In fact, you will formulate a much better test plan if you turn this idea on its head and consider the following rules proposed by Glen Myers in his book 'The Art of Software Testing'.

1. **Testing is a process of executing a program with the intent of finding an error.**

2. **A good test case is one that has a high probability of finding an as yet undiscovered error.**

3. **A successful test is one that uncovers an as yet undiscovered error.**

In other words, it is not sufficient to think up a few tests which you are fairly sure will not make your program crash or give a wrong result; you must use tests and test data which have been carefully thought out to test all parts of the program. How many times does a lecturer spend only a few minutes testing a project before it does something unexpected, to baffled cries of 'It's never done that before...' from the crestfallen student! This should never happen with a properly tested system.

Black box and white box testing

Black box testing involves performing tests without any knowledge of how the system actually works; its purpose is to test that the program performs all the functions that were originally specified, that all the input is correctly accepted, output correctly produced, and files correctly updated. It relates to the whole system and does not require a technical understanding of the system.

White box testing is carried out on each module of the program, with a knowledge of how the program works and what possible paths may be taken under different circumstances, so that all the logic of the program can be tested.

Quick Answer Questions

1. Who are the best people to carry out black box and white box testing?

2. If thorough white box testing is carried out, is black box testing really necessary?

QAQ Answers

1. The users are the obvious people to carry out black box testing, because they know exactly what they expect the system to do, and will have an insight into the sorts of errors and exceptions that the program should deal with. They will also be able to spot functions which have been omitted; for example, perhaps, owing to an oversight, a particular report has been left out or does not contain exactly the required information.

   The programmer or a knowledgeable colleague are the best people to carry out white box testing.

2. As mentioned above, black box testing will discover errors of omission; white box testing will only test what's there! The major problem with white box testing is that it is virtually impossible for it to be totally exhaustive: even a small program with only a few loops and conditions may have literally millions of possible routes through it. A combination of both types of testing is the best compromise.

```
21-6-1992               GILBERT AND SULLIVAN SOCIETY
         Page 1
                 1992  Subscriptions in Order of Entry

                    1@    F;
         OWMA:\Patrons.datA:\subs.data:subs.dat  1@fihI @uki
F~       1]JU    e1@    F;
         OWMA:\Patrons.dat  -16936800835000000000000.00
                   *;*u;          OWMA:\Patrons.datA:\subs
.data:subs  ;Fri#!;*
~*u
F;       F~i!;*
~*;*u;              OWMA:\Patrons.datA:\subs.data:su
bs.daty'=£    JW*A:\Subs.a:\   0.00
                   Bs

F+F      OWMA:\   *ui     F×kGF×
i
P
F+F;;Bs

F+F      OWMA:\Patrons.dat  -2018.19
                   Fzk

iD>;*u5Hv       GBX              OWMA:\Patrons.datA     0.
00
i;F×r           OWMA:\Patrons.datA  W
F;D~  -1216.19
              Kf    OWMA:\Patrons.datA:\subs.data:subs.daty'=£
```

Oh no! It's never done that before .....

Steps in software testing

1. Module testing

As you complete each module of your program, it needs to be thoroughly tested. Even if you can't test every combination of paths, you can test the important paths, the extreme cases, valid and invalid data, and so on. For the purposes of your project, you should aim to demonstrate that you have tested systematically and that your testing is **reasonably** exhaustive. A maximum of 20 to 30 pages of actual test runs which cover major processes and show a variety of test data (ie extreme, correct, incorrect) is quite sufficient.

A module such as M121_AddPatron, which checks for the existence of a patron already on the master file and accepts details of a new patron, is an example of a module which is extremely hard to test comprehensively. Different paths will be followed depending on the previous patron entered, whether or not this is the first patron on the file, whether or not the user changes their mind about adding the patron to the file having entered the details, whether they edit any fields before adding to the file, and so on.

You may start by using fairly random tests on such a module, but for the final test plan it is essential to write down on a piece of paper all the different test cases you need to test the various paths, carry out the tests systematically and have some way of verifying the results. You may already have a module which displays the contents of a file, or you may have to write one specially for test purposes.

Remember to test

- all computations in the module

- correct termination of all loops

- valid and invalid input data

- 'exception' data which will make the module follow a different execution path.

2. System testing

When all the modules have been written and the whole system put together, system testing can begin. Many of the tests may be the same ones which were performed to test individual modules. It is surprising, however, how often a module which seemed to be working perfectly at one stage goes wrong when it is integrated into the whole program.

At this stage, you should ideally test your system with a realistic volume of data. If the system is designed to hold details of 5000 stock items, and you have never tested it with more than 8, there is no way of knowing how it will perform after installation unless you test it. Obviously, you will not have the time to enter 5000 different records, and the AEB recommendation is to enter about 50 records as a sufficient demonstration of a working system's ability to handle larger volumes of data.

Drawing up a test plan

The test plan will form part of the Design documentation. To quote the AEB A Level Computing guidelines, it needs to be 'comprehensive without being tedious'. This is not easy to achieve, since really comprehensive testing of a substantial project could result in a fairly massive document.

For the module testing, draw up a test plan of preferably no more than two or three pages which shows that you have chosen your test data carefully, tested each module, and know what the results ought to be. The test plan for the first sample project can be seen at the end of the Design section in Part 2. The headings used are

Test no.	Module being tested	Purpose of test	Test data used	Expected result

You may well have to amend or add to your initial test plan as the program develops, but you will find it very helpful to have a written plan at all stages, even if you keep adjusting it.

Similarly, if you design your system tests **before** you start coding, you will be forced to think about how this phase will be carried out, what will have to be done to make system testing possible, and how to ensure that it will be successful. The earlier you can foresee any problems, the easier they will be to solve.

Presenting the test results

Your test results should be presented in an Appendix, and cross-referenced to your test plan. They will normally take the form of test runs, screen dumps and file dumps. You may need to explain exactly what data was input and use a highlighter pen or other means to show that files have been correctly updated. Be selective, and consider it a challenge to make it as easy as possible for a reader to confirm that test results were as expected. As a general rule, include the absolute minimum essential to get the point across.

You should aim for authenticity rather than neatness in your presentation of test results. Do not wordprocess your test output; the examiner cannot be sure that it is genuine, so hand in the original test runs, annotated and cross-referenced by hand. Likewise, there is little merit in presenting a table of tests performed with expected and actual results unless this is backed up with actual hardcopy output; however good your test data and test plan, you will not score more than half marks.

Summary

This chapter has covered

- *the types of testing you should carry out*

- *how to draw up a test plan*

- *how to present your results*

Further reading

1. *The Art of Software Testing* by G.Myers (Wiley, 1979)

2. *Software Engineering: A Practitioner's Approach* by Roger S.Pressman ((McGraw-Hill, 1982)

3. *The complete Guide to Software Testing* by William Hetzel (Collins)

Chapter 7 - The report

Objectives

By the end of this chapter you will have learned how to document your project.

It should include

- a title page
- a table of contents
- sections on:

    analysis

    design

    testing

    systems maintenance

- a user manual
- an appraisal of the project
- appendices showing for example

    input documents

    screen and report layouts

    file structures

    annotated program listings

    test runs

Introduction

The report that you hand in at the end of your project contains all the evidence of the work you have done over the past few months. No matter how careful your analysis, how appropriate the design, how clever the programming and how thorough the testing; if the written evidence is not there to prove it, you will not achieve a good mark.

It will take longer than you expect to complete the documentation. It will pay you to write the documentation in parallel with the other stages of the project and not leave it all to the end. Then, when you have finished the programming and testing, you will be able to go through it all, proof reading, adding a table of contents, page numbers, and appendices.

Should the documentation be wordprocessed?

The short answer is YES. It should also be thoroughly spellchecked, both using the spellchecking facility provided by the word processor, and by reading it through slowly and carefully. Remember that a spellchecker won't find misspellings like 'the' instead of 'then', or even 'curser' instead of 'cursor', as the manuals of one software firm will testify! If possible, allow yourself time to discover how to make text bold and italic, to use tabs properly, and to insert a page break where you need one. This document must do justice to the effort you have so far put into your project; it is all that the examiner will see, and even if you feel you have perhaps not achieved as much as you could have so far, a well-presented report will help.

How long should the documentation be?

Basically, it will have to be as many pages as it takes to do the job properly. The AEB guidelines suggest that project reports 'should not exceed 20 pages of A4 paper' with listings and test runs being added as appendices. You may find that you can comfortably fit your documentation into 20 pages of A4, (which can be interpreted as 40 sides) but if not, you can for example have the user manual as a separate document.

The guideline of 20 pages is designed to give you an idea of the size and scope of project that is expected at this level. You must be selective in what you include; for example, you do not need to include **all** your screen layout charts and report layout charts, just a couple of the more complex ones. Avoid duplicating information; if you have included a system chart in the Design section, for example, there is no need to reproduce it in the Systems Maintenance section. Just refer the reader to the relevant page.

Putting it all together

Your project documentation should be neatly bound in such a manner that it can be read without a major unbinding job, for example to look at a program listing on continuous stationery. A ring binder is too large and heavy to be conveniently posted, so investigate the shelves of W.H.Smith or any stationery shop to find something suitable.

The title page

The title page should include the title of the project, your name and centre, school or college. It could also include the date you submitted the project and your candidate number, if appropriate.

Table of contents

This is a must. Include in it the sections and numbered subsections, together with page numbers which will have to be added when the project is all put together. Every page in your project should be numbered for easy reference; you can add page numbers by hand at the end.

Analysis

A suggested framework for the Analysis section is given at the end of Chapter 2. Remember to include a write up of preparation for interview (such as a list of questions), or questionnaires with a summary of responses. The notes of any interviews that you have had with a user should also be written up and included here. Your own observations of the current system, and deductions, are worth including also. If your analysis included reading about other similar systems, or trying out other similar software packages, for example, then that can be written up here.

Design

Headings for the design section are given at the beginning of Chapter 3. Look carefully at these and make sure you have covered all aspects of the design in your documentation. Your test strategy and test data, with reasons for your choice, should be included in this section. You must aim to show that you have worked out what tests need to be performed and what results you expect. If you number the tests, it will make it easier to cross reference them to the actual test runs.

Testing

Testing is a vitally important part of the project. The test data and test plan should have already been documented in the Design section, but you shoud include a separate section called 'Testing' which will contain an analysis of the test plan to show that it does test all parts of the system. Then, in the Systems Maintenance section, you can refer to any unusual results or unsolved problems.

Test runs may be included in an appendix. The test runs should relate clearly to the test plan, and be presented in such a way that the reader can see at once what a specific page of output is designed to show. Devising appropriate tests, organising and cross-referencing screen dumps and printed output can take a great deal of time and ingenuity. There is no point including several pages of output with no explanation of what test it relates to or how the output proves that a certain section of the progam is working correctly. Make handwritten annotations on the output and use highlighter pen to show significant results.

It is not a good idea to import your test output into a wordprocessed document because there is no way for the examiner to tell if it is genuine or if it has been 'cooked'! For some projects you may need to send photographic evidence, or a tape or video film to show that the project works properly.

There is a great temptation to skimp on this section of the project; the feeling is 'Right! I've finished the programming and I'm pretty sure it all works. Here's a disk - you try it...'. Unfortunately the devising and implementation of the test plan is your job, not the examiner's!

System maintenance

This section is aimed at a programmer who would be maintaining or enhancing the system. It needs to include the following:

1. Schematic diagrams summarising how modules relate to each other (or a reference to diagrams already included in the design section).

2a. Where a program or suite of programs has been written, for each module in the system:

- a brief description
- module name
- modules called up
- calling modules

- variables list - with type, purpose, format and example content
- high level pseudocode or flowchart

2b. Where a package has been used:

- a brief description of each module in the system
- a summary of the capabilities of the package
- an explanation of the features you have used, and a description of exactly how you tailored the package to suit the user's requirements.

3. Limitations of the system.

4. Discussion of unresolved problems or odd test results.

5. Special operational details.

6a. You will also be awarded marks in this section for program code, if your project has involved writing a program. The listing should be a genuine printout rather than a wordprocessed document, and should be clearly annotated by hand wherever this helps to explain what is happening. It needs to be made easily understandable, for example by:

- using meaningful variable names
- stating the purpose of each variable unless it is self-explanatory
- using comments to state the purpose of each procedure
- using comments where necessary to explain the logic of a particular section
- grouping procedures in a logical order so that it is easy to find your way around a long program
- using indentation to clarify the extent of loops and condition statements
- using blank lines between procedures to separate them.

6b. If you have used a package which has generated code automatically, this code may be listed and included in an Appendix. Even though you have not written the code yourself, you should examine the modules carefully and make hand-written annotations on them where possible; for example to describe the purpose of each module generated. The inclusion of the code at least provides evidence that you did the work required to generate it!

In addition, with package-generated code, a disk directory should be included and related to the module hierarchy chart and the menu tree (found in the Design section). File extensions should be shown to be understood, as well as the amount of disk space required. You may also be able to show which files are needed for running the system and which would be used when modifying the system.

User manual

This section is aimed entirely at a non-technical user and should use ordinary English rather than 'computer-speak'. For example, do not say 'Boot up the system' when 'Switch on the computer' will achieve the same result.

Presentation is all-important here. Use whatever facilities your wordprocessor has to enhance the appearance of the document, spellcheck it carefully and read it through to make sure it flows well and makes sense. It should be a 'stand-alone' document and could even be bound separately from the rest of the project.

Your user manual should include:

- a table of contents
- an introduction, stating what the system is about and who it is for
- examples of actual screen displays such as menus, data input screens and ouput screens
- samples of printed output
- an explanation of what each option on a menu does
- any special instructions on how to input data; for example the format of a date field, or the range of accepted values in an amount field
- an explanation of any manual procedures such as batching or recording data manually
- error messages that may be displayed and what to do in that event
- error recovery procedures; for example what to do if you realise you have made a wrong data entry, or the power goes off in the middle of an update
- perhaps a hotline help number

If you have used a package, explain how to use the system you have created, rather than explaining how to use the software package in general terms.

Appraisal

Finally, your documentation should include a critical appraisal of the completed project. If the project has been written for a real user, it is a good idea to include the user's comments in this section, perhaps in the form of a letter written on official headed paper and signed by the user. If any suggestions have been made for amendment or improvement, include these as well, whether or not you have managed to incorporate the suggestions. Add your own suggestions for improvement and possibilities for future development.

Be honest about the shortcomings of the project; if it is not complete, maybe this is because it was over-ambitious and you should say so. You will not, however, score many marks for criticising the hardware, software, staff or lack of time. One of the skills to be learned in writing a project is to finish it on time in spite of all the difficulties you may encounter!

Summary

This chapter has covered the documentation of a computer project. You should now look at the documentation of the specimen projects in Parts 2 and 3 for an illustration of the points made.

PART 2

Specimen Project 1

Part 2 shows the report and appendices for the first specimen project,

Gilbert and Sullivan Society Patrons List

Gilbert and Sullivan Society
Patrons List

Submitted as an A-Level computing Project
by A. Student
Any College
April 199-

Gilbert and Sullivan Society Patrons List

Table of Contents

Section 1 - Analysis

1. Introduction

Number your sections and subsections

1.1 Background to the project

An introductory paragraph to set the scene is essential. It gets the reader involved, and doesn't leave him or her wondering what the project is about.

The local Gilbert and Sullivan Society is a thriving amateur Operatic Society with about 75 singing members and a number of patrons. The patrons are supporters of the Society - perhaps ex-members, or people interested in Gilbert and Sullivan operas - who make an annual donation of a minimum of £5.00 towards the Society's costs, the main expense being about £12,000 for an annual production at the local theatre.

In return for their support, all patrons are sent information about the Society's activities and receive a Priority Booking form so that they have the first choice of seats for the Autumn production. Also, their names appear in the programme as Patrons.

The Society maintains a list of the Patrons in alphabetical order of surname, and keeps a record of what each patron has donated each year.

1.2 Initial user request

If you have been given a reasonably clearly stated set of requirements, it is a good idea to copy them here

The Patrons Secretary, Mrs Joan Emsworth, is responsible for keeping all the records of patrons and their subscriptions (i.e. donations), and she suggested that it might be feasible to computerise this application. After an initial discussion the main requirements appeared to be as follows:-

A database of patrons is to be maintained in alphabetical order with the facility to add, change and delete records easily.

When a Patron makes a donation, this is to be recorded. A record is to be kept of previous donations.

Various printed reports are required:

i.   A list of patrons' names in alphabetical order for insertion into the programme for the Society's annual production of a Gilbert and Sullivan opera.

ii.   The donation made by each patron in the previous financial year, running from April 1 to March 31. This report should include a total of all donations at the bottom of the report as the total figure is required for the annual statement of accounts.

iii. A list of names and addresses, printed 'three up' on address label stationery.

2. The Investigation

2.1 The current system

Further investigation of the current system was made through an interview with the Patrons Secretary. A list of questions which was prepared prior to the interview, and a transcript of the interview is given below.

2.2 Questions to ask the Patrons Secretary

a.   How many patrons are there?

b.   etc

.....

2.3 Transcript of the interview

(Here you should include the questions from page 1 - 13, and the interview notes from pages 1 - 14 and 1 - 15, in the project write-up. To avoid repetition they have been omitted in this book).

2.4 Summary

i.   There are about 100 patrons, several of whom have been patrons for many years. Each year, about four or five new patrons are recruited and approximately the same number leave.

ii.   The data on the patrons is currently held on a card index file in alphabetical order of surname. Information held on each patron is:

- name, (surname first, followed by initials)

- name as it appears on the programme **or** 'wishes to remain anonymous'

- a note of the year as soon as the subscription is paid.

Two specimen card index records are shown in Appendix A, page 2 - 44. An extract from the 1991 programme from 'The Mikado' is shown on the same page. The Patrons Secretary explained that some patrons do not wish to have their name in the programme, and therefore a note of this has to be made on their card.

iii.   A reminder to pay subscriptions (ie donations) is sent out in February each year, together with a newsletter about the Society's activities (see Appendix A, page 2 - 45). Currently, someone else in the Society who has access to a wordprocessor has a computerised list of patrons' names and addresses, and prints out a complete set of mailing labels whenever required. Patrons are generally mailed four times each year; in addition to the February letter and/or reminder, they receive notice of the Annual General Meeting in April, a Priority Booking form in June, and a newsletter in December or January.

iv.   Patrons who do not pay the subscription are kept on file for a couple of years. They receive the mailings for the new financial year, and a reminder in the following February. If they do not pay for two years, they do not receive any

The following notes appear in the left margin alongside the text:

Marks will be awarded for your investigative skills, so you should show how you prepared for the interview and include your notes from the interview.

A summary of the findings is optional.

Data - how much? How often does it change?

What data is held?

Show copies of **actual** documents from the current system if possible

What processing is performed?

more mail and cease to be patrons.

v.   When a cheque is received by the Patrons Secretary, she notes the amount in a cash book which has duplicate (carbon copy) pages. The year (eg '92') is also noted on the card of the patron making the payment. At a convenient time, the amounts for a number of cheques are added up, the total entered in the book and the duplicate page torn out and given to the Treasurer, along with the cheques.

vi.   The programme for the annual production, which contains the list of patrons' names, is typeset using PageMaker software by another member of the Society. A list of changes to last year's patrons list is supplied by the Patrons Secretary.

vii.   The current Patrons Secretary, Mrs Emsworth, is shortly to give up the position and a new Patrons Secretary who owns an IBM PC is to take over the job.

2.5   Problems with the current system

1.   The main problem with the current system is that it is extremely time consuming, partly because of the duplication of effort involved. For example:

> When a patron changes address, or a new patron joins or one leaves, the card index file has to be changed, **and** the person doing the mailing labels has to be informed and make changes to her database of names and addresses. This could also lead to inconsistencies if the Patrons Secretary forgot to inform her assistant of the changes.

Some of this information is gleaned from the interview, but some can be deduced by thinking about the way things are done now.

> When a subscription is paid, the entry is made in the cash book **and** the card index file has to be updated.

2.   The whole card file has to be manually gone through to see who has not paid a subscription for two years, so that they can be removed from the mailing list.

3.   A note of any insertions to and deletions from the file has to be kept so that it can be given to the person who typesets the programme. These amendments are often handed over on scraps of paper during rehearsals and are sometimes mislaid or left in a pocket and put through the laundry...

3.   Requirements of the new system

3.1   General objectives

Objectives should be related to output.

The main objective of the new system is to save time for the Patrons Secretary. An additional benefit could be that the new system will be more accurate because it will involve less duplicated data entry.

3.2   Specific objectives

i.   In order to achieve the most efficient system possible, a database of some kind will be maintained holding information about each patron.

ii   All duplication of data entry should be eliminated. For example, when a patron pays a subscription this should be entered once only, and posted to the patrons file.

iii   Mailing labels will be printed and will no longer require a separate file of names and addresses to be maintained.

iv.   All manual sorting and searching of the database should be eliminated. A report will be produced of patrons who have allowed payments to lapse, making it much easier to keep track of people who are no longer subscribing to the Society. These patrons can then easily be deleted from the patrons file.

v.   The list of patrons' names for the programme will be output to a disk file for importing directly into PageMaker. Again, this will eliminate duplication of effort and possible transcription errors.

4.   Constraints and limitations

4.1   Hardware

The system must operate on a PC with hard disk, 3 ½" floppy drive and dot matrix printer, since that is the equipment owned by the new Patrons Secretary.

4.2   Software

The following software is available on the user's machine: SuperDB, Microsoft Works.

4.3   Cost

The system is not expected to incur any costs to the Society.

4.4   Timescale

Ideally, the system should be implemented by the end of February 1993, when the new Patrons Secretary takes over. This also coincides with the payment of the annual subscriptions.

5.   Recommendations

Notice that it is not specified WHAT software will be used - this is left to the Design stage.

It is proposed to install a new computerised system for the Patrons list, to replace the current manual system. The software will operate on the user's current equipment, and will be tested and installed by February 28, 1993.

6.   Summary - Data flow diagram

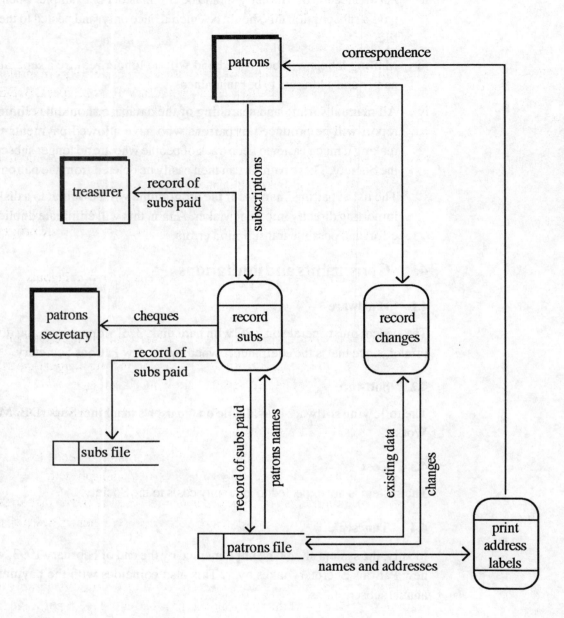

Section 2 - Design

1. Consideration of possible solutions

1.1 Using a database package

Since this is essentially a database application, one possible way of implementing the system is to use a database package such as dBase III+ or Super DB. DBase III+ has to be ruled out because it is not available within the College and is not one of the packages owned by the new Patrons Secretary.

Super DB would, however, be a possibility. It would have the following advantages:

- easy creation and maintenance of the patrons file
- ability to link a Subscriptions file to the Patrons file and to post subscriptions from one file to the other, with very little programming effort involved
- fast creation of customised input screens and report layouts
- the facility to print mailing labels.

1.2 Using a programming language to create a tailor-made system

Pascal is the only practical alternative here since it is the only language available for development of the system. It offers the following advantages:

- good random access file handling capabilities which will enable fast access to any information on the patrons file
- can send patrons names for theatre programme directly to a text file for importing into PageMaker, a desktop publishing system
- the program can be compiled and object code stored on disk so that it can be run on any PC without having to have any other software available.

2. Proposed solution

Although implementation using Super DB would require considerably less programming effort, I feel that the finished product will have a more professional appearance if it is written in Pascal, and will be easier to use. Turbo Pascal has good facilities for creating a customised user interface with pop-up windows for help messages and error messages, and I intend to exploit these capabilities.

An additional reason for choosing Pascal is that I am more familiar with it and will be better able to exploit its capabilities than would be possible in SuperDB, given the limited amount of time available for learning to use new software.

3. Output

Five different types of report are required for this system.

3.1 Mailing labels

Mailing labels will need to be produced for all patrons. The user will be given a choice of which set of labels to produce. Label stationery will be loaded into the printer and three 'dummy' labels printed to ensure that it is properly aligned, the operation being repeated until the user indicates that printing can proceed.

3.2 List of patrons for programme

This may be **either** a printed listing **or** a list of names sent as a text file to a specified disk, for importing directly into PageMaker. The user will be asked to specify which type of output she requires.

3.3 List of patrons' details

Output of patrons details such as name, address, subs paid, etc may be to **either** the screen **or** the printer. The user will be asked to specify which name to start at and if a printed list is requested, which name to stop at. If screen output is requested, the names will be displayed one at a time and the user can quit at any time.

3.4 Subscriptions (sequenced by patron)

This list will be printed from the patrons file, and will list all the subscriptions paid for the past three years. Patrons who have not paid a subscription for the last two years will have 5 asterisks printed next to their name for easy identification. The patrons secretary may then choose to delete these people from the patrons file.

3.5 Subscriptions in order of entry

This is a listing of all the subscriptions that have been paid during the year. It will have a total of all subs at the end and can be used in the preparation of the annual accounts.

A couple of sample print layouts is sufficient if space is limited.

Two sample report layouts are shown in Appendix D, pages 2 - 50 and 2 - 51.

4. Analysis of data requirements

A discussion of the data requirements similar to that found on page 1-25, 1-26 should be included in the report, to show that you have given careful thought to the chosen structure. (It has been omitted here to avoid repetition).

The following information needs to be held for each patron:

Name (surname followed by initials)   (eg JONES G)
Name as it appears in the theatre programme   (eg Gerald and Mary Jones)
Address (3 lines + postcode)
Year they became a patron
Subscription for current year, last year and the year before

The exact format of each data item is shown on the two file structure charts shown in Appendix B, pages 2-46 and 2-47.

5. Data validation

The following validation checks will be made on input data:

1. When adding a new patron, the patrons file will be looked up to see whether the patron is already on file, in which case an error message is displayed. This ensures that there will be no duplicate records on file.

2. When changing or deleting a patron, an error message will be displayed if the patron is not on file.

3. The field for 'Year they became a patron' will be checked as being a numeric field greater than 1951 and less than or equal the current year. This will help to ensure that the data is entered accurately, since no one has been a patron for more than 40 years.

4. When subscriptions are entered, the patron's name will be looked up from the patrons file to see that it exists. This will help to ensure that all subs are correctly posted to the right patron, since the most likely error is a spelling or punctuation mistake in the data entry rather than the entry of someone else's name.

All the validation checks to be carried out on the input data are also shown on the file structure charts in Appendix B, pages 2 - 46 and 2 - 47.

6. User interface design

There are three different types of user input to be considered.

6.1 Menu design

The user will have to make choices from various menus in the system for each function that they wish to perform, such as entering subscriptions, making changes to the patrons' details, or printing out reports and mailing labels. The following general rules will be applied.

- All menus within the system will have the same heading at the top of the screen, 'GILBERT AND SULLIVAN SOCIETY Patrons List' to identify the system.

- Each menu will have an individual heading which uniquely identifies it, such as 'Main Menu', 'Maintenance of Patrons File' and so on.

- Where a menu leads to a submenu, the heading of the submenu will show the choice that was made on the previous menu, so that the user will always have a clear idea of what option is currently operative. For example, if the user selects 'Maintenance of Patrons File' from the main menu, the next menu will be headed 'Maintenance of Patrons File'.

- All options on each menu will be numbered 1, 2, 3 etc except for Q for Quit being offered as the last option on each menu. This will take the user back to the previous level of menu.

If the number of pages
in the project is
limited, there is no
need to include every
screen layout chart -
one or two is sufficient

- All user entry will be validated as being one of the choices offered.

- Varied foreground and background colours will help to orient the user as to which 'level' of menu is currently being displayed. Colours are chosen for clarity and pleasing appearance.

A sample screen layout is shown in Appendix C, page 2 - 48.

A chart showing movement between menus is shown below.

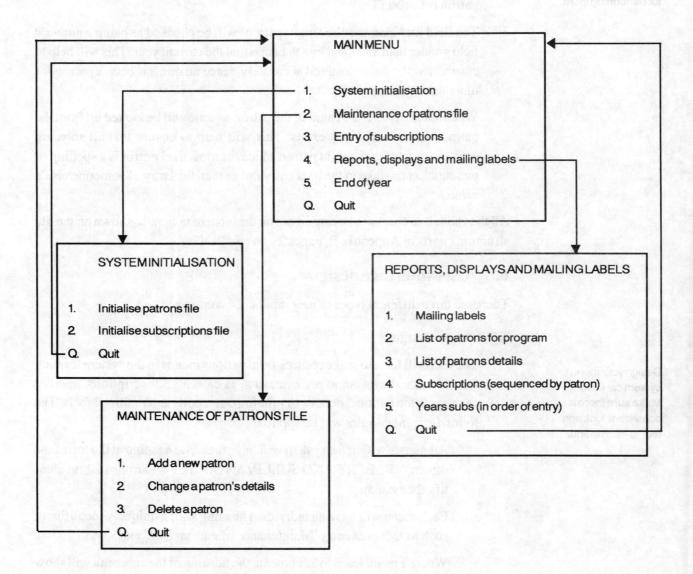

MAIN MENU

1. System initialisation
2. Maintenance of patrons file
3. Entry of subscriptions
4. Reports, displays and mailing labels
5. End of year
Q. Quit

SYSTEM INITIALISATION

1. Initialise patrons file
2. Initialise subscriptions file
Q. Quit

REPORTS, DISPLAYS AND MAILING LABELS

1. Mailing labels
2. List of patrons for program
3. List of patrons details
4. Subscriptions (sequenced by patron)
5. Years subs (in order of entry)
Q. Quit

MAINTENANCE OF PATRONS FILE

1. Add a new patron
2. Change a patron's details
3. Delete a patron
Q. Quit

6.2   Maintenance of Patrons file

The user will need to make additions, changes and deletions to the Patrons file. The following general rules will apply to this input:

- whatever the operation, the file will always be checked to see whether the patron exists on the file. Thus it will not be possible to add an existing patron, or delete a non-existing patron from the file

• the user will move forwards through the fields displayed on the screen by pressing <Enter>. Before a new record is added or changed, the user will be given an opportunity to go back through the fields making any more changes they wish. Similarly, the user will be asked to confirm a deletion after the patrons details have been displayed on the screen. (see Appendix C, page 2-49 for sample screen layout.)

6.3   Entry of subscriptions

These will be entered in batches of up to ten, with the number in the batch and the batch total being entered prior to individual transactions. The patrons file will be accessed to make sure that the patron exists, and the batch total will be calculated and compared with that entered by the user. If it is incorrect the user will be asked to edit the input or abandon the entry.

7.   File design and access methods

This is an online system with a relatively low volume of records on the master file (the patrons file contains about 100 patrons) and a low volume of transactions. (Only four or five patrons join or leave each year, and each patron pays one annual subscription). Ideally, the patrons file needs to be randomly accessed, both for lookup purposes and in order for it to be maintained easily.

Subscriptions could be entered directly on to the patrons file, but it would be preferable to enter them on to a separate subscriptions file, and the amount added to a 'Current Subscription' field on the patrons file. Then, if any query or error arises, the subscriptions (transaction) file can be checked against the original written entry in the cash book. A sequential file organisation is suitable here, with new subscription records being appended to the end of the file.

At the end of each financial year, a copy will be made on to a separate disk of the year's subscriptions, and a new Subs file initialised for the next financial year.

8.   Data structure design and data organisation

The simplest way of holding the patrons file so that it can be randomly accessed is to hold it as a 'relative file'. That is, each patron is given a number between say 1 and 100, or however many patrons there are, and this number acts as the key field. Patron number 23 is then stored in record number 23. However, this method has been rejected for this application because it would be inconvenient for the patrons secretary to have to remember or look up the patron's number. An alternative solution is to let the patron's surname and initial act as the key field. The question then arises of how to locate a patron with a given name. Hashing is a possibility here, with provision being made for 'collisions'. The disadvantage of this method is that it would then not be possible to print a list in alphabetical sequence of name (for mailing labels, or names in programme).

A third option is to organise the file as a binary tree. This is the method which has been chosen, as it will allow both fast access to any particular record, and an inorder

---

Sidebar notes (left margin):

This is an example of an 'on-line batch system'. (You do not really need to have this level of sophistication in your project; it is included here for teaching purposes).

Choosing the correct file design is probably the most crucial part of the project. You MUST justify your choice adequately.

For example, consider:

volume of master data

volume of transactions

hit rate

whether on-line queries or lookups are required

sequence of output

Does the format of the key field lend itself to relative file organisation? (In fact it would be quite acceptable here).

DISCUSS the various options and their suitability for this particular system 'traversal' of the tree will give the output sequenced alphabetically. If the tree is well balanced, at most 7 records will have to be read to find any patron on the file.

While there is always the possibility of two patrons having identical surnames and initials, the chances of this occurring with only 100 patrons on the file are small, and it would always be possible to use a patron's full first name if necessary.

9. Relationship between files

This application will use a master file and a transaction file, both keyed on patron's name and initial, as described in the previous two paragraphs. This is a typical example of a one-to-many relationship.

10. Security

While the information in this system is not of a highly confidential nature, and the system will be operated in the secure environment of the Patrons Secretary's home, it is nevertheless desirable to prevent an unauthorised person from tampering with the data. A password will therefore be requested and must be entered correctly by the user at the opening screen or all access will be denied. Proper backup procedures will be laid down in the user manual.

11. Charts showing overall system design

11.1 System outline chart

The overall system is illustrated in a system outline chart given below.

INPUT	PROCESSES
surname + initials	initialise patrons file
name for programme	initialise subs file
address	add new patron
Year they became a patron	change patron
subs (current)	delete patron
subs (previous 2 years)	enter subs
date of current year's sub	post subs to patrons file
	clear subs file at end of year
FILES	reset subs on patrons file at end of year
patrons	
subs	
	OUTPUT
	mailing labels
	list of patrons for programme
	list of patrons details

Side notes:

Frankly, this is a weakness in this project, not to be emulated! Better to allocate a unique code to each patron.

The relationship between files is discussed in more detail in the second project.

Security is discussed in more detail in the second project. It is an important topic and if you can incorporate passwords or different access levels for different users, for example, you should do so.

A system outline chart like the one shown here is a very useful summary of all the inputs, outputs, files and processes.

11.2 Systems flowcharts

11.2.1 The subscriptions subsystem

A systems flowchart can also be a useful representation of how the system works

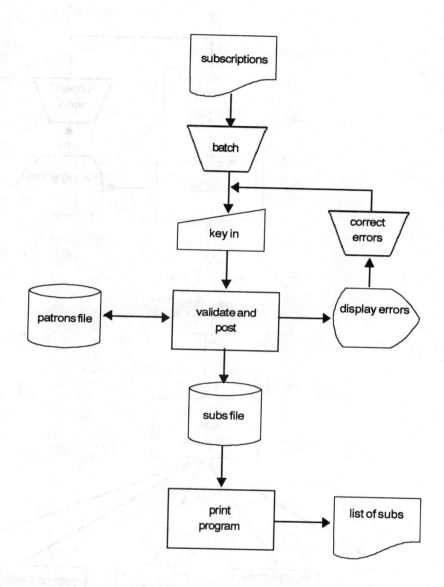

11.2.2 The patrons file subsystem

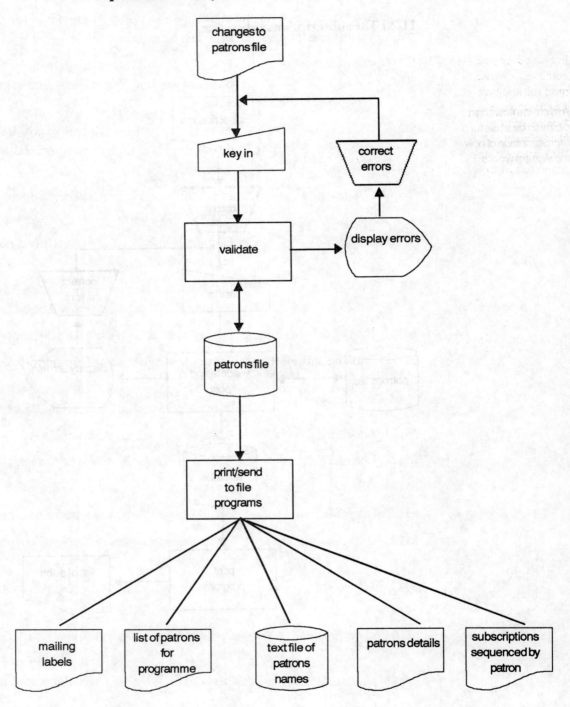

12. Program specifications

A hierarchy chart showing the main modules in the program is given on the next page. A brief description of each module is given below.

In this section you could include a list of modules and their functions, or put footnotes on the hierarchy chart. Detailed algorithms are not required here.

O1_OpeningScreen	Displays a graphics screen giving title 'Gilbert and Sullivan Society Patrons List' and asks for password.
O2_GetCurrentYear	Asks for current year, displays pop-up help window if F1 pressed. (Will be compared with date on Subs file).
O3_GetPathname	asks user for drive and directory on which data is stored; defaults to A:
M1_MainMenu	Displays main menu and accepts user choice, branching to appropriate routine.
M11_SysInitMenu	Displays menu to initialise either the Patrons file or the Subs file, accepts choice and branches.
M111_InitialisePatronsFile	Creates new patrons file with 100 empty records
M112_InitialiseSubsFile	Creates new subs file with one empty record
M12_MaintenanceMenu	Displays a menu to add, change or delete a record from the patrons file, accepts choice and branches.
M121_AddPatron	Allows the addition of a new patron
M122_ChangePatron	Allows a patron's details to be changed
M123_DeletePatron	Allows deletion of a patron's record
M124_OpenSubsFile	Open subs file and reads date from control record
M125_OpenPatronsFile	Opens patrons file and reads NextFree pointer from control record
M13_EntrySubs	Accept patrons subs in batches and posts to patrons file when batch is correct
M14_ReportsMenu	Displays menu of 5 reports, accepts user choice and branches.
M141_MailingLabels	Prints labels 3-up after user aligns stationery.
M142_PatronsForProg	Prints list of patrons names as they are to appear in the show programme

etc.

(The rest of the modules are omitted here, but in your project, include a list of ALL modules with a brief description in the Design section. More detailed descriptions belong in the Systems Maintenance section).

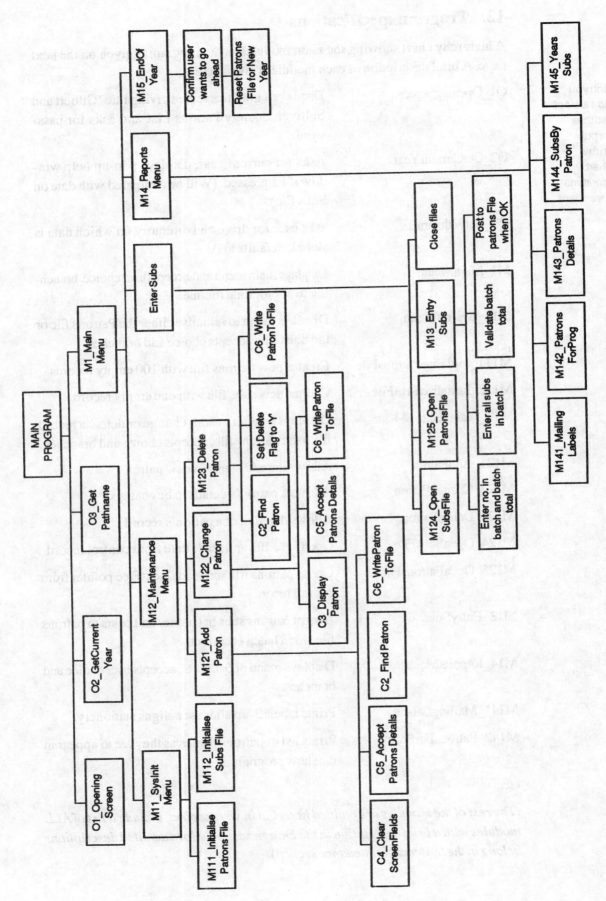

Hierarchy chart showing the main modules of the program

13. Test strategy

Two types of testing will be carried out.

13.1 Module testing

Each module will be tested as it is completed. The testing will be 'white box' testing, with test data being constructed to uncover any errors in:

- 'important' execution paths

- error handling paths

- the handling of 'extreme' data (eg data at the limit of a specified range), valid data and invalid data

13.2 System testing

You must demonstrate that you have tested *systematically* and that your tests are *reasonably* exhaustive.

This testing will be carried out when the system is complete, and is designed to test whether the software performs according to the user's expectations. This will be 'black box' testing, designed to test the functionality of the system, and to uncover any omissions or deficiencies in the way the system works. It will be carried out by the user using a test procedure defining specific test cases, and the user will also be invited to try any other tests they wish to ensure that all elements of the system are complete and working correctly. A realistic volume of data will be placed on the master file prior to the test to ensure that performance is satisfactory in terms of processing speed. Any omissions or inaccuracies in the user documentation will also be checked and corrected at this stage.

13.3 Test data

The following data will be put onto the patrons file. Further details of test data is given in the test plan which follows on page 2 - 22.

Specify the test data, with reasons for its selection. You will find this very useful when you test your project, as you will then know exactly what is on file and what the output from each test should therefore be.

Initial data entry		Edits made before adding to file
Name:	Lee R	
Year joined:	1992	Try entering 1998 (*should not be accepted; tests date validation*)
Name in programme:	Roger Lee	
Address:	The Lodge	
	Holbrook	
	Suffolk	
	IP5 4WE	
Name:	Cook P	Try entering 1890 (*should not be accepted; tests date validation*)
Year joined:	1990	
Name in programme:	Mr P.Cook	Alter to Anon (*tests editing of data field before accepting to file. Also, need at least 2 Anons to test 'Names for programme' module*)
Address:	5 Crescent Street	
	Norwich	
	NR6 5TY	

Initial data entry		Edits made before adding to file
Name:	Imran J	
Year joined:	1960	
Name in programme:	Mr J.Imran	
Address:	JJJ	135 Woodbridge Road
	JJJJJJJJJJJJJJJJJJJJJJJJJJJJJJ	Ipswich
	(tests effect of entering over-long field)	Suffolk
		IP9 7NB

Name:	Hawes M	
Year joined:		
Name in programme:		Mr & Mrs M Hawes
Address:		587 Barrack Rd
(tests effect of missing out address initially)		Woodbridge
		Suffolk IP9 7NB

Name:	Tanjit M	
Year joined:	1982	
Name in programme:	Mr M Tanjit	Mrs M. Tanjit
Address:	28 Castle Rd	
	Framlingham	
	Suffolk	
	FR3 5SD	

Name:	Young A B	change to Young C
Year joined:	1985	*(tests effect of altering the key field*
Name in programme:	anon	*before accepting the data)*
Address:	Convent Rd	
	Sudbury	
	Suffolk IP9 6CX	

Name:	johns r	
Year joined:	1951	
Name in programme:	Mr R.Johns	Mr and Mrs R.Johns
Address:	Fire Station	
	Needham Market	
	Suffolk	
	IP9 15RE	

Name:	Roach H	No changes.
Year joined:	1981	
Name in programme:	ANON	*(tests use of uppercase)*
Name on label:	Mr and Mrs H.Roach	
Address:	70 Corinthian Ave	
	Colchester	
	Essex	

To test the entry of subscriptions, the following data will be used:

Number of entries: 6

Batch total :   £60

date	surname & initials	subscription	
28-14-92			*(should display error message, invalid date)*
28-07-92	Imran K		*(should not be accepted because not on patrons file)*
28-07-92	Imran j	10.00	*(valid)*
28-07-92	cook p	abc	*(Should not accept invalid sub)*
\<enter\>	cook p	10.00	*(should accept previous date)*
30-07-92	johns r	5.00	
\<enter\>	lee r	5.00	
\<enter\>	tanjit m	10.00	
\<enter\>	hawes m	10.00	

(batch total wrong; error message should be displayed.)

Change batch total to £50 *(should be accepted)*

13.4 Test plan

The detailed test plan for the module testing is given on the following two pages.

The system testing will use the same tests, but 50 records will be placed on the file prior to the tests. System initialisation will not be tested at this stage.

Do not attempt to add more than 50 test data records; this is adequate for a project. Fewer may be quite acceptable.

Module test plan

test	module	purpose	test data	expected result
1	O1_OpeningScreen	test password check	'abc', 'Patience'	only 'Patience' allows user to continue
2	O1_GetCurrentYear	test F1 key press	press F1	window display
3	O1_GetCurrentYear	test date validation	192w	not accepted
4	O2_GetPathname	test valid path	b:	file opened OK
5	O2_GetPathname	test default path	press <Enter>	file opened OK
6	O2_GetPathname	test invalid path	k	error message
7	M1_MainMenu	test valid option	1,2,3,4,5,q,Q	correct option selected
8	M1_MainMenu	test invalid option	a,6	not accepted
9	M11_SysInitMenu	test valid option	1,2,3,q,Q	correct option selected
10	M11_SysInitMenu	test invalid option	<Enter>, F1, 4	not accepted
11	M111_InitialisePatronsFile	file initialisation	Y or y to proceed	file initialised
12	M111_InitialisePatronsFile	check disk routine	disk not in drive	error message
13	M112_InitialiseSubsFile	file initialisation	Y or y to proceed	file initialised
14	M112_InitialiseSubsFile	check disk routine	disk not in drive	error message
15	M12_MaintenanceMenu	test valid option	1,2,3,q,Q	correct option selected
16	M12_MaintenanceMenu	test invalid option	8,z	not accepted
17	M121_AddPatron	add new patron	see prev. page	data written to file
18	M121_AddPatron	try to add existing patron	Young C	error message
19	M122_ChangePatron	change existing patron's data	Tanjit M	specified fields changed
20	M122_ChangePatron	try to change non-existent patron	Trent F	error message
21	M123_DeletePatron	delete existing patron	Young C	deleted
22	M123_DeletePatron	try to delete non-existent patron	Young C	error message
23	M13_EntrySubs	test date validation	23-6-92, qwerty	pop-up window message

test	module	purpose	test data	expected result
24	M13_EntrySubs	test batch total check	£60 instead of £50	error message
25	M13_EntrySubs	enter valid batch	see page 2-21	accepted and posted
26	M13A_PostSubs	correct posting of subs	same as above	correctly posted
27	M14_ReportsMenu	test valid option	1,2,3,4,5,q,Q	correct option selected
28	M14_ReportsMenu	test invalid option	6,d,<Enter>	not accepted
29	M141_MailingLabels	test label print	choose option 1	all labels printed
30	M142_PatronsForProg	send to file	choose option F	all except Charles, Raymond
31	M142_PatronsForProg	send to printer	choose option P	all except above printed
32	M143_PatronsDetails	test screen display	start at T	Tanjit M displayed
33	M143_PatronsDetails	test print option, all names	<Enter> for names	all names printed
34	M143_PatronsDetails	start and end at different names	I to start, Johns R to end	Imran and Johns printed
35	M144_SubsByPatron	test headings, date	complete file	all patrons with subs as entered
36	M145_YearsSubs	test print details	see page G7	all subs printed as entered
37	M15_EndOfYear	test end of year routine	enter Y	subs moved to previous year
38	M143_PatronsForProg	system test with 50 records	<Enter> for names	all 50 names printed

Note: The above tests also test the sub-modules:

A1-A9 (utility routines)

B1 - B6 (window routines)

C1 - C6 (traversing the binary tree to find patron, displaying details)

D1 - D9 (used in the print and display routines)

For the final system test, 50 names are to be added and printed out. This will also test the efficiency of the file structure with a realistic amount of data on the file.

Section 3 - Testing

Analysis of testing

Generally you will have at least 10, and more likely between 20 and 30 pages of test runs in the Appendix, ALL cross referenced to the test plan.

It proved very difficult to construct test data and a test plan which would test ALL the possible paths in the program, since there are literally millions of different combinations of paths. This was especially true of the modules M121_AddPatron and M121_ChangePatron, and numerous unexpected errors kept surfacing as different combinations of edits were made before accepting the record and posting it to the file.

However, the test data and test runs were carefully designed to check for all possible errors and I believe that these modules now work perfectly.

The test plan systematically goes through each option on the menu and the test data is designed to check that all validations are correctly performed, using a combination of valid and invalid data.

The actual test runs are shown in Appendix E, cross-referenced to the test plan and annotated by hand to point out the various error messages resulting from invalid data entry and so on.

In a few exceptional cases like this one, you can ask the lecturer to 'sign off' the test as working correctly. Use this sparingly; in general, hard evidence of a working system is required!

Results of some tests, for example test 7 where an invalid option (a or 6) is selected from the main menu, cannot be shown as the option is simply not accepted and the cursor remains at the same place waiting for the user to enter a valid option. However my supervisor will verify that all tests worked correctly.

For the system test, 50 records were added to the file and no noticeable delay occurred when records were being looked up on the patrons file.

A discussion of the test results is given in the Systems Maintenance section on page 2-28.

Section 4 - System Maintenance

1. System overview

The Gilbert and Sullivan Society Patrons List is basically a database system written in Pascal as a series of modules. The database contains two files. The first is referred to as the Patrons file and contains one record for each patron which holds details such as name, address etc. The second file is the Subs file, and holds a record for each subscription paid during the year. It may also contain 'adjustment' records if any errors were made in entering subscriptions which subsequently need to be corrected.

Access to the system is only allowed after the correct password is entered. If an incorrect password is entered, the user is automatically returned to the operating system prompt.

The system is menu-driven, allowing the user to make choices at each stage from a menu displayed on the screen. The menu 'tree' is shown on page 2 - 12. Maintenance routines allow additions and changes to, and deletions from the patrons file. Subscriptions are entered in batches of up to ten, with batch checks being performed and no batch being posted to the patrons file until it is correct. Once a new batch has been entered, validated and posted, it is appended to the end of the subs file. Reports and mailing labels can be produced whenever they are needed. End of year routines are provided to clear the subs file ready for the new year, and on the patrons file to move 'last years subs' to 'previous year's subs' and move 'current subs' to 'last year's subs'.

The patrons file is organised as a binary tree which allows fast random access as well as processing in key sequence using an 'inorder traversal'; useful for reports which are sequenced on patron's name (which acts as the key field).

Please refer to pages 2 - 12 to 2 - 18 for an overview of the system.

2. Disk space requirements

The following table shows the disk space requirements of the various files in the system:

File name	Directory	Description	Size
GSPatron.pas	root	Source code	69K
GSPatron.exe	root	Executable code	57K
(various)	BGI	graphics routines	178K
Patrons.dat	root	patrons file (100 records)	17K
Subs.dat	root	subs file (100 records)	6K

3. Detailed algorithm design

The program is modular in design and as far as possible each module uses its own local variables. However there are a number of global variables and these are documented in the program listing which can be found in Appendix F.

On the following pages, each module is described and pseudocode given.

Module name:	**M1_MainMenu**
Brief description:	Clears screen and displays main menu. Accepts user choice and branches accordingly.
Called from:	Main program
Modules called:	A7_GSTitle, M11SysInitMenu, M12MaintenanceMenu, M125OpenPatronsFile, M124OpenSubsFile, M13_EntrySubs, M14ReportsMenu, M15_EndOfYear.
Local variables:	choice : char (user's choice)
	DateError : char (will be set to S for 'Start again' if user wishes to abort if the date on the subs file does not match current year)
Screen layout:	Chart number 1 (see Appendix C)

You can use flowcharts or structure diagrams, max. one page per module, if you prefer, instead of pseudocode.

Processing steps:
```
repeat
   display title
   display menu
   accept and validate choice
   call appropriate module
until user selects q for quit.
end of procedure.
```

Module name:	**M121_AddPatron**
Brief description:	Allows the addition of a new patron to the patrons file.
Called from:	M12_MaintenanceMenu
Modules called:	A3_ReadField, A6_WriteXY, A7_GSTitle, A8_GetOneChar, A9_ClearAllFields, C1DisplayPText, C2_FindPatron, C3_DisplayPatron, C4_ClearScreenFields, C5_AcceptPatronsDetails, C6_WritePatronToFile
Local variables:	FirstTimeThrough : boolean (set to true initially, false if user wants to edit data before accepting)
	ErrorFound : boolean; (set to true if patron on file, allows for name change before accepting data)
	Present : boolean (set to true in C2_FindPatron if patron on file)
	ptrToRec : integer (passed from C2_FindPatron, giving position of record if found)
	reply : (user enters Y if OK to add)
	PName : (patrons name as entered by user)
	nch : no of chars read in A3_ReadField)

Screen layout: Chart number 4 (see Appendix C)

Input file: Patrons.dat

Output: Patrons.dat (updated)

Processing steps:

```
set Present = false {indicates  patron not already on file}
display screen headings
while name <> 'X'
     clear all fields in input record except name
     set FirstTimeThrough = true
     clear all fields on screen display
     display the screen text
     clear the name field
     repeat
        set errorfound = false
        set reply = 'Y'  {this is the 'OK to add' indicator}
        read name and convert to uppercase
        if name <> 'X' then
          if this is a different name
             {after a reply of 'N' to 'OK to add?'}
             {or a new record is being added, first time through}
             look up patrons name on file
             clear all fields in input record except name
             clear all fields on screen display
             set FirstTimeThrough = true
          endif
          if patron is already on file then
             display patrons details on screen
             display an error message
             set ErrorFound = true
             get any keypress from user to continue
             clear all fields on screen
          else
             if FirstTimeThrough then
               clear all fields in input record except name
             endif
             accept all patrons details
             display message 'OK to add?' and get reply
             set FirstTimeThrough = false
             endif {patron on file}
          endif {name<>'X'}
     until reply ='Y' or ErrorFound
     if ErrorFound = false and name <> 'X' then
         set left and right pointers = -1
         write the record in correct location
         clear screen fields
endwhile
end of procedure
```

(For reasons of space, no more algorithms are given here. In your project, you should give an overview of algorithm design for EVERY module. It is very time consuming and rather tedious so do not leave it all to be done at the last minute.)

The trained eye (and you can bet the examiner has one!) will observe that the descriptive comments explaining the purpose of each procedure tend to tail off after the first few pages of the listing. NOT GOOD! You will lose marks for this omission so spend time making sure the listing is properly commented right the way through.

4. Complete annotated listings

The listings for the program are given in Appendix F, page 2 - 59.

5. Discussion of test results

Test runs and results cross referenced to the test plan on pages 2 - 22 and 2 - 23 are given in Appendix E, starting at page 2 - 52. The following points are noted:

1. Dates entered are not fully validated. Thus it is possible to enter a date 30-02-92, for example. While not critical in this application, perhaps this could be added as an enhancement.

2. If pop-up windows are called repeatedly, say 20 times, the program crashes. I have not been able to determine why. Again, it is not really critical in this application.

3. In retrospect, it might be better to use the <Tab> and <Shift Tab> keys to move between fields in the patrons file maintenance routines, using <Enter> to signal the end of data entry. This would require A2_ReadString to be upgraded to cater for these keypresses, and the module to be used for all data entry.

4. The opening screen routine requires the use of the graphics utilities within Turbo Pascal. For convenience, these have been stored in a separate directory (\BGI) on the floppy disk holding the source and object code. If the program is run from the C drive, an adjustment needs to be made to the line

    PathToDriver := 'a: \bgi';

    in the routine O1_OpeningScreen.

5. If an attempt is made to enter subscriptions before there are any patrons on the master file, the program does not allow the user to 'escape' without entering a valid patron's name, so the system has to be rebooted. This is not a serious deficiency since in practice the master file would always be created before entering subscriptions.

6. If the printer is not on-line when a user attempts to print a report, the program will abort with a run-time error. This is rather irritating and could be overcome by checking the printer status before printing.

All errors which surfaced during testing have been corrected and all tests have produced the expected results in the final systems test.

Section 5 - User Manual

Your user manual may be presented as a completely separate document, or as one section, as shown here.

Either way, it should have its own table of contents

Table of contents

Gilbert and Sullivan Society

Patrons List

User Manual

Introduction

Always start with an introduction

Welcome to GSPatron - a tailor made system to take care of all the administrative functions of the Patrons Secretary of the Gilbert and Sullivan Society.

The program includes the following functions:

- *additions or changes to, and deletions from the Patrons list*
- *recording of subscriptions as they are paid*
- *printing of mailing labels*
- *printing all details of each patron*
- *printing a list of patrons names as they appear in the show programme*
- *sending the above list to a file on floppy disk for importing into PageMaker*
- *printing subscriptions either in order of entry or sequenced by patron, highlighting patrons who have not paid a sub for two or more years*
- *end of year routines to get ready for the new financial year.*

Installing GSPatron

Try to avoid using technical language. You may have to specify some operating system commands, but try to keep them simple.

The program runs on any IBM compatible PC, and you will need a floppy disk drive (3½" or 5 ¼"), and a printer to print reports and mailing labels. Although the program will run quite satisfactorily from a floppy disk, you may prefer to install it on your hard disk, if you have one. To do this, follow the steps below to create a directory called GS and load the program into it:

1. Enter **c:** to log on to the C drive and enter **cd** to go to the root directory. Then enter **md gs** to Make the new Directory. Type **cd gs** to Change to the Directory GS.

2. Enter **copy a:gspatron.exe** and press **<Enter>** (ie the Enter key). This will copy the program to the new directory on the C drive.

3. Make a copy of the original disk using **diskcopy** or **xcopy**.

   eg   **xcopy a: b:**   to copy from drive a to drive b

   or   **xcopy a: a:**   if you have only one floppy disk drive.

Put the original disk away, and use the new disk to store your data on. (It contains the graphics driver without which the opening screen cannot be displayed). This disk should always be inserted in the floppy drive when you run the program, whether you are running from the hard disk or the floppy disk.

You are now ready to start running the program.

Making backups

It is a good idea to have a paragraph on backup and/or security

The importance of having a backup copy of your data files cannot be over-emphasised. After you have made additions or changes to the patrons file, or entered subscriptions paid, you should make a new backup of the floppy disk. You will probably find it convenient to have one backup copy on your hard disk and a second backup on a floppy disk which is stored away from the machine.

To create a directory on the hard disk for your backup files:-

> Enter **c:** to log on to the C drive and enter **cd** to go to the root directory. Then enter **md gsback** to Make the new Directory.

Each time you want to make a backup from A: to C:\GSBACK, enter

> **copy a:*.* c:\gsback**

To make a second backup copy on to another floppy disk, insert the floppy disk in drive A and enter

> **copy c:\gsback*.* a:**

Getting started

To start the program running from the hard disk,

1.	Enter **cd \gs** to change to the directory GS on the hard disk, or enter **A:** if you are running the program from a floppy disk in drive A. Press <Enter>.

2.	Enter **gspatron.** You will then see an opening screen,

Security measures are somewhat basic here! They could obviously be improved.

Enter the password, 'Patience', and the screen will display

```
Enter current year (eg 1992) :

(Press F1 if you need advice on this)
```

Normally you will enter the current financial year here, as most subscriptions will be paid in March or April for the current year. When you initially load data onto the system, you may wish to enter last years subscriptions and in that case you would enter last year (eg 1991) here.

You will then be asked to specify which drive your data is kept on, as follows:

```
Please specify drive and directory for data
     eg c:\patrons (default is a:\)
```

If your data is on drive A (the floppy disk drive), simply press <Enter> here.

The opening menu now appears.

Use screen dumps to
show the user exactly
what he or she will see
on the screen

```
      GILBERT AND SULLIVAN SOCIETY
              Patrons List


                  Main Menu

         1. System Initialisation

         2. Maintenance of Patrons file

         3. Entry of subscriptions

         4. Reports, displays and mailing labels

         5. End of Year

         Q. Quit


         Please enter your choice:   6
```

1.   System Initialisation

Systematically
describe each menu
option

You should choose this option when you first use the system. You should
initialise both the Patrons file and the Subscriptions file, selecting each option
in turn from the following on the System Initialisation screen:

```
      GILBERT AND SULLIVAN SOCIETY
              Patrons List


            System Initialisation


         1. Initialise Patrons file

         2. Initialise Subscriptions file
            for new financial year

         Q. Quit to main menu



         Please enter your choice:
```

2. Maintenance of patrons file

Choosing this option will cause another menu to be displayed:

```
              GILBERT AND SULLIVAN SOCIETY
                     Patrons List

              Maintenance of Patrons file

              1. Add a new patron

              2. Change a patron's details

              3. Delete a patron

              Q. Quit to main menu




              Please enter your choice:
```

Adding patrons to the file

You should start by adding new patrons to the file. Because of the way the file is constructed, the program will work more efficiently if you do NOT add patrons in alphabetical order. Start from somewhere near the middle of the list, and pick randomly from the current card index or printed list until all patrons have been added.

If you make a mistake when typing in data, you may use the backspace key to delete the wrong characters. Use the <Enter> key to go to the next item. If you are already, say, on the Bankers Order item and want to change a line of address, simply continue with the data entry until the message 'OK to add?' appears. Enter N for No and you will be given a chance to re-enter any incorrect items, pressing <Enter> to step over any items you do not wish to change. When you are satisfied everything is correct, answer Y to the 'OK to add?' prompt.

The data entry screen is shown on the next page.

GILBERT AND SULLIVAN SOCIETY
Patrons List

Add a new patron

Surname followed by initials: Russell H███████████ Year joined: 1987
enter x to return to Maintenance menu

Name as it appears on programme: Mrs H. Russell███████████
(enter Anon if name is not to appear)

Address   32 Orchard Close██████████
           Mayfield█████████████
           Ipswich████████████
Postcode   IP6 4ER█

Subscription (1992):   Sub (1991):   Sub (1990):

                    OK to add? (Y/N):

Explain what each field is on a data entry screen, and describe any limitations there are on data entry

Notes:

1. *It doesn't matter whether you use uppercase or lowercase for the surname and initials; it will automatically be converted to uppercase. Enter x or X instead of a name, and press <Enter> to quit to the menu.*

2. *'Year joined' is an optional field; it cannot be before 1951. This is the year that the person first became a patron, and is for reference purposes only.*

3. *'Name as it appears on programme' shows how the patron wishes their name to appear in the show programme. If Anon (upper or lower case) is entered, the name will not appear on the relevant list.*

4. *You cannot enter anything into the Subs fields; amounts will be automatically posted to these fields through the 'Entry of Subscriptions'.*

Changing or deleting a patron

These options produce similar screens to the 'Additions' screen.

3.   Entry of subscriptions

When you receive cheques or cash from patrons, you will still need to enter the amounts manually into your cash book, as in the current system.

Subscriptions are entered into the computer in 'batches' of up to ten at a time. When you have received ten subscriptions and entered them manually into the cash book, total them up and write the total down. (You may of course have less than ten on a page.) At the top of the 'Entry of Subscriptions' screen, shown below, you will enter the number of subs recorded on the page (normally 10), and the total amount.

You must then enter the details of each subscription (you will not be allowed to enter the name of a patron who does not exist on the patrons file). A word of warning here; you **must** add patrons to the master file using the 'Maintenance of Patrons file' option from the main menu before you attempt to add subscriptions, or you will not be able to complete the entry of subscriptions and you will have to reboot the system (or turn your computer off and on again).

If several subscriptions were made on the same date, you do not have to keep re-entering the date. Simply press <Enter>, and the date of the previous subscription in the batch will be automatically entered for you.

Posting subscriptions

If the computer agrees with your batch total, you will be given the option to either Edit, Post or Abandon. If all is correct, post the subscriptions, and they will be recorded permanently on your data disk. If you have made an error and the batch total is incorrect, you will have to either find and correct the error or abandon this particular batch; the computer will not allow you to post until the total is correct.

Correcting errors

It is very important to tell the user how to put right any errors that may have been made in data entry.

If you later discover that you have, for example, recorded a subscription against the wrong patron, enter a corresponding negative subscription against that patron and correctly credit the right person. Make the same entries in your cash book.

```
              GILBERT AND SULLIVAN SOCIETY
                      Patrons List

                  Entry of Subscriptions

     Number of Entries in Batch (Max 10): 6        Batch Total: £50

         Date        Surname and initials          Subscription
     eg 25-04-92
        28-07-92     Imran J                        10.00
        28-07-92     Cook P                         10.00
        30-07-92     Johns R                        5.00
        30-07-92     Lee R                          5.00
        30-07-92     Tanjit M                       10.00
        30-07-92     Hawes M                        10.00
```

4. Reports, displays and mailing labels

Choosing this option will cause another menu to appear, as shown below:

```
          GILBERT AND SULLIVAN SOCIETY
                  Patrons List

       Reports, Displays and Mailing Labels

       1. Mailing labels

       2. List of Patrons for programme

       3. List of patrons' details

       4. Subscriptions (sequenced by patron)

       5. Year's subscriptions (in order of entry)

       Q. Quit


       Please enter your choice:
```

Mailing labels

Mailing labels can be produced for all patrons. They will be printed three per row, on sticky label stationery such as 'Butterfly' copier labels. One row of 'dummy' labels will be printed first in order for you to be able to line up the stationery correctly. The screen will display the question

Are labels lined up correctly?

and when you answer **Y** the label printing will start. If you answer **N** then another row of dummy labels will be printed.

Sample output is shown below.

Show examples of output. The ones shown here are just reduced photocopies of the original output. In your project, it is a good idea to include actual output as proof that it does actually do what you say it does!

```
xxxxxxxxxxxxxxxxxxxxxxxx    xxxxxxxxxxxxxxxxxxxxxxxx    xxxxxxxxxxxxxxxxxxxxxxxx
xxxxxxxxxxxxxxxxxxxxxxxx    xxxxxxxxxxxxxxxxxxxxxxxx    xxxxxxxxxxxxxxxxxxxxxxxx
xxxxxxxxxxxxxxxxxxxxxxxx    xxxxxxxxxxxxxxxxxxxxxxxx    xxxxxxxxxxxxxxxxxxxxxxxx
xxxxxxxxxxxxxxxxxxxxxxxx    xxxxxxxxxxxxxxxxxxxxxxxx    xxxxxxxxxxxxxxxxxxxxxxxx


COOK P                      HAWES M                     IMRAN J
5 Crescent Street           587 Barrack Rd              135 Woodbridge Road
Norwich                     Woodbridge                  Ipswich
                            Suffolk                     Suffolk
NR6 5TY                     IP9 7NB                     IP9 7NB



JOHNS R                     LEE R                       ROACH H
Fire Station                The Lodge                   70 Corinthian Ave
Needham Market              Holbrook                    Colchester
Suffolk                     Suffolk                     Essex
IP9 15RE                    IP5 4WE
```

List of patrons for programme

If you choose this option, the screen will display the question

```
Output to file or printer? (F or P):
```

If you enter **P**, you will get a printed list of patrons names as they are to appear in the show programme, excluding any who wish to remain anonymous. If you enter **F**, a message will be displayed:

```
Names will be written to a:\PNames.dat
```

(or c:\PNames.dat if your data is held on the c drive).

This is useful if the person typesetting the programme wishes to import the list directly from disk into the desktop publishing system (eg PageMaker).

Sample output is shown below:

```
15-8-1992                    GILBERT AND SULLIVAN SOCIETY              Page 1
                          LIST OF PATRONS' NAMES FOR PROGRAMME

                             Mr P.Cook
                             Mike & Jane Hawes
                             J.Imran
                             Mr and Mrs R.Johns
                             Roger Lee
                             Mrs M.Tanjit

END OF REPORT
```

List of patrons' details

This list will show all the information held for each patron. You will be given the option of displaying the list on the screen (for any given range of names) or sending the list to the printer.

Sample output is shown below:

```
4-9-1992                     GILBERT AND SULLIVAN SOCIETY              Page 1
                             LIST OF PATRONS' DETAILS

Name                         Name in Programme              Mailing labels
COOK P                         Mr P.Cook
                                                            5 Crescent Street
                                                            Norwich

                                                            NR6 5TY

Year joined      Sub (1992) Sub (1991)  Sub (1990)
1990             15.00      0.00        0.00

****************************************************************************

END OF REPORT
```

Subscriptions (sequenced by patron)

State the purpose of a report if it is not immediately obvious.

This report is useful for seeing who has not paid their subs for one, two or three years. Sample output is shown below:

```
15-8-1992            GILBERT AND SULLIVAN SOCIETY            Page 1
                 Subscriptions 1992, 1991 and 1990

              Name            1992       1991       1990
              COOK P         15.00       0.00       0.00
              HAWES M        15.00       0.00       0.00
              IMRAN J        20.00       0.00       0.00
              JOHNS R        10.00       0.00       0.00
              LEE R          10.00       0.00       0.00
        ***** ROACH H         0.00       0.00       0.00
              TANJIT M       30.00       0.00       0.00
                          --------   --------   --------
                   Total   100.00       0.00       0.00
```

Year's subscriptions (in order of entry)

Sample output is shown below:

```
15-8-1992            GILBERT AND SULLIVAN SOCIETY            Page 1
                 1992   Subscriptions in Order of Entry

              Date       Name                   Amount
              28-07-92   IMRAN J                 10.00
              28-07-92   HAWES M                  5.00
              28-07-92   COOK P                   5.00
              30-07-92   JOHNS R                  5.00
              30-07-92   LEE R                    5.00
              28-07-92   IMRAN J                 10.00
              28-07-92   COOK P                  10.00
              30-07-92   JOHNS R                  5.00
              30-07-92   LEE R                    5.00
              30-07-92   TANJIT M                10.00
              30-07-92   HAWES M                 10.00
                                              ------
                               Total            80.00
```

5.   End of Year

At the end of the financial year, you should choose this option. It will move 'Current Subs' to 'Previous Years Subs' on the Patrons file, and leave all the Current subs at zero, ready for the new year. You should also make a backup copy of the subscriptions file, put it away safely, and then run the 'System Initialisation' option to initialise a new Subs file. DO NOT RE-INITIALISE THE PATRONS FILE.

Error messages

Your user documentation should include a list of all the error messages which could occur (the ones you programmed, and possibly some operating system errors)

The following is a list of error messages that may appear when you run the program, and the action you should take in each case.

Message	**Action**
Graphics Error. Enter full path to BGI driver or type <Ctrl-Break> to quit	You may be running the program from drive B; rather than drive A. Enter b:\bgi as the pathname for the BGI (graphics) driver. Otherwise, check the installation instructions at the start of this manual and ensure that you have a directory BGI on the floppy disk.
cannot create file - check disk in drive A	Check the disk is correctly inserted, and not write-protected.
incorrect drive name - please restart program	You entered a non-existent drive name after the opening title screen was displayed. Restart the program.
Error: patron of this name already on file	You are attempting to add a new patron with the same name as one already on file. Try a different name.
Error: no patron of this name found	You are attempting to change or delete a non-existent patron. Check the name you have entered - surname followed by initials.
Error: Check Batch Total. Press E to Edit or A to abandon	After entering a batch of subs, the batch total was found to be incorrect. Edit either the batch total or the offending subscription.
CAUTION: Date entered does not match the date on Subs file. Do you wish to continue or start again?	The subs file contains a date which you specified when the file was initialised. You are now attempting to add subs for a different year. Check your dates, or perhaps you have loaded the wrong floppy disk (ie one for a previous year). If you are deliberately entering subs for a previous year, ignore this message and continue. Otherwise, restart the program.
101 Disk write error.	This means your floppy disk is full. You will have to delete some files from your disk before continuing.

Program limitations

You may experience problems if you are using a printer other than a dot matrix printer, for example a laser printer. Also, if you use different label stationery from that specified, the spacing may not be correct. In either case, contact system support.

System support

In the event of any problems, please contact A.Student, 0978-463889.

Section 6 - Appraisal

1.   Performance in relation to objectives

The program works satisfactorily and has achieved the objectives as originally specified.

User feedback is essential; try to get a letter on official headed paper, signed by the user, stating good points and weak ones too, for inclusion in the appraisal. If you have made amendments in response to user feedback, mention them here.

- an easily maintainable database of patrons has been created

- subscriptions can be recorded whenever they are paid

- required reports are printed

- a list of patrons name can be written to a file for easily importing into PageMaker when the programme is produced

- mailing labels can be printed.

The Patrons Secretary of the Gilbert and Sullivan Society has seen it running and is generally pleased with the system and finds it easy to use. The main criticism is the format of the name on the mailing labels which does need to be changed, and I intend to do this shortly. The system will be put into use next February when the new Patrons Secretary takes over.

2.   Suggestions for improvement

Some aspects of the system could be improved. For example

Write a thoughtful appraisal and be honest about shortcomings. You may still lose marks for design faults but at least you will earn marks for the appraisal!

- having to enter patrons in random order when the system is first set up is rather clumsy. This is needed to ensure a balanced binary tree, and if the user does enter the names in alphabetical order, the program will not work nearly so efficiently. There is no easy way around this problem.

- If the user specifies an incorrect drive name for the data files, the program does not immediately check this; it is checked when an attempt is made to open a file after an option has been chosen from the menu. It would be better to check it immediately and give the user a chance to re-enter the correct drive.

- Dates are not validated very thoroughly. Thus a user could enter 30-02-92, for example. A date validation routine could be included.

- It could be useful, when entering subscriptions, to be able to press a function key to have a list of patrons' names displayed in a pop-up window, so that the exact format of name and initials can be easily verified.

- As mentioned above, there needs to be separate fields for surname, initials and title so that the name on the mailing labels can be printed as for example, 'Mr P.Cook', and not 'Cook,P'. The key for each record will then consist of the two fields Surname and Initials. It can be expressed using the **concat** function in Turbo Pascal, for example

```
KeyField := concat (Surname, Initials)
```

3.   Further development

Make some
suggestions for future
enhancements or
additions, with an
indication of how they
could be implemented.

The password routine is at present very basic. The password cannot be changed and is coded into the program. Further modules need to be added to encrypt the password and store it on a password file, and to enable the user to change the password at any time.

Some aspects of the program could be more flexible. For example, the user could be asked how many labels are to be printed across the page, so that different label stationery can be used.

At present although the date that a patron joined is held, this item is not really used. Since the Society is very dependent on the goodwill of its patrons, a report could be printed of people who had been patrons for ten, twenty, thirty years etc, and some kind of personal 'Congratulations' card would then be posted to them, expressing the hope that they would continue as a patron for many more years.

Appendices

for

Gilbert and Sullivan Society Patrons List

Contents

Input documents produced by the patrons secretary

(You should include actual documents in your project)

John Imran
135 Woodbridge Rd
Ipswich
 Suffolk
  IP9 7NB
J. Imran in programme
89 90 91

Mrs H. Purdie
27 Leggatt Drive
Ipswich
 Suffolk
  IP8 4HJ

No name in programme

88 89 90

1. Card index records of patrons

LIST OF PATRONS 1992

...rcher

Dora Bilton
Mr P. Birchnall
Ken Bird
John Black

...ridges
...ristow-Smith

...own

...Collins

...rman
...arnett

H. Hambling & Co Ltd
Mr B.E. Harris
Phil Hartley
Mike and Jane Hawes
Norman Hollis
S. Hubbins
J. Imran
Mr & Mrs K. Jeffery
Mr and Mrs R. Johns
Mr and Mrs V. Kapoor
Mavis Lay
Mr D. le Mare
Roger Lee
Joy Leek
Gordon Lonsdale
Mr and Mrs E. Lopez
Sir Charles Lord
Paul Loveday
Mr and Mrs J. MacManus
Bill MacMillan
Greg Malloy

Jeff Marsh
T. Martin and Sons
Martin Matthews
Mrs S. McLaughlin
Hamish McPhee
Rose Moffatt
Miss F. Nightingale
Robert Nixon
Bertram B Norman
Northgate Nurseries
Mr and Mrs Keith Osborn
Jane Osborne
Mrs P. Overall
Ron Owens
Mr and Mrs J. Oxborrow
Mrs J. Parmee
Mr M. Patel
A. Prescott
Kathie and Fred Pretty
Miss M. Price
Rachel Proudfoot
Harriet Purdie
Purnell Building Supplies Ltd
Lou Rainbird
Mr and Mrs J.M. Rosehall
Miss Louise Sadler
Mrs Q. Saker
Mrs T Salcombe
Mrs R.J. Slade
Valerie Smith
Doug Spencer
Barbara Starke
Sheila Sutherland
Mrs M. Tanjit
Andy Tennyson
Archie Tew
Peter Thackeray
Mrs J. Thadani
Richard Turpin
Chris and Angie Tweed
John Tye
W. Underwood
Capt. J. Waller
Greg Westley
Walt Whatling
T. Wilkinson
Mrs K. Williamson
Mrs K. Wright

also those wishing to remain anonymous

2. List of patrons in 'Mikado' programme

REPLY SLIP (Please detach)

To: THE PATRONS SECRETARY

     GILBERT & SULLIVAN SOCIETY

     156 DALES ROAD

     MAYTOWN MA3 3XZ

I enclose my subscription for the year commencing April 1st.

NAME ....

(Block letters please)

ADDRESS   ....

           ....

           ....Postcode................

Date   ....

NOTES

1.   The minimum subscription is £5.00. Please make cheques payable to
     the Gilbert and Sullivan Society.

2.   All patrons will receive full information regarding the annual stage
     production and concerts taking place during the year.

3.   Patrons will be notified when booking opens and will be able to take
     advantage of priority booking facilities.

4.   Any patron who does not wish to have his or her name mentioned in
     the programme should make a special request to this effect to the
     Patrons Secretary.

5.   Patrons who would prefer to pay their annual subscription by
     banker's order are asked to inform the Patrons Secretary.

February reminder sent to patrons

File Structure

File name	PATRONS FILE	External file ID	PATRONS.DAT
File Organisation	Random (BINARY TREE)	Key fields	P_NAME (Patrons surname + initials)
Record length			

Used by:

Program name	Description	Program name	Description
GS PATRON	G & S Patrons List Project		

General file description

Master file holding details of each patron

Record name	General record description
PatronsRec	Data record

Field description	Field name	Format	Dec pl.	Validation check
Surname + Initials	P_Name	String(25)		
Name in programme	P_NameInProg	" (30)		
Address Line 1	P_Address1	" (25)		
Address Line 2	P_Address2	" (25)		
Address Line 3	P_Address3	" (25)		
Postcode	P_Postcode	" (8)		
Year joined	P_YearJoined	" (4)		Numeric, >1950
This years subs	P_SubCurrent	Real		
Last years subs	P_SubLastYear	Real		
Sub 2 years ago	P_Sub2YrsAgo	Real		
Left pointer (for tree)	P_Left	Integer		
Right pointer (for tree)	P_Right	Integer		
Delete flag	P_Deleted	Char		

File Structure

File name SUBSCRIPTIONS FILE		External file ID SUBS.DAT	
File Organisation SERIAL		Key fields NONE	
Record length			

Used by:

Program name	Description	Program name	Description
GSPATRON	GoS Patrons List Project		

General file description Holds the subs paid by patrons, in the order in which they are entered. New subs are added to the end of the file.

Record name	General record description
SUBS REC	Data record

Field description	Field name	Format	Dec pl.	Validation check
Name (surname+initials)	S_Name	String(25)		
Amount of sub	S-Amount	Real		
Date paid	S-Date	String(8)		Format dd-mm-yy

Screen Layout

Program/System: G&S Patrons List	Chart number: 1
Designed by: AS.	Layout name: MAIN MENU

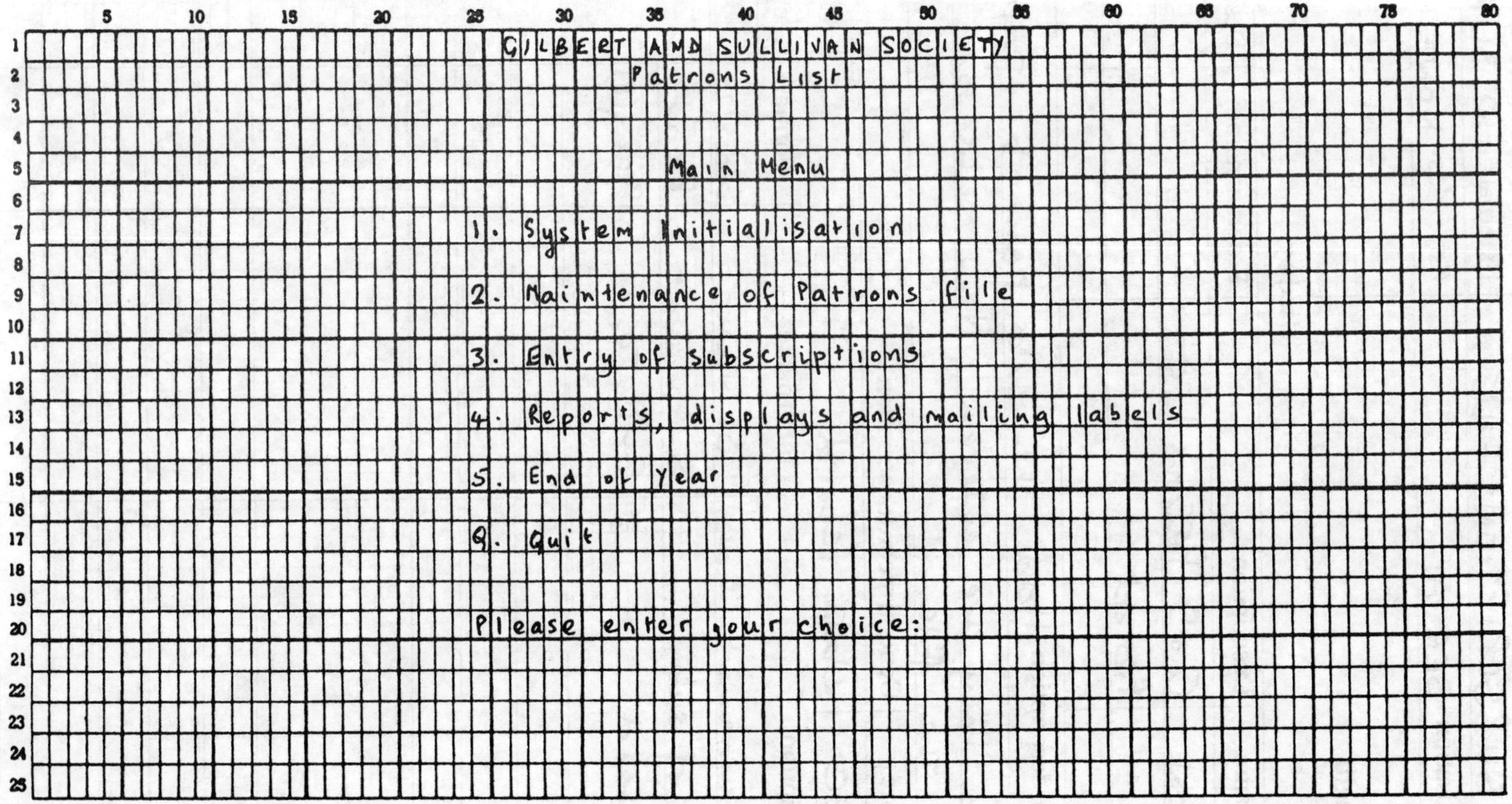
GILBERT AND SULLIVAN SOCIETY
Patrons List
Main Menu
1. System Initialisation
2. Maintenance of Patrons file
3. Entry of subscriptions
4. Reports, displays and mailing labels
5. End of Year
Q. Quit
Please enter your choice:

Screen Layout

Program/System: G & S Patrons List	Chart number: 4
Designed by: KS	Layout name: Add Patron

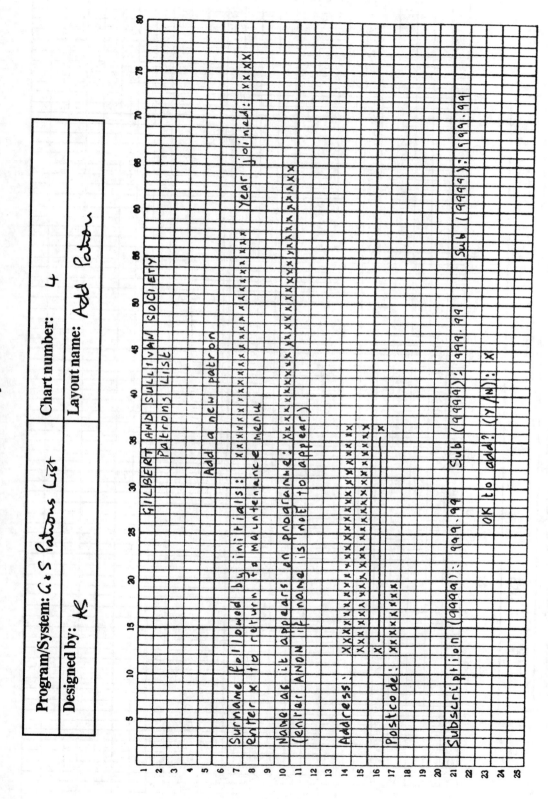

Report Layout

Program/System: G & S Patrons List	Chart number: 4
Designed by: KS	Layout name: PATRONS DETAILS

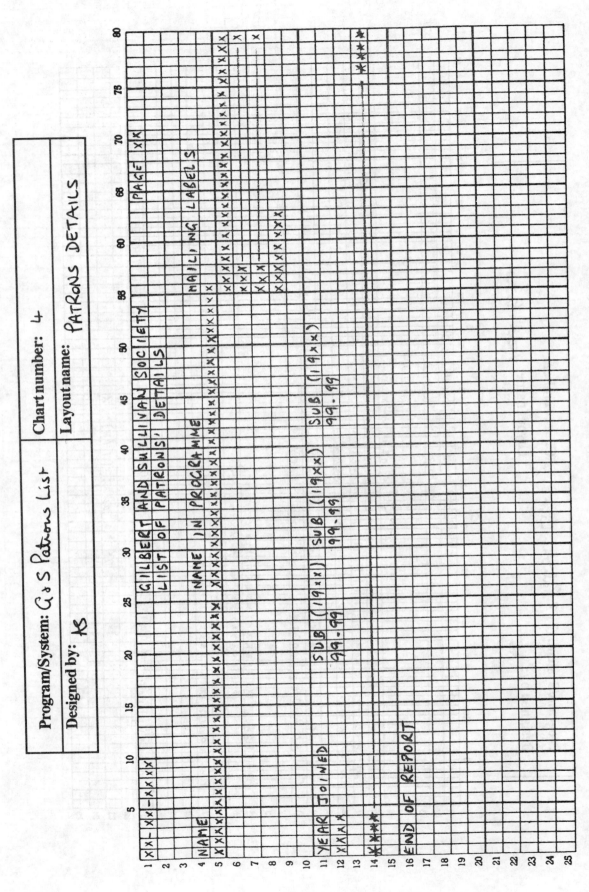

Report Layout

Program/System: G & S Patrons List	Chart number: 3
Designed by: KS	Layout name: SUBS BY PATRON

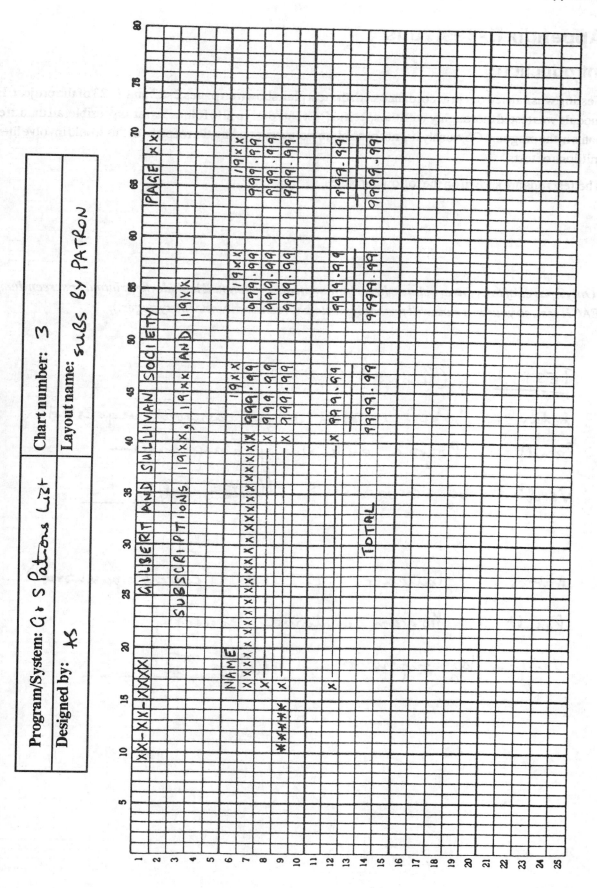

Appendix E - Test runs

Introduction

Testing was carried out in accordance with the test plan shown on pages 2 - 22 and 2 - 23 of the project. Each module was tested thoroughly with the specified test data designed to follow, as far as possible, all the different paths in the program. Obviously it is not possible to test every combination of paths as this would involve literally millions of tests.

The test runs are shown on the following pages.

(Only 7 pages of test runs are shown here. In your project you should include the printout or screen dump for EACH test, so your test runs will probably run to between twenty and thirty pages.)

TEST 1   (Password Check)

Action : 'abc' entered when password requested

Result : Program exits to operating system.

Verified by supervisor : <u>Matthew Todd</u>

Action : 'Patience' entered (correct password)

Result : Program continues correctly

Verified by supervisor : <u>Matthew Todd</u>

Test 2 (Test F1 keypress in 01-Get Current Year)

Action: Press F1 when date requested

Result: Window display

(see screen dump below)

```
                         GILBERT AND SULLIVAN SOCIETY
                                 Patrons List


              Enter current year (eg 1992) :

           ┌──────────────────────────────────────────────────────────┐
           │                                                          │
           │                                                          │
           │    Enter the financial year as 4 digits.                 │
           │                                                          │
           │    e.g. For April 1 1992 - March 30 1993, enter 1992     │
           │                                                          │
           │    This date is checked against the date on the Subscriptions file │
           │                                                          │
           │    Press any key to continue                             │
           │                                                          │
           │                                                          │
           └──────────────────────────────────────────────────────────┘
```

pop-up window appears on screen

<u>Test 18</u>   (Try to add existing patron)

Action: Enter Young C   (already on file)

Result: error message
  (see screen dump below)

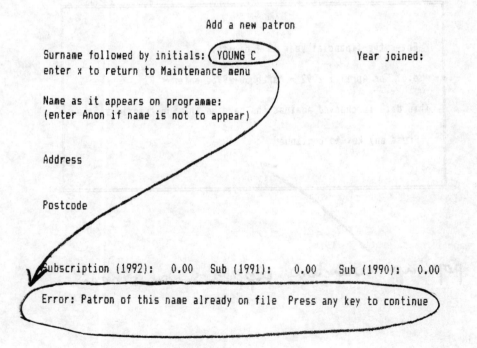

```
                        GILBERT AND SULLIVAN SOCIETY
                               Patrons List


                              Add a new patron

  Surname followed by initials: YOUNG C              Year joined:
  enter x to return to Maintenance menu

  Name as it appears on programme:
  (enter Anon if name is not to appear)


  Address


  Postcode


  Subscription (1992):   0.00   Sub (1991):   0.00   Sub (1990):   0.00

  Error: Patron of this name already on file  Press any key to continue
```

```
                    GILBERT AND SULLIVAN SOCIETY
                         Patrons List


                      Delete a patron's details

Surname followed by initials: ( YOUNG C )          Year joined: 1985
enter x to return to Maintenance menu
```

TEST 21 (Delete patron)

```
Name as it appears on programme: ANON
(enter Anon if name is not to appear)



Address    Convent Rd
           Sudbury
           Suffolk
Postcode   IP9 6CX




Subscription (1992):   0.00   Sub (1991):   0.00   Sub (1990):   0.00

               OK to delete? (Y/N):
```

↗ Enter Y

TEST 22

```
                    GILBERT AND SULLIVAN SOCIETY
                         Patrons List


                      Delete a patron's details

Surname followed by initials:  Young C███████████████  Year joined: ████
enter x to return to Maintenance menu

Name as it appears on programme: ███████████████████████
(enter Anon if name is not to appear)
```

(Try to delete non-existent patron)

```
Address    █████████████████████
           █████████████████████
           █████████████████████
Postcode   ███████




Subscription (1992):         Sub (1991):          Sub (1990):

( Error: No patron of this name found )    Press any key to continue
```

← Patron deleted in Test 21

Test 24 - Test Batch Total check.

GILBERT AND SULLIVAN SOCIETY
Patrons List

Entry of Subscriptions

Number of Entries in Batch (Max 10): 6   Batch Total: £60

should be £50

Date	Surname and initials	Subscription
eg 25-04-92		
28-07-92	Imran j	10.00
28-07-92	cook p	10.00
30-07-92	johns r	5.00
30-07-92	lee r	5.00
30-07-92	tanjit m	10.00
30-07-92	hawes m	10.00

Error: Check Batch Total. Press E to Edit or A to Abandon

Test 34 (Print patrons' details for patrons
between I and Johns R)

2 names printed

```
15-8-1992              GILBERT AND SULLIVAN SOCIETY        Page 1
                       LIST OF PATRONS' DETAILS

Name                   Name in Programme              Mailing labels
IMRAN J                   J.Imran
                                                      135 Woodbridge Road
                                                      Ipswich
                                                      Suffolk
                                                      IP9 7NB

Year joined     Sub (1992) Sub (1991)  Sub (1990)
1960              20.00      0.00         0.00

************************************************************************

Name                   Name in Programme              Mailing labels
JOHNS R                  Mr and Mrs R.Johns
                                                      Fire Station
                                                      Needham Market
                                                      Suffolk
                                                      IP9 15RE

Year joined     Sub (1992) Sub (1991)  Sub (1990)
1951              10.00      0.00         0.00

************************************************************************

END OF REPORT
```

Test 38   (System test with 50 records)

4-9-1992   GILBERT AND SULLIVAN SOCIETY   Page 1
                       LIST OF PATRONS' NAMES FOR PROGRAMME

                              Mr J.Archer
                              Dora Bilton
                              Ken Bird
                              John Black
                              Mr P.Cook
                              Mr B.E.Harris
                              Phil Hartley
                              Mike & Jane Hawes
                              Norman Hollis
                              S.Hubbins
                              J.Imran
                              Mr and Mrs R.Johns
                              Mr and Mrs V.Kapoor
                              Roger Lee
                              Greg Malloy
                              T.Martin and Sons
                              Mrs S.McLaughlin
                              Hamish McPhee
                              Robert Nixon
                              Mr and Mrs Keith Osborn
                              Mrs P.Overall
                              Mr and Mrs J.Oxborrow
                              Mr M.Patel
                              Kathie and Fred Pretty
                              Rachel Proudfoot
                              Harriet Purdie
                              Lou Rainbird
                              Mr and Mrs J.M.Rosehall
                              Louise Sadler
                              Mrs Q.Saker
                              Mrs R.J.Slade
                              Valerie Smith
                              Barbara Starke
                              Sheila Sutherland
                              Mrs M.Tanjit
                              Andy Tennyson
                              Archie Tew
                              Peter Thackeray
                              Mrs J.Thadani
                              John Tye
                              W.Underwood
                              Capt.J.Walller
                              Mrs K.Wright

          END OF REPORT

Appendix F - Complete annotated listings

The following is a complete listing of the source code for GSPatron.

```
Program GSPatron;
{written by: P.Heathcote}
{May 1992}

{ This program was written as a specimen project called
  The Gilbert and Sullivan Patrons List. Its purpose is
  to keep track of all the details on patrons of the G & S
  Society, and subscriptions paid. Mailing labels and
  various other reports are produced. }

uses dos,crt,printer,graph;    {call in standard Turbo Pascal units }
const space25= '                         ';
      space30= '                              ';
type
   string30  = string[30];
   string25  = string[25];
   string8   = string[8];
   string80  = string[80];
   string4   = string[4];
   string3   = string[3];
   string1   = string[1];

   PatronsRecType = record
       case PControlRec : boolean of
           true: ( PC_NextFree    : integer );

           false:( P_Name         : string25;  {25 char}
                   P_NameInProg    : string30;  {30 ch}
                   P_Address1      : string25;
                   P_Address2      : string25;
                   P_Address3      : string25;
                   P_Postcode      : string8;   { 8 ch}
                   P_YearJoined    : string4;   { 4 ch}
                   P_SubCurrent    : real;
                   P_SubLastYear   : real;
                   P_Sub2YrsAgo    : real;
                   P_Left          : integer; {tree pointers}
                   P_Right         : integer;
                   P_Deleted       : char;
end;

   SubsRecType = record
       case SControlRec:boolean of
           true  : ( SC_currentYear  : integer);

           false : ( S_Name          : string25;     {25 ch}
                     S_Amount        : real;
                     S_Date          : string8);     { 8 ch}
   end;
```

Control record (first record on file) points to location of next free space on The file

) ← used to indicate that patron has been deleted

```
        FileOfPatrons = file of PatronsRecType;
        FileOfSubs    = file of SubsRecType;

        LabelType = record
          name        : string25;                          {25 ch}
          address1    : string25;                          {25 ch}
          address2    : string25;                          {25 ch}
          address3    : string25;                          {25 ch}
          postcode    : string25;                          { 8 ch}
        end;

{Global variables}
var
      ProgNames       : text;   {text file type}
      PatronsRec      : PatronsRecType;
      PInputRec       : PatronsRecType;
      SubsRec         : SubsRecType;
      PatronsFile     : FileOfPatrons;
      SubsFile        : FileOfSubs;
      PathName        : string;       {pathname for data files, default is a:}
      PControlRec     : boolean;
      SControlRec     : boolean;
      CurrentYear     : integer;
      p               : integer;  {points to the root of the binary tree}
      nextfree        : integer;  {points to the next free record position}
      code            : integer;  {used in Turbo function Val}
      char1,char2     : char;     {passed to A8_GetOneChar from many procs}
      LastYear        : integer;
      YearBefore      : integer;
      year,month      : word;     {system date displayed on various reports}
      day,dayOfWeek   : word;
      pageno          : integer;  {displayed at the top of various reports}
      linecount       : integer;
      reportchoice    : char;     {choice from report menu}
      choiceofMore    : char;     {more names to be displayed on screen}
      fpchoice        : char;     {programme names to go to file or printer}
      spchoice        : char;     {patrons details to screen or printer}
      startname       : string25; {first name to display details of}
      endname         : string25; {last name to display details of}
      SubsFilePtr     : integer;
      TotalCurrent    : real;        {total subscription for this year}
      TotalLastYear,
      Total2YrsAgo    : real;        { and for 2 previous years}
      LabelArray      : array [1..3] of labelType;
      NIn             : integer;  {used in printing 3-up labels}
      labelchoice     : char;     {choice of which set of labels}
      iocode          : integer;  {used in Turbo I/O routines}
      password        : string8;
```

```pascal
{Procedures A1 - A9 are utility routines called from various modules}

PROCEDURE A1_Continue(x,y:integer);
{accepts any key without echo on screen}
var   character : char;
begin
  gotoxy(x,y);
  write('Press any key to continue');
  character:=readkey;
end; {Continue}

FUNCTION A2_ReadString(inx,iny:integer;var f1:boolean): string;
{ This function acts as a 'filter' which
  detects when the F1 key is pressed by the end user to get extra
  information }
var
    character : char;
    finished : boolean;
    extended : char;
    entry      : string;
    index      : integer;
begin
    finished := false;
    index := 0;
    entry := '';
    while (finished = false) or (entry = '') do
      begin
        gotoxy(inx,iny);
        character := readkey;
        case ord(character) of
          0    : begin
                   extended := readkey;
                   case ord(extended) of
                     59 : begin                 { This detects the F1 key}
                            F1:=True;
                            exit;
                          end;
                   end; {end of case}
                 end; {end of 0 loop}

          13   : finished := true; {This is the return key, and means that the
                        user has finished entering the string}

          8    : begin             { 8 is the ascii code for backspace}
                   If index > 0 then
                     begin
                       delete(entry,index,1);
                       index:=index-1;
                       write (chr(8)+' '+chr(8));
                       inx:=inx-1;
                     end
                   else
                     begin
                       sound(220);
                       delay(200);
```

[handwritten annotation:] This routine is called from 02-Get Current Year

[handwritten annotation:] Readkey returns 0 if a special key (eg function key) has been pressed — call Readkey again to see which key

```
                                 nosound;
                          end;
            end;

               else
                   begin
                      write(character);
                      entry := entry + character;
                      index := index + 1;
                      inx:=inx+1;
                      finished := false;
                   end; {end of else statement}
               end; {end of case statement}
          end;{end of while loop}
          A2_ReadString := entry;
end;{end of function}
```

accepts any length of string

```
PROCEDURE A3_Readfield(var textstring:string;
                       SLength:integer;var n:integer);
{ Reads a field, padding out with blanks to a specified length.
  This ensures that data in the reports all lines up correctly. }
const space=' ';
var
    counter:integer;
begin
    n:=0;      { n>0 tells us that at least one character has been read}
    for counter:=1 to SLength do
       if eoln then textstring[counter]:=space
       else
         begin
            read(textstring[counter]);
            n:=n+1;
         end;
    readln;
    textstring[0] := chr(slength);
end; {A3_ReadField}
```

sets The stringlength to SLength before returning to calling module

```
PROCEDURE A4_StripBlanks(var s:string);
{ Strips any trailing blanks from a number entered by the user.
 This is necessary for the Val function to return a legal value. }
begin
    while(s[Length(s)] = ' ') do
      delete(s,length(s),1);
end; {A4_StripBlanks}
```

```
FUNCTION A5_UpCaseStr(s:string):string;
{Converts a string to uppercase}
var
    i,j    :integer;
begin
    j:=ord(s[0]);
    for i:=1 to j do
      s[i]:=upcase(s[i]);
    A5_UpCaseStr := s;
end; {A5_UpCaseStr}
```

determine The length of the string

```
PROCEDURE A6_WriteXY(x,y:integer;DisplayText:string80);
begin
   gotoxy(x,y);    {call standard Turbo function}
   write(DisplayText);
end; {A6_WriteXY}

PROCEDURE A7_GSTitle(textcolour,backgroundcolour:byte);
Begin
   Textbackground(backgroundcolour);
   Textcolor(textcolour);
   clrscr;      {clear screen}
   A6_WriteXY(27,1,'GILBERT AND SULLIVAN SOCIETY');
   A6_WriteXY(34,2,'Patrons List');
end; {A7_GSTitle}
```

← *standard screen heading*

```
PROCEDURE A8_GetOneChar(x,y:integer;var choice:char;char1,char2: char);
{reads one character and checks it is either char1 or char2}
begin
   repeat
     gotoxy(x,y);
     choice:=readkey;
     write(choice);
     choice:=upcase(choice);
   until choice in [char1,char2];
end; {GetYN}

PROCEDURE A9_ClearAllFields(var recname:PatronsRecType);
{Clears all fields except the key field NAME}
begin
  with recname do
    begin
        P_NameInProg        := space30;
        P_Address1          := space25;
        P_Address2          := space25;
        P_Address3          := space25;
        P_Postcode          := '        ';
        P_YearJoined        := '      ';
        P_SubCurrent        := 0.0;
        P_SubLastYear       := 0.0;
        P_Sub2YrsAgo        := 0.0;
        P_Deleted:=' ';
    end; {with}
end; {A9_ClearAllFields}


{ ********* WINDOW ROUTINES *********** }

PROCEDURE B11_WindowNumber1(var reply:char);
{called from M13_EntrySubs via B1_WindowDisplay }
begin
  A6_WriteXY(7,4,'Date must be in format');
  A6_WriteXY(14,6,'dd-mm-yy');
  A6_WriteXY(5,8,'e.g. 01-05-92 NOT 1-5-92');
  A1_Continue(7,10);
end;
```

} (pop up window)

```
PROCEDURE B12_WindowNumber2(var reply:char);
{ called from M124_OpenSubsFile via B1_WindowDisplay }
begin
      A6_WriteXY(4,4,
        'CAUTION: Date entered does not match the date on Subs file.');
      A6_WriteXY(10,6,'Do you wish to Continue or Start again (S or C)?: ');
      A8_GetOneChar(wherex,wherey,reply,'C','S');
end;
```

2nd pop-up window

```
PROCEDURE B13_WindowNumber3(var reply:char);
{ called from O1_GetCurrentYear via B1_WindowDisplay}
begin
   A6_WriteXY(7,4,'Enter the financial year as 4 digits.');
   A6_WriteXY(7,6,'e.g. For April 1 1992 - March 30 1993, enter 1992');
   A6_WriteXY(5,8,'This date is checked against the date on the Subscriptions
file');
   A1_Continue(7,10);
end;
```

3rd pop-up window

```
PROCEDURE B1_WindowDisplay(x1,y1,x2,y2,
                           foreground,background,WindowNumber:integer;
                           var reply:char);
   const maxwin=1;
type
   ScreenType = record
      Pos   : Array[1..80,1..25] of record
         ch :char;
         at :byte;
         end;
      Cursx,
      cursy : byte;
      end;

   WindowPtr = ^WindowType;
   WindowType = record
      Scr  : ScreenType;
      WinX1,
      WinY1,
      WinX2,
      WinY2  : byte;
      end;

var
   ch              : char;
   i               : integer;
   ActiveWin       : WindowPtr;
   Windo           : array [0..maxwin] of windowPtr;
   CurrentWindow   : integer;
   line            :integer;

Function B2_VidSeg  : word;
{checks the type of screen, colour or monochrome}
Begin
```

Pop up Window routines

```
      if mem[$0000:$0449] = 7 then
         B2_VidSeg := $B000
      else
         B2_VidSeg := $B800;
end;


(**********************************************)


PROCEDURE B3_FastBox(x1,y1,x2,y2,fg,bg : byte);
{ draws a double box around the inside of the window }
var
   i : byte;
   s : string[1];
begin
   TextColor(fg);
   TextBackground(bg);
   clrscr;
   s:= #205; {double horizontal line -}
   for i := x1+1 to x2 do
      begin
         gotoxy(i,y1);
         write(s);
      end;
   for i := x1+1 to x2 do
      begin
         gotoxy(i,y2+1);
         write(s);
      end;

   s:= #186;       {double vertical line |}
   for i := y1 to y2 do
      begin
          gotoxy(x1+1,i);
          write(s);
      end;
  for i:= y1 to y2 do
      begin
         gotoxy(x2,i);
         write(s);
      end;

   s := #201;           { top left corner + }
   gotoxy(x1+1,y1);
   write(s);
   s := #187;           { top right corner + }
    gotoxy(x2,y1);
    write(s);
   s := #200;           { bottom left corner + }
    gotoxy(x1+1,y2+1);
    write(s);
   s := #188;
    gotoxy(x2,y2+1);
    write(s);
end;
```

```
Procedure B4_SetUpWindows;
var
  i : integer;
begin
   New(ActiveWin);
   for i:=0 to maxwin  do
      New(Windo[i]);

   with ActiveWin^ do
   begin
      WinX1 := 1;
      WinY1 := 1;
      WinX2 := 80;
      WinY2 := 25;
      With scr do
      begin
         CursX := WhereX;
         CursY := WhereY;
      end;
   end;


   ActiveWin := Ptr(B2_VidSeg,$0000);
   CurrentWindow := 0;
   With Windo[CurrentWindow]^ do
   begin
      WinX1 := 1;
      WinY1 := 1;
      WinX2 := 80;
      WinY2 := 25;
      with scr do
      begin
         CursX := 1;
         CursY := 1;
      end;
   end;
end;
   (*******************************)

   Procedure B5_OpenWindow;
   begin
   If CurrentWindow < MaxWin then
      Begin
         Windo[CurrentWindow]^.Scr := ActiveWin^.Scr;
         Windo[CurrentWindow]^.Scr.CursX := WhereX;
         Windo[CurrentWindow]^.Scr.CursY := WhereY;

         CurrentWindow := CurrentWindow + 1;
         With Windo[CurrentWindow]^ do
           begin
             WinX1 := x1;
             WinX2 := x2;
             WinY1 := y1;
             WinY2 := y2;
```

```
            with Scr do
              begin
                CursX := 1;
                CursY := 1;
              end;
            Window(WinX1,WinY1,WinX2,WinY2);
            B3_FastBox(1,1,WinX2-WinX1,WinY2-WinY1,cyan,Black);
            TextColor(Yellow);
            TextBackGround(Black);
          end;
      end;
    end;


    (********************************)

    PROCEDURE B6_CloseWindow;
    var
      i : integer;
    begin
    if CurrentWindow > 0 then
        begin
            Windo[CurrentWindow]^.Scr.CursX := WhereX;
            Windo[CurrentWindow]^.Scr.CursY := WhereY;

            CurrentWindow := CurrentWindow - 1;
            ActiveWin^.Scr := Windo[CurrentWindow]^.Scr;
            with Windo[CurrentWindow]^ do
                begin
                    Window(WinX1,WinY1,WinX2,WinY2);
                    gotoxy(Scr.cursx,Scr.CursY);
                end;

        end;
        for i:=0 to maxwin  do
          dispose(windo[i]);

    end;

    (******  Start of B1_WindowDisplay  *******)

Begin
  B4_SetUpWindows;
  B5_OpenWindow;
  case WindowNumber of
    1: B11_WindowNumber1(reply);
    2: B12_WindowNumber2(reply);
    3: B13_WindowNumber3(reply);
  end; {case}
  B6_CloseWindow;
  textcolor(foreground);          {restore the original colours}
  textbackground(background);
end;
```

```
PROCEDURE C1_DisplayPText;
begin
  textcolor(yellow);
  A6_WriteXY(59,7,'Year joined:');
  A6_WriteXY(3,10,'Name as it appears on programme: ');
  textcolor(lightgray);
  A6_WriteXY(3,11,'(enter Anon if name is not to appear)');
  textcolor(yellow);
  A6_WriteXY(3,14,'Address');
  A6_WriteXY(3,17,'Postcode');
  A6_WriteXY(3,21,'Subscription (');
  gotoxy(17,21);
  write(CurrentYear);
  A6_WriteXY(21,21,'):');
  A6_WriteXY(33,21,'Sub (');
  LastYear:=currentYear-1;
  gotoxy(38,21);
  write(LastYear);
  A6_WriteXY(42,21,'):');
  A6_WriteXY(56,21,'Sub (');
  YearBefore:=LastYear-1;
  gotoxy(61,21);
  write(YearBefore);
  A6_WriteXY(65,21,'):');

end;{C1_DisplayPtext}
```

Displays the text for the Additions, changes and deletions on patrons file

```
PROCEDURE C2_FindPatron(name:string25; var ptrToRec:integer;
                                       var present:boolean);


begin
  with PatronsRec do
    begin
      present:=true;
      P_Deleted :=' ';
      if p=-1 then
        begin
          present:=false
        end
      else
        begin
          ptrToRec:=p;
          seek(PatronsFile,ptrToRec);
          read(PatronsFile,PatronsRec);
        while (((P_Name <> name) or (P_deleted='Y')) and (present=true))  do
          if (P_Left=-1) and (P_Right=-1) then
              present:=false
          else
            begin
              if P_Name > name
              then ptrToRec:=P_Left
              else ptrToRec:=P_Right;
              if ptrtoRec=-1 then present:=false
              else
```

Performs a search of the binary tree and returns Present = True if patron found on file

```
                        begin
                           seek(PatronsFile,ptrToRec);
                           read(PatronsFile,PatronsRec);
                        end;{if}
                     end; {else}
                  {endwhile}
               end; {else}
         end;{with}
end;{C2_FindPatron}


PROCEDURE C3_DisplayPatron;
begin
  with PatronsRec do
     begin
       textcolor(white);
       gotoxy(34,7);   write(P_Name);
       gotoxy(72,7);   write(P_YearJoined);
       gotoxy(36,10);  write(P_NameInProg);
       gotoxy(13,14);  write(P_Address1);
       gotoxy(13,15);  write(P_Address2);
       gotoxy(13,16);  write(P_Address3);
       gotoxy(13,17);  write(P_Postcode);
       gotoxy(24,21);  write(P_SubCurrent:6:2);
       gotoxy(46,21);  write(P_SubLastYear:6:2);
       gotoxy(68,21);  write(P_Sub2YrsAgo:6:2);
     end;{with}
end; {C3_DisplayPatron}
```

Displays patron's record on screen

```
PROCEDURE C4_ClearScreenFields;
begin
  textcolor(cyan);
  A6_WriteXY(72,7,'____');                              {date joined}
  A6_WriteXY(36,10,'_____'); {name in prog}
  A6_WriteXY(13,14,'_____');        {address1}
  A6_WriteXY(13,15,'_____');
  A6_WriteXY(13,16,'_____');
  A6_WriteXY(13,17,'_____');
  A6_WriteXY(24,21,'      ');                       {subs}
  A6_WriteXY(46,21,'      ');
  A6_WriteXY(68,21,'      ');
  textcolor(white);
  gotoxy(1,23);
  clreol;
end; {clear screen fields}
```

Clears all fields on the screen ready for data entry

```
PROCEDURE C5_AcceptPatronsDetails(FirstTimeThrough:boolean);
var
   YearJoinedInt: integer;
   valcode      : integer;
   nch          : integer;  {no of chars read in ReadField}
   InField      : string;
Begin
  with PInputRec do
```

```
      begin
        PatronsRec.PControlRec:=false;
        P_Name:=PatronsRec.P_Name;
        repeat
         gotoxy(72,7);
         A3_ReadField(InField,4,nch);
         P_YearJoined:=InField;
         val(P_YearJoined,YearJoinedInt,valcode);
        until(valcode=0)and(YearJoinedInt>1950) or (P_YearJoined='    ');
        if nch<>0 then PatronsRec.P_YearJoined:=P_YearJoined;
        gotoxy(36,10);
        A3_ReadField(InField,30,nch);
        P_NameInProg := InField;
        If A5_UpCaseStr(P_NameInProg)='ANON              ' then
        P_NameInProg:=A5_UpCaseStr(P_NameInProg);
        If nch <> 0
           then PatronsRec.P_NameInProg:=P_NameInProg;
        gotoxy(13,14);
        A3_ReadField(InField,25,nch);
        P_Address1 := InField;
        if nch <> 0
           then PatronsRec.P_Address1:=P_Address1;
        gotoxy(13,15);
        A3_ReadField(InField,25,nch);
        P_Address2 := InField;
        if nch <> 0
           then PatronsRec.P_Address2:=P_Address2;
        gotoxy(13,16);
        A3_ReadField(InField,25,nch);
        P_Address3 := InField;
        if  nch <> 0
           then PatronsRec.P_Address3:=P_Address3;
        gotoxy(13,17);
        A3_ReadField(InField,8,nch);
        P_Postcode := InField;
        If nch <> 0
           then PatronsRec.P_Postcode:=P_Postcode;
     end;{with}
end; {C5_AcceptPatronsDetails}

PROCEDURE C6_WritePatronToFile;
var    back : integer;
begin
{ write the new record to the next free space on the file}
   seek(PatronsFile, NextFree);
   write(PatronsFile, PatronsRec);

             { search for the insertion point in the tree }
             { P is a pointer to the root of the tree,
               set in OpenPatronsFile }

   back := -1;   { Back points to the previous node visited }

   while p <> -1 do
     begin
```

validates date of joining ↓

← *nch = number of __characters__*
nch = 0 if user skips over field (either leaving it blank or leaving previous contents)

```
        back := p;
        seek (PatronsFile,p);
        read(PatronsFile, PatronsRec);
        if (PatronsRec.P_Name) > (PInputRec.P_Name)
           then
               p := PatronsRec.P_Left
           else
               p := PatronsRec.P_Right;
        {endif}
      end; {while}

          { insertion point has been found; now adjust the pointer
            in the previous node to point to new node }
          { If we are at the root, there is of course no previous node }

    if back <> -1   { meaning that we have not just created the root}
       then
         begin
          seek (PatronsFile, back);
          read (PatronsFile, PatronsRec);
          if PatronsRec.P_Name > PInputRec.P_Name
              then  PatronsRec.P_left := NextFree
              else  PatronsRec.P_right := NextFree;
          {endif}
          seek(PatronsFile,back);
          write(PatronsFile,PatronsRec);
         end; {if}
            { Now update control record}
    PControlRec:=true;
    nextFree :=nextFree + 1;
    PatronsRec.PC_NextFree := nextFree;
    seek(PatronsFile,0);
    write (PatronsFile,PatronsRec);
    writeln;
    p:=1; {and update the pointer to the root}
end; {C6_WritePatronToFile}

PROCEDURE D1_WriteDetails;
begin
    ChoiceofMore:='M';
    with PatronsRec do
        begin
          if (P_Name>=Startname) and (P_Name<=Endname)
             and (P_Deleted<>'Y')
            then
            begin
              A7_GSTitle(yellow,blue);
              A6_WriteXY(1,4,'Name');
              A6_WriteXY(24,4,'Name in Programme');
              A6_WriteXY(56,4,'Mailing labels');
              gotoxy(1,5);   write(P_Name);
              gotoxy(24,5);  write(P_NameInProg);
              gotoxy(56,6);  write(P_Address1);
              gotoxy(56,7);  write(P_Address2);
              gotoxy(56,8);  write(P_Address3);
```

[handwritten annotation pointing to ChoiceofMore:='M';] user enters 'M' for 'More' if they want details on next patron. This routine displays on screen details of one patron at a time. User enters 'Q' for Quit if no more details required.

```
                    gotoxy(56,9); write(P_Postcode);
                    A6_WriteXY(1,12,'Year joined                    Sub (');
                    gotoxy(43,12);
                    write(currentYear);
                    write(')');
                    LastYear:=CurrentYear-1;
                    YearBefore:=LastYear-1;
                    write('  Sub (',Lastyear,')');
                    write('   Sub (',YearBefore,')');
                    gotoxy(1,13);    write(P_YearJoined);
                    gotoxy(37,13); write(P_SubCurrent:6:2);
                    gotoxy(49,13); write(P_SubLastYear:6:2);
                    gotoxy(61,13); write(P_Sub2YrsAgo:6:2);

            {Following lines are for test purposes only}

                    A6_WriteXY(1,16,'Left          Right');
                    gotoxy(1,17);   write(P_Left,'               ', P_Right);
                    gotoxy(21,17); write(P_Deleted);
            {end of test lines}

                    A6_WriteXY(26,20,'Press M for more, Q to Quit ');
                    A6_WriteXY(26,21,'(No need to press Enter) ');
                    repeat
                    gotoxy(51,21);
                    choiceOfMore:=Readkey;
                    write(ChoiceOfMore);
                    until upcase(ChoiceofMore) in ['M','Q'];
                    if(upcase(choiceofmore)='Q') then endname:='A';
                end; {if name in range}
            end; {with}
            end;{D1_WriteDetails}

PROCEDURE D2_Print3Labels;
begin
    writeln(lst,' ',labelArray[1].name,' ',labelArray[2].name,
        ' ',labelArray[3].name);
    writeln(lst,' ',labelArray[1].address1,'  ',
        labelArray[2].address1,'  ',labelArray[3].Address1);
    writeln(lst,' ',labelArray[1].address2,'  ',
        labelArray[2].address2,'  ',labelArray[3].Address2);
    writeln(lst,' ',labelArray[1].address3,'  ',
        labelArray[2].address3,'  ',labelArray[3].Address3);
    writeln(lst,' ',labelArray[1].postcode,'              ',
        labelArray[2].postcode,'              ',
        labelArray[3].Postcode);
    writeln(lst);
    writeln(lst);
    writeln(lst);
end;
```

These lines will be deleted from working system.

Mailing Label print

```
PROCEDURE D3_PrintMailingLabels;
var i:integer;
begin
   with PatronsRec do
   begin
       NIn := NIn + 1;
       LabelArray[NIn].name     := P_Name;
       LabelArray[NIn].address1 := P_Address1;
       LabelArray[NIn].address2 := P_Address2;
       LabelArray[NIn].address3 := P_Address3;
       LabelArray[NIn].postcode := P_Postcode;
   end;   {with}
   if NIn=3 then
      begin
         D2_Print3Labels;
         NIn:=0;
         {Fill array with spaces}
         for i:=1 to 3 do
            begin
               with labelArray[i] do
                  begin
                     name:= space25;
                     address1:=space25;
                     address2:=space25;
                     address3:=space25;
                     postcode:='         ';
                  end; {with}
            end; {for}
      end; {if}
end; {D3_PrintMailingLabels}
```

Gets 3 labels ready in an array & Then calls The print routine

```
PROCEDURE D4_PrintSubsByPatron;
var stars  : string[5];
Begin
with PatronsRec do
   begin
     if (P_Deleted<>'Y')
       then
         begin
           if linecount>=50 then
             begin
               write(lst,#12);   {form feed}
               write(lst,'      ',day:2,'-',month,'-',year);
               write(lst,'         ');
               write(lst,'GILBERT AND SULLIVAN SOCIETY');
               writeln(lst,'         Page ',pageno);
               writeln(lst);
               write(lst,'                         ');
               writeln(lst,'Subscriptions ',currentYear,', ',currentYear-1,
                        ' and ',CurrentYear-2);
               writeln(lst);
               write(lst,'                Name');
               write(lst,'                         ',currentYear);
               writeln(lst,'        ',currentYear-1,'          ',currentYear-2);
               linecount:=5;
```

*Prints subs in order of patron, highlighting patrons who have not paid a sub for 2 years (by printing **** next to their names)*

```
                pageno:=pageno+1;
            end; {if linecount>=50}        ← check for lapsed
        if(P_SubCurrent=0.0) and(P_SubLastYear=0)        subscriptions
            then stars:='*****' else stars:='     ';
        write(lst,'            ',stars,' ',P_Name);
        write(lst,' ',P_SubCurrent:6:2,'        ',P_SubLastYear:6:2);
        writeln(lst,'        ',P_Sub2YrsAgo:6:2);
        TotalCurrent:=TotalCurrent+P_SubCurrent;
        TotalLastYear:=TotalLastYear + P_SubLastYear;
        Total2YrsAgo:=Total2YrsAgo+P_Sub2YrsAgo;
        linecount:=linecount+1;
    end; {with}
end;
end; {D4_PrintSubsByPatron}


PROCEDURE D5_PrintNamesForProg;
const space55='                                                      ';
begin

with PatronsRec do
    begin
        if (P_Deleted<>'Y')
            then
                begin
                    if linecount>=50 then
                        begin
                            write(lst,#12);   {form feed}
                            write(lst,day:2,'-',month,'-',year);
                            write(lst,'                ');
                            write(lst,'GILBERT AND SULLIVAN SOCIETY');
                            write(lst,'          Page ',pageno);
                            writeln(lst);
                            write(lst,'                        ');
                            writeln(lst,'LIST OF PATRONS'' NAMES FOR PROGRAMME');
                            writeln(lst);
                            linecount:=4;
                            pageno:=pageno+1;
                        end; {if linecount>=50}
                    if (P_NameInProg <>'ANON                        ')
                    then writeln(lst,space25,P_NameInProg);
                    linecount:=linecount+1;
            end; {with}
end;
end; {D5_PrintNamesForProg}



PROCEDURE D6_NamesToFile;
{ sends programme names to a text file for importing
 into PageMaker }

    Begin
    with PatronsRec do
        begin
            if (P_Deleted<>'Y')
                then
```

Prints all names except those "wishing to remain anonymous"

Same, but sends name to a file instead of to the printer

```
          begin
            if (P_NameInProg<>'ANON                               ') then
              writeln(ProgNames,P_NameInProg);
       end; {with}
end;


  end; {D6_NamesToFile}


PROCEDURE D7_PrintDetails;
const space55='
```

Prints all details of patrons within name range specified by user in M143_PatronsDetails

```
';

begin
    with PatronsRec do
        begin
          if (P_Name>=Startname) and (P_Name<=Endname)
              and (P_Deleted<>'Y')
            then
            begin
              if linecount>=50 then
                begin
                   write(lst,#12);   {form feed}
                   write(lst,day:2,'-',month,'-',year);
                   write(lst,'                     ');
                   write(lst,'GILBERT AND SULLIVAN SOCIETY');
                   write(lst,'           Page ',pageno);
                   writeln(lst);
                   write(lst,'                              ');
                   writeln(lst,'LIST OF PATRONS'' DETAILS');
                   writeln(lst);
                   linecount:=4;
                   pageno:=pageno+1;
                 end; {if linecount>=50}
              write(lst,'Name                     ');
              write(lst,'Name in Programme          ');
              writeln(lst,'Mailing labels');
              writeln(lst,P_Name,P_NameInProg);
              writeln(lst,space55,P_Address1);
              writeln(lst,space55,P_Address2);
              writeln(lst,space55,P_Address3);
              writeln(lst,space55,P_Postcode);
              writeln(lst);
              write(lst,'Year joined        ',
                   'Sub (',currentYear:4,')');
              LastYear:=CurrentYear-1;
              YearBefore := LastYear - 1;
              write(lst,' Sub (',Lastyear:4,')');
              writeln(lst,'  Sub (',YearBefore:4,')');
              write(lst,P_YearJoined,'             ');
              write(lst,P_SubCurrent:6:2,'      ');
              write(lst,P_SubLastYear:6:2,'       ');
              writeln(lst,P_Sub2YrsAgo:6:2);
              writeln(lst);
              write(lst,'*****************************************');
              writeln(lst,'*********************************');
```

```
              writeln(lst);
              linecount:=linecount+12;
           end; {if name in range}
        end; {with}
    end;{D7_PrintDetails}


PROCEDURE D8_ScreenTraverse(p:integer);
{Traverses the binary tree and displays patrons' details }


begin    {D8_ScreenTraverse}
      if (p<>-1) and (upcase(ChoiceofMore)='M') then
        begin
          seek(patronsFile,p);
          read(PatronsFile, PatronsRec);
          D8_ScreenTraverse(patronsRec.P_Left);
          seek(patronsFile,p);
          read(PatronsFile, PatronsRec);
          if (patronsrec.P_Deleted<>'Y') then D1_WriteDetails;
          D8_ScreenTraverse(PatronsRec.P_Right);
        end;
end; {D8_ScreenTraverse}


PROCEDURE D9_PrintTraverse(p:integer);
{ Traverses the binary tree and prints a specified report }
begin    {D9_PrintTraverse}
      if (p<>-1) then
        begin
          seek(patronsFile,p);
          read(PatronsFile, PatronsRec);
          D9_PrintTraverse(patronsRec.P_Left);
          seek(patronsFile,p);
          read(PatronsFile, PatronsRec);
          if Patronsrec.P_Deleted<>'Y' then
            case reportchoice of
                '1': D3_PrintMailingLabels;
                '2': D5_PrintNamesForProg;
                '3': D7_PrintDetails;
                '4': D4_PrintSubsByPatron;
                '8': D6_NamesToFile;
            end; {case}
          D9_PrintTraverse(PatronsRec.P_Right);
        end;

end;  {D9_PrintTraverse}




PROCEDURE M111_InitialisePatronsFile;
var choice, default  : char;
    code             : integer;
    iocode           : integer;
    count            : integer;
    PFileName        : string;
    PRecNo           : integer;
```

Handwritten annotations:

Tree traversal — calls routine which displays patrons details on screen

Similar to above, but calls one of 5 reports depending on the menu choice made in M14_ Reports Menu (ie report choice)

Initialises patrons file, creating a control record and 100 empty data records

```
begin
    A7_GSTitle(black,cyan);
    PFileName:=pathname + 'patrons.dat'; {set default name}
    A6_WriteXY(29,5,'Initialise Patrons File');
    A6_WriteXY(25,7,'THIS PROCEDURE SHOULD BE CARRIED OUT');
    A6_WriteXY(23,8,'ONLY WHEN THE SYSTEM IS FIRST INSTALLED');
    A6_WriteXY(20,10,'Do you wish to proceed? (Y/N):');
    A8_GetOneChar(51,10,choice,'Y','N');
    if         (choice)='N' then exit;
    A6_WriteXY(29,14,'Initialising.... please wait');

    {disable automatic IO checking with the compiler directive $I-,
    which has to be written in curly brackets as shown}
    {$I-}
    assign (PatronsFile,PFileName);
```

← *This will prevent program crashing if file cannot be opened.*

```
    rewrite(PatronsFile);
    {ioresult is a reserved word in Turbo Pascal}
    {it returns a code depending on the result of the IO operation}
    iocode:=ioresult;
    case iocode of
        0    : rewrite(PatronsFile);
        1,2,3    : begin
                    Window(2,23,79,24);
                    Textcolor(black);
                    Textbackground(red);
                    clrscr;
                    A6_WriteXY(16,23,
                        'Incorrect drive name - please restart the program.   ');
                    A1_Continue(16,24);
                    window(1,1,80,25);
                    exit;
                end;
        else
        begin
            A6_WriteXY(16,17,'cannot create file - check disk in Drive A');
            A1_Continue(16,18);
        end;
    end; {case}
```

← *Turn on automatic I/o checking again*

```
    {$I+}
    {ioresult =0 when operation is successful}

    {now create control record}
    PRecNo:=0;
    PControlRec:=true;
    PatronsRec.PC_NextFree:=1;
    seek(PatronsFile,PRecNo);
    write(PatronsFile,PatronsRec);

    { now create 100 empty patrons records}
    PControlRec:=false;
    A9_ClearAllFields(PatronsRec);
    PatronsRec.P_Name:=space25;
    PatronsRec.P_Left:=-1;
```

```
      PatronsRec.P_Right:=-1;
      PControlRec:=False;
      for count:=1 to 100 do
        begin
           seek(PatronsFile,count);
           write(PatronsFile,PatronsRec);
        end;{for}
      close(PatronsFile);

end; {M111_InitialisePatronsFile}


PROCEDURE M112_InitialiseSubsFile;
var choice, default     : char;
    SCurrentYear        : integer;
    CurrentYearString   : string;
    code                : integer;
    iocode              : integer;
    SFileName           : string;
    SRecNo              : integer;
    nch                 : integer;  {no of chars read in ReadField}
begin
   A7_GSTitle(black,cyan);
   SFileName:= pathname + 'subs.dat'; {set file name}
   A6_WriteXY(25,5,'Initialise Subscriptions File');
   A6_WriteXY(21,7,'THIS PROCEDURE SHOULD BE CARRIED OUT');
   A6_WriteXY(19,8,'ONLY WHEN THE SYSTEM IS FIRST INSTALLED,');
   A6_WriteXY(19,9,'OR AT THE END OF THE FINANCIAL YEAR.');
   A6_WriteXY(19,10,'MAKE SURE YOU HAVE A BACKUP ON A SEPARATE DISK');
   A6_WriteXY(19,11,'BEFORE PROCEEDING.');
   A6_WriteXY(16,13,'Do you wish to proceed? (Y/N):');
   A8_GetOneChar(47,13,choice,'Y','N');
   if        (choice)='N' then exit;
  {disable automatic IO checking with the compiler directive $I-,
      which has to be written in curly brackets as shown}
      {$I-}
      assign (SubsFile,SFileName);
        rewrite(SubsFile);
        {ioresult is a reserved word in Turbo Pascal}
        {it returns a code depending on the result of the IO operation}
        iocode:=ioresult;
        case iocode of
           0    : rewrite(SubsFile);
           1,2,3   : begin
                   Window(2,23,79,24);
                   Textcolor(black);
                   Textbackground(red);
                   clrscr;
                   A6_WriteXY(16,23,
                     'Incorrect drive name - please restart the program.  ');
                   A1_Continue(16,24);
                   window(1,1,80,25);
                   exit;
                end;
           else
```

Initialises The Subs file, writing current year to control record.

Checks for various errors such as wrong drive name (entered by user in O3_GetPathname)

```
            begin
                A6_WriteXY(16,17,'cannot create file - check disk in Drive A');
                A1_Continue(16,18);
                exit;
            end;
        end; {case}
    {$I+}
    A6_WriteXY(16,21,'Enter subscriptions year (eg 1992) : ');
    repeat
        gotoxy(54,21);
        A3_ReadField(CurrentYearString,4,nch);
        A4_StripBlanks(CurrentYearString);
        val(currentyearstring,SCurrentYear,code);
    until(code=0)and(currentyear>1990) ;
    {ioresult =0 when operation is successful}

    {now create control record}
    SRecNo:=0;
    SControlRec:=true;
    SubsRec.SC_CurrentYear:=SCurrentYear;
    seek(SubsFile,SRecNo);
    write(SubsFile,SubsRec);

    { now create 1 empty SUBS record}

    SControlRec:=false;
    SubsRec.S_Name:=space25;
    SubsRec.S_Amount:=0.0;
    SubsRec.S_date :='          ';
    seek(SubsFile,1);
    write(SubsFile,SubsRec);
    close(subsFile);
end; {M112_InitialiseSubsFile}

PROCEDURE M11_SysInitMenu;
var choice:char;
begin
  choice := 'x';
  repeat
  A7_GSTitle(black,cyan);
  A6_WriteXY(31,5,'System Initialisation');
  A6_WriteXY(26,8,'1. Initialise Patrons file');
  A6_WriteXY(26,10,'2. Initialise Subscriptions file');
  A6_WriteXY(29,11,'for new financial year');
  A6_WriteXY(26,13,'Q. Quit to main menu');
  A6_writeXY(25,20,'Please enter your choice:');
  repeat
    gotoxy(52,20);
    choice:= readkey;
    write(choice);
  until choice in ['1'..'2','Q','q'];
  write(choice);
  case choice of
      '1'      : M111_InitialisePatronsFile;
      '2'      : M112_InitialiseSubsFile;
```

Displays menu for system initialisation — can create new Patrons file or subs file

```
      'Q','q' : exit;
    end; {case}
  until upcase(choice) ='Q'
end; {M11_SysInitMenu}


PROCEDURE M121_AddPatron;
var
    FirstTimeThrough    : boolean;
    errorFound          : boolean;
    present             : boolean;
    ptrToRec            : integer;
    reply               : char;
    PName               : string;
    nch                 : integer;   {no of chars read in ReadField}
begin
  present:=false;
  PName[1]:=' ';
      A7_GSTitle(yellow,blue);
      A6_WriteXY(32,5,'Add a new patron');
      A6_WriteXY(3,7,'Surname followed by initials:');
      textcolor(lightgray);
      A6_WriteXY(3,8,'enter x to return to Maintenance menu');
      textcolor(white);
      gotoxy(34,7);
  while (upcase(PName[1]) <> 'X') do
  begin
      A6_WriteXY(34,7,'_____'); {clear name}
      A9_ClearAllFields(PInputRec);
      FirstTimeThrough := true;
      C4_ClearScreenFields;
      C1_DisplayPtext;
      PInputRec.P_Name:=space25;
       repeat                   {until ok to add}
       errorFound:=false;
       reply:='Y';
       repeat
         gotoxy(34,7);
         A3_ReadField(Pname,25,nch);
         PName := A5_UpCaseStr(PName);
         if nch <> 0
           then PInputRec.P_Name:=Pname;
      until PInputRec.P_Name<>space25;
      if (Upcase(PName[1])<>'X')  then
      begin
        if  (Patronsrec.P_Name<>PInputrec.P_name)  then
          begin
            C2_FindPatron(PInputRec.P_Name,ptrToRec,present);
            A9_ClearAllFields(PatronsRec);
            C4_ClearScreenFields;
            FirstTimeThrough:=True;
          end;
        PatronsRec.P_Name:=PInputRec.P_Name;
        if present then
          begin
```

Adds a new patron to the file after checking that he/she is not already on file

```
                C1_DisplayPtext;
                C4_ClearScreenFields;
                C3_DisplayPatron;
                window(2,23,79,24);
                textbackground(red);
                clrscr;
                A6_WriteXY(2,1,'Error: Patron of this name already on file');
                A1_Continue(46,1);
                ErrorFound:=true;
                gotoxy(1,23);
                window(1,1,80,25);
                textbackground(blue);
                C4_ClearScreenFields;
                gotoxy(1,23);
                clreol;
                gotoxy(1,24);
                clreol;
                textcolor(cyan);
                A6_WriteXY(34,7,'_____'); {clear name}
                textcolor(white);
              end
            else
              begin
                C1_DisplayPtext;
                if FirstTimeThrough then A9_ClearAllFields(PatronsRec);
                C5_AcceptPatronsDetails(FirstTimeThrough);
                A6_WriteXY(26,23,'OK to add? (Y/N): ');
                A8_GetOneChar(wherex,wherey,reply,'Y','N');
                FirstTimeThrough:=false;
                gotoxy(26,23);
                clreol;
              end;
            {end if record present}
        end; {if upcase(name)<>'X'}
      until (upcase(reply)='Y') or (errorfound);
            if (upcase(pname[1])<>'X')and (errorfound=false)
            then
              begin
                PatronsRec.P_Left:=-1;
                PatronsRec.P_Right:=-1;
                C6_WritePatronToFile;
                C4_ClearScreenFields;
              end;
    end; {while}
end;{M121_AddPatron}


PROCEDURE M122_ChangePatron;
var
    FirstTimeThrough : boolean;
    errorFound       : boolean;
    present          : boolean;
    ptrToRec         : integer;
    reply            : char;
    PName            : string;
    nch              : integer;   {no of chars read in ReadField}
```

Changes existing patron's record - eg change of address etc

```
begin
  present:=false;
  FirstTimeThrough :=false;
  PName[1]:=' ';
      A7_GSTitle(yellow,blue);
      A6_WriteXY(30,5,'Change a patron''s details');
      A6_WriteXY(3,7,'Surname followed by initials:');
      textcolor(cyan);
      A6_WriteXY(34,7,'_____'); {clear name}
      textcolor(lightgray);
      A6_WriteXY(3,8,'enter x to return to Maintenance menu');
      textcolor(white);
      gotoxy(34,7);
  while (upcase(PName[1]) <> 'X') do
    begin
    A6_WriteXY(34,7,'_____'); {clear name}
    C4_ClearScreenFields;
    C1_DisplayPtext;
    PInputRec.P_Name:=space25;
    repeat
      errorFound:=false;
      repeat
        gotoxy(34,7);
         A6_WriteXY(34,7,'_____');} {clear name}
        gotoxy(34,7);
        A3_ReadField(Pname,25,nch);   ← User enters patrons name....
        PName := A5_UpCaseStr(PName);
        if nch <> 0
           then PInputRec.P_Name:=Pname;
      until PInputRec.P_Name<>space25;
      if (Upcase(PName[1])<>'X')  then
      begin
        if  (Patronsrec.P_Name<>PInputrec.P_name)  then
            C2_FindPatron(PInputRec.P_Name,ptrToRec,present);
        PatronsRec.P_Name:=PInputRec.P_Name;
        if present then              ← If patron is on file then all
          begin                         details are displayed ...
            C1_DisplayPtext;   ←
            C4_ClearScreenFields;
            C3_DisplayPatron;            ← user enters changes...
             C5_AcceptPatronsDetails(FirstTimeThrough);
             A6_WriteXY(26,23,'OK to change? (Y/N): ');
             A8_GetOneChar(wherex,wherey,reply,'Y','N');  ← and confirms
             gotoxy(26,23);
             clreol;                   whether to go ahead and
          end                          change the record.
        else {record not found}
          begin
             window(2,23,79,24);
             textbackground(red);
             clrscr;
             A6_WriteXY(2,1,'Error: No patron of this name found');
             A1_Continue(46,1);
             ErrorFound:=true;
             window(1,1,80,25);
```

```
            textbackground(blue);
            C4_ClearScreenFields;
            gotoxy(1,23);
            clreol;
            gotoxy(1,24);
            clreol;
            textcolor(cyan);
            A6_WriteXY(34,7,'_____');  {clear name}
            textcolor(white);
          end;

          {end if record not found}
      end; {if upcase(name)<>'X'}
    until (upcase(reply)='Y')or (errorfound)
                  or (upcase(pname[1])='X');
    if (upcase(pname[1])<>'X')and (errorfound=false)
            then
              begin
                  seek(patronsfile,PtrToRec);
                  write(patronsfile,patronsrec);
                  C4_ClearScreenFields;
              end;
    end; {while}
end; {M122_ChangePatron}


PROCEDURE M123_DeletePatron;
var
    errorFound    : boolean;
    present       : boolean;
    ptrToRec      : integer;
    reply         : char;
    PName         : string;
    nch           : integer;   {no of chars read in ReadField}
begin
  present:=false;
  PName[1]:=' ';
      A7_GSTitle(yellow,blue);
      A6_WriteXY(30,5,'Delete a patron''s details');
      A6_WriteXY(3,7,'Surname followed by initials:');
      textcolor(lightgray);
      A6_WriteXY(3,8,'enter x to return to Maintenance menu');
      textcolor(white);
      gotoxy(34,7);
  while (upcase(PName[1]) <> 'X') do
    begin
    A6_WriteXY(34,7,'_____');  {clear name}
    C4_ClearScreenFields;
    C1_DisplayPtext;
    PInputRec.P_Name:=space25;
    repeat
      errorFound:=false;
      repeat
        gotoxy(34,7);
        A6_WriteXY(34,7,'_____');  {clear name}
        gotoxy(34,7);
```

Deletes existing patron

```
      A3_ReadField(Pname,25,nch);
      PName := A5_UpCaseStr(PName);
      if nch <> 0
         then PInputRec.P_Name:=Pname;
   until PInputRec.P_Name<>space25;
   if (Upcase(PName[1])<>'X')   then
   begin
      present:=false;
      if  (Patronsrec.P_Name<>PInputrec.P_name)  then
          C2_FindPatron(PInputRec.P_Name,ptrToRec,present);
      PatronsRec.P_Name:=PInputRec.P_Name;
      if present then
        begin
          C1_DisplayPtext;
          C4_ClearScreenFields;
          C3_DisplayPatron;
           A6_WriteXY(26,23,'OK to delete? (Y/N): ');
           A8_GetOneChar(wherex,wherey,reply,'Y','N');
           gotoxy(26,23);
           clreol;
        end
      else {record not found}
        begin
          window(2,23,79,24);
          textbackground(red);
          clrscr;
          A6_WriteXY(2,1,'Error: No patron of this name found');
          A1_Continue(46,1);
          ErrorFound:=true;
          window(1,1,80,25);
          textbackground(blue);
          C4_ClearScreenFields;
          gotoxy(1,23);
          clreol;
          gotoxy(1,24);
          clreol;
          textcolor(cyan);
          A6_WriteXY(34,7,'_____'); {clear name}
          textcolor(white);
        end;

      {end if record not found}
    end; {if upcase(name)<>'X'}
  until (upcase(reply)='Y')or (errorfound)
             or (upcase(pname[1])='X');
  if (upcase(pname[1])<>'X')and (errorfound=false)
         then
           begin
               seek(patronsfile,PtrToRec);
               PatronsRec.P_Deleted:='Y';
               write(patronsfile,patronsrec);
               C4_ClearScreenFields;
           end;
    end; {while}
end; {M123_DeletePatron}
```

user enters name which is converted to upper case

If patron is on file all details are displayed

and user confirms that record is to be deleted.

If patron is not on file an error message is displayed.

```
PROCEDURE M124_OpenSubsFile(var reply:char);
begin
   assign(SubsFile, pathname + 'Subs.dat');
   {$I-}
   repeat
   reset(SubsFile);
   {ioresult is a reserved word in Turbo Pascal}
   {it returns a code depending on the result of the IO operation}
   iocode:=ioresult;
   case iocode of
           0     : reset(SubsFile);
           1,2,3 : begin
                     Window(2,23,79,24);
                     Textcolor(black);
                     Textbackground(red);
                     clrscr;
                     A6_WriteXY(16,23,
                        'Incorrect drive name - please restart the program.   ');
                     A1_Continue(16,24);
                     window(1,1,80,25);
                     exit;
                   end;


           else
           begin
             Window(2,23,79,24);
                     Textcolor(black);
                     Textbackground(red);
                     clrscr;
                     A6_WriteXY(16,23,
                        'Cannot open file - check disk in specified drive');
                     A1_Continue(16,24);
                     window(1,1,80,25);
           end;
   end; {case}
   until iocode=0;
   {$I+}

   {Read the Control Record to check the date}
   subsfilePtr:=0;
   SControlRec:=true;
   reply :='x';
   seek(subsfile,0);
   read(SubsFile,SubsRec);
   if(SubsRec.SC_CurrentYear<>CurrentYear) then
     begin
       B1_WindowDisplay(7,7,71,16,yellow,lightgray,2,reply);
       if reply='S' then exit;
     end;
   {Carry on}
   SubsFilePtr := FileSize(SubsFile)-1;

end;
```

Opens the subscriptions file, checking for various errors

positions pointer at the first empty record. (File starts off with one empty data record) ←

```
PROCEDURE M125_OpenPatronsFile;
begin
    assign(PatronsFile,pathname + 'Patrons.dat');
    {$I-};
    repeat
    reset (PatronsFile);
    {ioresult is a reserved word in Turbo Pascal}
    {it returns a code depending on the result of the IO operation}
    iocode:=ioresult;
    case iocode of
            0      : reset (PatronsFile);
            1,2,3  : begin
                     Window(2,23,79,24);
                     Textcolor(black);
                     Textbackground(red);
                     clrscr;
                     A6_WriteXY(16,23,
                        'Incorrect drive name - please restart the program.   ');
                     A1_Continue(16,24);
                     window(1,1,80,25);
                     exit;
                   end;
          else
          begin
             Window(2,23,79,24);
             Textcolor(black);
             Textbackground(red);
             clrscr;
             window(1,1,80,25);
             A6_WriteXY(16,23,
                'cannot open file - check disk in specified drive ');
             A1_Continue(16,24);
             window(1,1,80,25);

          end;
    end; {case}
    until iocode=0;
       {$I+}
    PControlRec:=true;
    seek (PatronsFile,0);
    read(PatronsFile, PatronsRec);
    NextFree := PatronsRec.PC_NextFree;
    { if next_free is 1, the tree is empty,
              otherwise the root is at record 1.
              Set up a pointer P to the root accordingly. }

    if   NextFree = 1 then p:=-1
    else p:=1;
end; {Open_PatronsFile}


PROCEDURE M12_MaintenanceMenu;
var
    choice   : char;
begin
  choice := 'x';
```

[handwritten annotation: Opens patrons file]

[handwritten annotation: reads The control record to get The position of the next free record, checking for an empty file.]

```
  repeat
    A7_GSTitle(black,cyan);
    A6_WriteXY(26,5,'Maintenance of Patrons file');
    A6_WriteXY(26,8,'1. Add a new patron');
    A6_WriteXY(26,10,'2. Change a patron''s details');
    A6_WriteXY(26,12,'3. Delete a patron');
    A6_WriteXY(26,14,'Q. Quit to main menu');
    A6_WriteXY(25,20,'Please enter your choice:');
    repeat
      gotoxy(52,20);
      choice:=readkey;
      write(choice);
    until choice in ['1'..'3','Q','q'];
    case choice of
        '1'       : begin
                        M125_OpenPatronsFile;
                        if iocode<>0 then exit;
                        M121_AddPatron;
                        Close(PatronsFile);
                    end;
        '2'       : begin
                        M125_OpenPatronsFile;
                        if iocode<>0 then exit;
                        M122_ChangePatron;
                        close(PatronsFile);
                    end;
        '3'       : begin
                        M125_OpenPatronsFile;
                        if iocode<>0 then exit;
                        M123_DeletePatron;
                        Close(PatronsFile);
                    end;
        'Q','q' : exit;
    end; {case}
  until upcase(choice)='Q';
end; {MaintenanceMenu}


PROCEDURE M13_EntrySubs;
var
    MoreBatches       : char;
    ptrTorec          : integer;
    present           : boolean;
    code1, code2,
    code3             : integer;
    reply             : char;
    SubsString        : string;
    NumEntriesStr     : string;
    NumEntries        : integer;
    BatchTotalStr     : string;
    BatchTotal        : real;
    BatchTotalIn      : real;
    CalcTotal         : real;
    InSubsarray       : array[1..10] of SubsRecType;
    i                 : integer;
```

Routine for entry of patrons subscriptions in batches

```
    EditOrPost          : char;
    day,month,year      : integer;
    DayStr,MonthStr     : string;
    YearStr             : string;
    dateStr             : string;
    DateValid           : boolean;
    NameIn              : string;
    SubsIn              : real;
    DateIn              : string;
    PrevDate            :string;
    nch                 : integer;      {no of chars read in ReadField}
PROCEDURE M13A_PostSubs;
var i       : integer;
begin
 gotoxy(2,23);
 write('POSTING SUBS......');
 seek (SubsFile, SubsFilePtr);
 for i:=1 to NumEntries do
   begin
     C2_FindPatron(InSubsArray[i].S_Name,ptrToRec,Present);
    PatronsRec.P_SubCurrent:=PatronsRec.P_SubCurrent + InSubsArray[i].S_Amount;
     seek(patronsFile,PtrToRec);
     write(PatronsFile,PatronsRec);

     { and write to Subs File}
     SubsRec:=InSubsArray[i];
     write(SubsFile,SubsRec);
   end;
 gotoxy(2,23);
 clreol;
end;   {M13A_PostSubs}


{************ BEGIN M13_ENTRY_SUBS ********************}

begin
  repeat           {until No More Batches }
   A7_GSTitle(yellow,blue);
   A6_WriteXY(28,4,'Entry of Subscriptions');
   A6_WriteXY(6,6,'Number of Entries in Batch (Max 10):');
   A6_WriteXY(51,6,'Batch Total: £');
   A6_WriteXY(6,8,'Date       Surname and initials        Subscription');
   A6_WriteXY(2,9,'eg 25-04-92');
   textcolor(white);
   for i:=1 to 10 do
     begin
       InSubsArray[i].S_Date := '';
       InSubsArray[i].S_Name := space25;
       InSubsArray[i].S_Amount :=0;
     end;
   repeat
     gotoxy(43,6);
     readln(NumEntriesStr);
     A4_StripBlanks(NumEntriesStr);
     val(NumEntriesStr,NumEntries,code);
   until (code=0) and (NumEntries in [1..10]);
```

Each patron is looked up and the subs amount added to their current subs field.

The batch of records is held in an array in memory until the batch total is correct. Then the user can 'post' the batch to the patrons file (M13A_PostSubs)

```
repeat    {until EditOrPost = A or P}
  repeat
    gotoxy(65,6);
    readln(BatchTotalStr);
    A4_StripBlanks(BatchTotalStr);
    val(BatchTotalStr,BatchTotalIn,code);
  until(code=0) or (BatchTotalStr='');
  if (BatchTotalStr<>'') then BatchTotal := BatchTotalIn;
  CalcTotal:=0.0;
  PrevDate := InSubsArray[1].S_Date;
  for i:=1 to NumEntries do
    begin
      DateStr:=PrevDate;
      NameIn:=space25;
      SubsIn:=0;
      {get date}
      repeat
        gotoxy(5,i+9);
        readln(datestr);
        if (datestr='') and (InSubsArray[i].S_date='') then
          begin
            datestr:= PrevDate;
            gotoxy(5,i+9);
            write(prevdate);
          end;
        Daystr:=Copy(Datestr,1,2);
        val(Daystr,day,code1);
        monthstr:=Copy(DateStr,4,2);
        val(MonthStr,Month,code2);
        YearStr:=Copy(DateStr,7,2);
        val(YearStr,Year,code3);
        Datevalid:=false;
        if ((code1=0) and (code2=0) and (code3=0) or (datestr=''))
        and ((day in [1..31]) and (month in [1..12]) and (year in [00..99])
           or (datestr='')) then DateValid:=true;
        if not datevalid then
            B1_WindowDisplay(14,7,51,19,white,blue,1,reply);
{the last parameter but one identifies this particular window}

if (datestr='') and (InSubsArray[i].S_Date='') then datevalid:=false;
      until DateValid;
    if(datestr<>'')then
      begin
        InSubsArray[i].S_Date:=datestr;
        PrevDate := InSubsArray[i].S_Date;
      end;

    {get name and look it up on Patrons file}

    reply:='C';
    repeat
      gotoxy(16,i+9);
      A3_ReadField(NameIn,25,nch);
      NameIn:=A5_UpCaseStr(NameIn);
      if nch <> 0 then
```

(handwritten annotations:)

← can either 'Abandon' or 'Post'.

All numeric fields are read in as strings so that program can't crash with invalid characters

← pop-up window appears with error message if invalid date is entered

```
            begin
              InSubsArray[i].S_Name:=NameIn;
              C2_FindPatron(InSubsArray[i].S_Name,ptrToRec,Present);
            end;
        if not present then
            begin
                window(2,23,79,24);
                textbackground(red);
                clrscr;
                A6_WriteXY(2,1,'Error: No patron of this name. ');
                A1_Continue(33,1);
                window(1,1,80,25);
                textbackground(blue);
                gotoxy(1,23);
                clreol;
                gotoxy(1,24);
                clreol;
                gotoxy(16,i+9);
                write(space25);
            end;
          if InSubsArray[i].S_Name = space25 then present:=false;
        until (present=true);

        {get Subscription}
        repeat
            gotoxy(46,i+9);
            Readln(SubsString);
            A4_StripBlanks(SubsString);
            val(SubsString,SubsIn,code);
        until (code=0) or (SubsString='');
        if (SubsIn<>0) then InSubsArray[i].S_Amount:=SubsIn;
    end; {for}


    for i:=1 to NumEntries do
    begin
          CalcTotal:=CalcTotal+InSubsArray[i].S_Amount;
    end; {for}
    if (CalcTotal<>BatchTotal) then
      begin
        window(2,23,79,24);
        textbackground(red);
        clrscr;
    A6_WriteXY(2,1,'Error: Check Batch Total. Press E to Edit or A to Abandon
');
        A8_GetOneChar(wherex,wherey,EditOrPost,'E','A');
        window(1,1,80,25);
        textbackground(blue);
        gotoxy(1,23);
        clreol;
        gotoxy(1,24);
        clreol;

    end
    else
      begin
```

← checks that patron is on file

← checks batch total

```
            window(2,23,79,24);
            textbackground(green);
            clrscr;
            A6_WriteXY(2,1,'Press E to Edit, P to Post or A to Abandon ');
            repeat
              gotoxy(45,1);
              readln(EditOrPost);
            until Upcase(EditOrPost) in ['E','P','A'];
            window(1,1,80,25);
            textbackground(blue);
            gotoxy(1,23);
            clreol;
            gotoxy(1,24);
            clreol;
          end; {if}
      until (Upcase(EditOrPost)= 'A') or (Upcase(EditorPost)='P');

      if (upcase(EditOrPost)='P') then M13A_PostSubs;
      A6_WriteXY(22,23,'Enter another batch? (Y/N): ');
      A8_GetOneChar(wherex,wherey,MoreBatches,'Y','N');

    until UpCase(MoreBatches) = 'N';
end;

PROCEDURE M141_MailingLabels;
const x25 = 'xxxxxxxxxxxxxxxxxxxxxxxxx';
      x8  = '        ';
var
      i      : integer;
      reply  : char;
begin
    {Fill array with x's}
    for i:=1 to 3 do
      begin
        with labelArray[i] do
        begin
          name     := x25;
          address1:= x25;
          address2:= x25;
          address3:= x25;
          postcode:= x8;
        end; {with}
      end; {for}
  A7_GSTitle(blue,yellow);
  {Print a test set of labels}
  repeat
    D2_Print3Labels;
    A6_WriteXY(25,10,'Are the labels correctly lined up? ');
    A8_GetOneChar(wherex,wherey,reply,'Y','N');
  until reply='Y';
  NIn:=0;
  D9_PrintTraverse(p);
  {Print the final row of labels}
  If NIn <> 0 then D2_Print3Labels;
end;{M141_MailingLabels}
```

This gives the user a row of 3 'dummy' labels filled with x's to check that labels are correctly positioned in the printer. If labels are not aligned, another row can be printed

```
PROCEDURE M142_PatronsForProg;
{Names can either be printed or sent to a file for
 importing into PageMaker, according to user's choice }

begin
  getdate(year,month,day,dayofWeek);
  A7_GSTitle(yellow,blue);
  A6_WriteXY(19,5,'List of Patrons'' Names for Programme');
  A6_WriteXY(11,9,'Output to file or printer? (F or P): ');
  A8_GetOneChar(49,9,fpchoice,'F','P');
  if upcase(fpchoice)='F'then
    begin
      assign(ProgNames,pathname + 'Pnames.dat');
      rewrite(ProgNames);
      gotoxy(20,16);
      Writeln('Names will be written to ',pathname,'PNames.Dat...');
      ReportChoice:='8';
      D9_PrintTraverse(p);
      close(Prognames);
      A6_WriteXY(27,18,'Transfer complete.');
      A1_Continue(25,21);
    end
    else
      begin
        linecount:=50;
        pageno:=1;
        D9_PrintTraverse(p);
        writeln(lst);
        writeln(lst,'END OF REPORT');
      end;

end;     {M142_PatronsForProg}


PROCEDURE M143_PatronsDetails;
{ asks user where in the list of names to start,
 and if printout requested, where to stop.
  If screen display selected, names will be
  displayed one at a time so user can quit any time }

var InputField : string;
    nch        : integer;

begin
  getdate(year,month,day,dayofWeek);
  A7_GSTitle(yellow,blue);
  A6_WriteXY(29,5,'List of Patrons'' Details');
  A6_WriteXY(11,7,'Output to screen or printer? (S or P): ');
  A8_GetOneChar(49,7,spchoice,'S','P');
  A6_WriteXY(11,9,'Enter name to start at:');
  A6_WriteXY(11,10,'(Press Enter to start at the first name)');
  gotoxy(34,9);
  readln(startname);
  StartName:=A5_UpCaseStr(startname);
  if upcase(spchoice)='S'then
```

[handwritten annotation:] Sends names to file if user enters 'F'

[handwritten annotation:] ↑ informs user of the DOS file name

[handwritten annotation:] otherwise, sends names to the printer

```
      begin
          endname:='zzzzz';
          choiceofMore:='M';
          D8_ScreenTraverse(p);
          A1_Continue(25,23);
      end
      else
          begin
            A6_WriteXY(11,12,'Enter name to finish at:');
            A6_WriteXY(11,13,'Press Enter to end at last name');
            gotoxy(36,12);
            A3_Readfield(InputField,25,nch);
            endname := InputField;
            endname:=A5_UpCaseStr(endname);
            if endname=space25 then endname:='zzzzzzzzzzzzzzzzzzzzzzzzz';
            linecount:=50;
            pageno:=1;
            D9_PrintTraverse(p);
            writeln(lst);
            writeln(lst,'END OF REPORT');
          end;
      {end screen/print choice}
end;    {M143_PatronsDetails}


PROCEDURE M144_SubsByPatron;
{ calls routine to print subs as recorded on patrons file}
begin
  TotalCurrent:=0.0;
  TotalLastYear:=0.0;
  Total2YrsAgo:=0.0;
  getdate(year,month,day,dayofWeek);
  linecount:=50;
  pageno:=1;
  D9_PrintTraverse(p);
  write(lst,'                                       ');
    writeln(lst,'————      ————        ————');
  write(lst,'                                  ');
  writeln(lst,'Total         ',TotalCurrent:7:2,'      ',
              TotalLastYear:7:2,'      ',Total2YrsAgo:7:2);
end;    {M144_SubsByPatron}


PROCEDURE M145_YearsSubs;
{Prints subs from Subs file in order of entry}
Const   space55='
Var
  TotalSubs    : real;
  ReportYear   : integer;
begin
    TotalSubs := 0.0;
    ReportYear := SubsRec.SC_CurrentYear;
    GetDate(year,month,day,DayOfWeek);
    LineCount:=50;
    PageNo := 1;
    with SubsRec do
    begin
```

Default endname is high ASCII character string zzzzz

```
      while not eof(SubsFile) do
        begin
        read(SubsFile,SubsRec);
        if linecount>=50 then
          begin
            write(lst,#12);   {form feed}
            write(lst,day:2,'-',month,'-',year);
            write(lst,'                    ');
            write(lst,'GILBERT AND SULLIVAN SOCIETY');
            write(lst,'            Page ',pageno);
            writeln(lst);
            write(lst,'                    ');
            writeln(lst,ReportYear,'  Subscriptions in Order of Entry');
            writeln(lst);
            write(lst,'                            Date     Name');
            writeln(lst,'                         Amount');
            linecount:=6;
            pageno:=pageno+1;
          end; {if linecount>=50}
        TotalSubs:=TotalSubs+S_Amount;
        writeln(lst,'                          ',S_Date,'  ',
              S_Name,'   ',S_Amount:6:2);
        linecount:=linecount+1;
        end;{while not eof}
      end; {with}
      write(lst,space55);
        writeln(lst,' ———');
      write(lst,'                                        Total');
      write(lst,'            ',TotalSubs:7:2);
end;   {M145_YearsSubs}

PROCEDURE M14_ReportsMenu;
var
  dateError:char;
begin
  repeat
    A7_GSTitle(black,cyan);   {clear screen and display title}
    A6_WriteXY(23,5,'Reports, Displays and Mailing Labels');
    A6_WriteXY(25,7,'1. Mailing labels');
    A6_WriteXY(25,9,'2. List of Patrons for programme');
    A6_WriteXY(25,11,'3. List of patrons'' details');
    A6_WriteXY(25,13,'4. Subscriptions (sequenced by patron)');
    A6_WriteXY(25,15,'5. Year''s subscriptions (in order of entry)');
    A6_WriteXY(25,17,'Q. Quit');
    A6_WriteXY(25,20,'Please enter your choice:');
    repeat
      gotoxy(52,20);
      reportchoice:=readkey;
      write(reportchoice);
    until reportchoice in ['1'..'5','Q','q'];
    case reportchoice of
        '1'      : begin
                     M125_OpenPatronsFile;
                     if iocode<>0 then exit;
                     M141_MailingLabels;
```

Submenu displayed listing all reports

```
                                 close (PatronsFile);
                         end;
         '2'     : begin
                         M125_OpenPatronsFile;
                         if iocode<>0 then exit;
                         M142_PatronsForProg;
                         close (PatronsFile);
                 end;
         '3'     : begin
                         M125_OpenPatronsFile;
                         if iocode<>0 then exit;
                         M143_PatronsDetails;
                         close (PatronsFile);
                 end;
         '4'     : begin
                         M125_OpenPatronsFile;
                         if iocode<>0 then exit;
                         M144_SubsByPatron;
                         close (PatronsFile);
                 end;
         '5'     : begin
                         M124_OpenSubsFile(DateError);
                         if iocode<>0 then exit;
                         If DateError='S' then exit;
                         M145_YearsSubs;
                         close (SubsFile);
                 end;
      'Q','q' : exit;
   end; {case}
 until upcase(reportchoice)='Q';
end; {ReportsMenu}

PROCEDURE M15_EndOfYear;
var recpointer  : integer;
    reply       : char;
begin
   A7_GSTitle(yellow,black);
   A6_WriteXY(36,5,'End of Year');
   A6_WriteXY(11,7,'This procedure will reset all subscriptions to zero, ');
   A6_WriteXY(11,8,'ready for the new financial year. ');
   A6_WriteXY(11,10,'Are you sure you want to continue? ');
   readln(reply);
   If upcase(reply)<>'Y' then exit;
   A7_GSTitle(yellow,black);
   A6_WriteXY(27,6,'Working, please wait....');
   M125_OpenPatronsFile;
   recpointer := 1;
   with PatronsRec do
   begin
     while not eof(PatronsFile) do
     begin
       seek(patronsFile,Recpointer);
       read(patronsFile,PatronsRec);
       P_Sub2YrsAgo:= P_SubLastYear;
       P_SubLastYear:= P_SubCurrent;
```

End of Year routine

Moves subs to previous year on patrons file

```
        P_SubCurrent:=0.0;
        seek(PatronsFile,RecPointer);
        write(PatronsFile,PatronsRec);
        RecPointer:=RecPointer+1;
    end;{while}
end; {with}
M124_OpenSubsFile(reply);
Textcolor(yellow);
TextBackground(Black);
seek(subsFile,0);
read(subsFile,subsRec); {to get the date on the control record}
A6_WriteXY(11,8,
    'The Patrons file has been reset for the new financial year.');
A6_WriteXY(11,10,
        'You should now make a backup of the Subs file, A:Subs.Dat');
A6_WriteXY(11,11,'on to a separate disk, label it "SUBS ');
    write(SubsRec.SC_CurrentYear,'"');
A6_WriteXY(wherex, wherey,' and put it safely away.');
A6_WriteXY(11,13,'Then choose Option 1 "System Initialisation"');
A6_WriteXY(11,14,'from the Main Menu, to initialise a new subs file');
A1_Continue(25,20);
close(PatronsFile);
end; {EndOfYear}


PROCEDURE M1_MainMenu;
var
    choice          : char;
    DateError       : char;
begin
    repeat
    A7_GSTitle(yellow,lightgray);    {clear screen and display title}
    A6_WriteXY(36,5,'Main Menu');
    A6_WriteXY(25,7,'1. System Initialisation');
    A6_WriteXY(25,9,'2. Maintenance of Patrons file');
    A6_WriteXY(25,11,'3. Entry of subscriptions');
    A6_WriteXY(25,13,'4. Reports, displays and mailing labels');
    A6_WriteXY(25,15,'5. End of Year');
    A6_WriteXY(25,17,'Q. Quit');
    A6_WriteXY(25,20,'Please enter your choice:');
    repeat
        gotoxy(52,20);
        choice:=readkey;
        write(choice);
    until choice in ['1'..'5','Q','q'];
    case choice of
        '1'     : M11_SysInitMenu;
        '2'     : M12_MaintenanceMenu;
        '3'     : begin
                    M125_OpenPatronsFile;
                    if iocode<>0 then exit;
                    M124_OpenSubsFile(dateError);
                    if dateError<>'S' then
                    M13_EntrySubs;
                    close(PatronsFile);
                    close(SubsFile);
                end;
```

Handwritten annotations:
- Makes current subs equal to zero
- Tells user to initialise a new subs file for the new financial year.
- Opening menu

```
   '4'       : M14_ReportsMenu;
   '5'       : M15_EndofYear;
   'Q','q' : exit;
  end; {case}
 until upcase(choice)='Q';
end; {M1_MainMenu}


PROCEDURE O1_OpeningScreen;
var
   GraphDriver   : integer;
   GraphMode     : integer;
   ErrorCode     : integer;
   PathToDriver  : string;
   ch            : char;
begin
   PathToDriver:='a:\bgi';
   repeat
   GraphDriver := Detect;
   InitGraph(GraphDriver,GraphMode,PathToDriver);
   ErrorCode := GraphResult;
   if ErrorCode<>grOK then
   begin
     writeln('Graphics Error:', GraphErrorMsg(ErrorCode));
     if ErrorCode = grFileNotFound then   { Can't find driver file }
     begin
      Writeln('Enter full path to BGI driver or type <Ctrl-Break> to quit:');
       Readln(PathToDriver);
       Writeln;
     end
     else
     begin
       writeln('Program Aborted');
       Halt(1);
     end; {if}                          {some other error; terminate}
   end;
  until ErrorCode = grOK;
  SetColor(lightblue);
  Rectangle(2,2,GetMaxX-2,GetMaxY-2);
  SetTextJustify(CenterText,CenterText);
  SetTextStyle(GothicFont,HorizDir,7);
  SetColor(cyan);
  OutTextXY(GetMaxX div 2, 60,
    'Gilbert & Sullivan');
  OutTextXY(GetMaxX div 2, 160,'Society');
  OutTextXY(GetMaxX div 2+1, 160,'Society');
  OutTextXY(GetMaxX div 2, 260, 'Patrons List');
  OuttextXy(GetMaxX div 2 +1,60,'Gilbert & Sullivan');
  OutTextXY(GetMaxX div 2+1, 260, 'Patrons List');
  SetTextStyle(SansSerifFont,horizdir,2);
  SetColor(red);
  OutTextXY(GetMaxX div 2,430,'Please enter password:');
  textcolor(black);          {so it won't show on the screen}
  gotoxy(2,2);               {just inside border}
  readln(password);
  RestoreCRTMode;
end;  {O1_OpeningScreen}
```

The bgi directory holds the Turbo Pascal graphics routines. Without these routines the opening screen cannot be displayed.

printing each word twice slightly offset makes it stand out better

```
PROCEDURE O2_GetCurrentYear;
var
    CurrentYearString  : string;
    F1Pressed          : boolean;
    xcoord,ycoord      : integer;
begin
    A7_GSTitle(black,cyan);
    A6_WriteXY(10,5,'Enter current year (eg 1992) : ');
    A6_WriteXY(10,10,'(Press F1 if you need advice on this)');
    repeat
      gotoxy(44,5);
      xcoord:=wherex;
      ycoord:=wherey;
      F1Pressed:=false;
      CurrentYearString := A2_ReadString(xcoord,ycoord,F1Pressed);
      A4_StripBlanks(CurrentYearString);
      if F1Pressed then
        begin
         B1_WindowDisplay(5,7,75,19,black,cyan,3,char1);
         code:=1;
        end
      else
       val(currentyearstring,currentYear,code);
    until(code=0)and(currentyear>1990) ;
    gotoxy(10,10);
    ClrEol;
end; {O2_GetCurrentYear}
```

← calls Pop-up Window routine

```
PROCEDURE O3_GetPathname;
begin
  A6_WriteXY(10,10,'Please specify drive and directory for data');
  A6_WriteXY(10,12,'eg c:\patrons (default is a:\)  ');
  readln(pathname);
  if(pathname='') then pathname:='A:\';
end; {O3_GetPathname}


{ ********************************************** }
{ ************* Main Program ***************** }
{ ********************************************** }

Begin
   O1_OpeningScreen;
   if password<>'Patience' then exit;
   O2_GetCurrentYear;
   O3_GetPathname;
   M1_MainMenu;
   window(1,1,80,25);
   textcolor(white);
   textbackground(black);
   clrscr;
 end.
```

} MAIN PROGRAM

PART 3

Specimen Project 2

Part 3 shows the report for the second specimen project, ' Short Course Database'.

SHORT COURSE DATABASE

Submitted as an A-Level computing Project
by B. Student
Xxx College
April 199-

Short Course Database

Table of Contents

Every section should
be clearly identified
with a heading.

Section 1 - Analysis

1. Introduction

XXX College is a large educational establishment located within Anytown, serving not only the residents of the town but also a large number of students from the surrounding rural area. It is the largest supplier of adult education in the area, also running a large number of business and summer courses in addition to links with schools and employers.

You must include an
introduction.
Background
information about the
organisation can be
included if relevant.
Then give an overview
of what the project is
about.

As part of an expanding short course programme, the Computing Section runs a programme of one- and two-day courses for clients from business, industry and local government departments. The Computing Section keeps its own records of courses run and who has taught on them, hours worked, income and profit from each course.

The present manual record keeping system is cumbersome and cannot provide all the facts required by senior management without a lot of work on the part of the organiser, Mr Morris. A suggestion has been made to me by Mr Morris that some sort of computer system for keeping records would be useful.

2. The Investigation

2.1 Preparing for interview

In order to find out exactly how the current system works, and what the new system would need to do, I arranged to interview Mr Morris, and prepared the following list of questions in advance.

Check page 1.10; do
the questions cover all
the relevant points in
the analysis of a
system?

1. What sort of facts do management want about the short course programme?

2. Are any reports currently produced that I could look at?

3. How is the data recorded at present?

4. Are there any input documents that I could look at?

5. How many courses are run every week?

6. Does data need to be kept about each student on a course?

7. Does the data need to be kept secure, so that only authorised people can look at it?

8. What are the problems with the current system?

9. What are the objectives of the new system?

10. What hardware and software is available?

2.2 Transcript of the interview

These are the notes of an interview between Mr Morris and myself which took place on October 1, 1991.

Marks will be awarded for your investigative skills, so you should show how you prepared for the interview and include your notes from the interview.

Self: I would like to find out more about the short course programme, and what the objectives of a computerised system would be. Can you tell me, what sort of facts does the management need about these courses?

Mr M: Well, there are various people who want information about short courses. Mr Hodges, for example, keeps the budget for the Computing Section so he needs to know how much profit we are making on each course. Then he knows how much he can spend on new hardware and software, training courses for our own staff and so on. The Head of Department (or Head of School as he is known at this College) needs statistics on how many hours of staff time are spent on these courses and whether that is increasing or decreasing, so that he can plan staff requirements for next year. Also, all the members of staff who teach on the courses need to know how much preparation time they have been allocated for each course, and how many hours teaching time they spent on each course. That's because a lot of this work is done on overtime so they have to keep a record of all the hours they teach in the year.

Self: Surely they know how many hours they taught on a course?

Mr M: You would think so, but unfortunately most teachers are pretty busy and don't write down the information at the time, and a few months later they can't even remember which courses they taught on! It would be really useful if a report could be produced whenever it was needed of exactly what hours any member of staff had taught on which courses.

Self: Are there any reports produced now that I could look at?

Show copies of **actual** documents from the current system if possible

Mr M: No, not really. All the information is got from a 'costing sheet' and I've got one here to show you. *(see page 3 - 10)*. I fill in one of these for each course that is run. Basically it shows how many people were on the course, how much they were charged and how much profit was made. Several copies of this sheet are made; I keep one, the Head of School has a copy on file, one goes to the Finance Department and so on.

Self: There's nothing on the costing sheet to show who taught on the course. Where does that information come from?

Mr M: Ah, yes. I decide who will teach on the courses, and how much preparation time is required, after negotiating with the staff concerned, and then I just note the information down on a piece of paper and keep it in my filing cabinet. Each member of staff is supposed to note down his own hours as well, to record on their personal timetables, but they often forget and come to me for the information, if I can lay my hands on it!

Self:	How many courses are run every week?
Mr M:	About two, on average. All the courses are either one day or two days. Well, occasionally they could be one and a half or three, I suppose. Each course has a maximum of ten students, and if there are more than six, we double-staff it, at least for part of the time. They're each paying about £120 a day so we have to make it good!
Self:	Wow! It sounds very profitable.
Mr M:	Yes, but there are a lot of hidden costs like the building itself, the equipment, new software coming out all the time, staff time and so on. We have to have about 3 or 4 students to break even. Now, have you got all the information you need?
Self:	Could there ever be more than two people teaching on a course?
Mr M:	Ah, good point. Yes; in fact it could be as many as four, perhaps even five. Different people come in to double staff, and sometimes someone else altogether gets the credit for preparation of the course, if they originally wrote the course manual. Each student on these courses is given a complete set of course notes, prepared in advance.
Self:	Does preparation have to be recorded separately from teaching time, then? And is double-staffing something else again?
Mr M:	We don't differentiate at the moment. No, I think keep it simple, record everything as 'hours taught'.

Make sure you understand exactly what data needs to be collected...

Self:	*(Looking at the costing sheet again)* Do I need to record all the information on the costing sheet?
Mr M:	Well, let's think. I don't actually use all this information, but I suppose it could be needed in the future. You definitely don't need to keep 'Grade', short courses are not given a Grade. Mode of Attendance and Venue are not necessary either for this system.
Self:	Can you tell me what reports you would need?
Mr M:	It would be useful to have a report showing for each course separately, total fees received and total course costs, and also showing profit, or what is called 'contribution to capital funds' on the costing sheet. I would need to be able to specify what range of dates to include in the report. That's the information which Mr Hodges needs for his budget, and the Head of School also sometimes asks for that information. It's possible he may ask for a breakdown of costs in the future, but if you are storing that information the system could be extended to cope with that.

... and that there are no misunderstandings over what output is required

A second report is needed for the Head of School showing basically the number of short courses that have been taught in a given period, with the duration of each and the number of taught hours on each, with totals at the bottom.

Identify the problem(s) to be solved.

Self: Is that report in addition to the one showing the hours for one particular member of staff?

Mr M: Yes.

Self: Do you think there should be some sort of security measures such as a password, to keep people from accidentally or deliberately destroying data?

Mr M: I haven't really thought about that. Is it possible to do that? I suppose it would be a good idea.

Self: I'll give that some thought, then. What hardware and software do you have available for this?

Mr M: The standard College PCs, and I would think some kind of database would be ideal - any of the standard College packages.

Have you noticed that no questions have been asked regarding the order that courses should appear on the reports? This oversight could lead to problems later on!

Self: OK, thanks very much. I'll draw up some sample reports and perhaps you could check them to see whether I've really understood what's needed.

Mr M: Good idea. Goodbye for now.

2.3 Summary description of the current system

About seventy or eighty short courses are run each year by the Computer Section. For each short course run, a costing sheet is filled in by Mr Morris, and a separate note kept of the hours worked by each individual member of staff on the course. From time to time information about short courses is needed by various people, as summarised in the data flow diagram on the next page.

2.4   Data flow diagram of the existing system

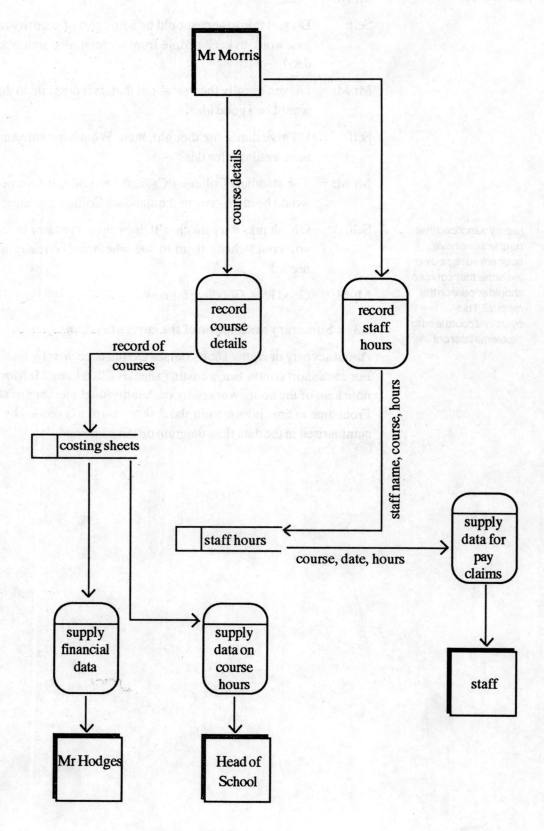

2.5   Problems with the current system

Identify the problem(s) to be solved.

At present there is no system in place for keeping records of short courses run, apart from the file of costing sheets. It is time-consuming to go through each of these sheets to find out, for example, how many courses have been run in a specific time period, and what profit was made. In addition, the costing sheets provide no information on hours taught by individual staff members, and this information is needed when making overtime claims.

If staff members forget to record the hours of preparation and teaching time on the courses they have taught on, they have to rely on Mr Morris to provide the information. As he can be difficult to get hold of (often teaching, etc) this can result in delays in submitting overtime claims.

3.   Objectives of the new system

State the objectives clearly. They usually relate to the output.

1.   A database is required which will provide the following information:

   i.   A report on the total number of hours taught by any staff member in a given time period.

   ii.   A management report showing for each course in a given time period, course code, date, title, course duration in hours, number of students, and showing totals for staff hours, number of students and number of courses

Further discussion of WHY these three reports are needed in this system could be included here.

   iii.   A second management report showing for each course, total fees, total costs and profit, with overall totals at the end.

2.   It should be easy to add, change or delete data on the database.

3.   Additional information may be needed from the database, such as for example a breakdown of course costs, or a comparison of this year's course hours or profits with last year's. The system should hold the necessary data and allow for additional reports to be added at a later date.

4.   The system needs to be secure so that an unauthorised person cannot access the data, since the computer on which the system will be installed is accessible by many people in the Computer Section staffroom. Some limited access rights need to be given to staff who wish to look up the hours they have worked on particular courses.

4.   Constraints and limitations

4.1   Hardware

The system must operate on a PC with hard disk, 3 ½" floppy drive and dot matrix printer.

4.2   Software

The following software is available on the user's machine: SuperDB, Microsoft Works, Paradox, Supercalc, Turbo Pascal.

Specimen Costing Sheet

Include copies of
actual documents
whenever possible

Notice that not ALL the
information on this
sheet is needed in the
system; it is up to you
to establish exactly
what IS needed.

XXX COLLEGE

SHORT COURSE COSTING (1991/92) - UNIT/SCHOOL: __COMPUTING__

COURSE TITLE: __PageMaker__   COURSE CODE: __XED 101__

DURATION: __12__ Weeks/Days/Hours   GRADE: _____

MODE OF ATTENDANCE: __P/T Day__

VENUE: __College__   NUMBER OF STUDENTS: __5__

DATES: START: __16 Nov 91__   FINISH: __17 Nov 91__

A   FEES RECEIVED: __990.00__

B1. LECTURING STAFF

__14__ hours X £ __27.00__ per lecturer hour   __378.00__

B2   OVERHEADS

a. ON-Site (25% of lecturing staff costs) __94.50__

b. OFF-Site (10% of Lecturing staff costs) __94.50__

SUB -TOTAL (B1 + B2)   __472.50__

C.   NON-STANDARD COURSE COSTS

1.   Advertising and Publicity __100.00__

2.   Other non-standard course costs __127.50__   __227.50__

TOTAL COURSE COSTS (B + C)   __700.00__   __700.00__

CONTRIBUTION TO CAPITAL FUNDS   __290.00__

D.   FEES TO BE CHARGED *(Delete as necessary)*

Per student __198.00__   Block fee __——__

Tutor: __F. Morris.__   Head of Unit./School: __CJ Scott__

Date: __5.11.91__   Date: __5/11/91__

Section 2 - Design

1. Consideration of possible solutions

1.1 Using a database package

Present a clear evaluation of alternative methods of solution.

The system could be implemented using a database package such as MicroSoft Works, Paradox or Super DB, all of which are available within the College.

The advantages of using a database would be

- easy creation and maintenance of the file of short courses

- fast creation of customised input screens and report layouts

- quicker to develop the system because less programming effort involved

- ability to make 'off the cuff' queries in response to information requests from management

- easy to implement security measures giving different levels of user access

1.2 Using a programming language to create a tailor-made system

Pascal is the only practical alternative here since it is the only language available for development of the system. Although it would be possible to use Pascal, it would take much longer to implement and would not give the flexibility to the user that can be achieved with a database package. Spontaneous requests for information would require extra programs to be written. Since management are quite likely to come up with new queries at any time ('Ah, Frank - how much have we spent on advertising short courses this year?') it is important that the new system should provide this ability.

1.3 Improving the current manual system

The manual system could be improved by redesigning the costing sheet, so that on the reverse side there was room to record hours taught by each staff member. Mr Morris could record the information regarding hours, costs and profit in tabular form in a separate book (or on a spreadsheet) at the same time as he fills in the costing sheet, so that this information is readily available in a convenient form for the Head of School and Mr Hodges.

The problem with this solution is that it does not allow for any extra information to be supplied easily should there be a need for it, and totals still have to be calculated manually. It does not solve the problem of the information regarding hours taught on various courses not being easily accessible by all members of staff.

Also, redesigning the costing sheet is not easy to implement because this particular form is used throughout the College and the Administration might not agree to the proposed changes.

2. Proposed solution

I propose to use the database package Paradox to create a customised system for maintaining a database of short courses, and printing the reports as specified. Since the user, Mr Morris, has some familiarity with Paradox he should be able to use the database to answer any other queries that may arise regarding short courses.

Paradox incorporates a 4GL called the Paradox Personal Programmer which enables a complete customised menu-driven system to be quickly developed. I believe the facilities for system development offered by Paradox are superior to those found in MS Works or SuperDB.

3. Output design

If you consider the output first, it will be easier to see exactly what input data is required, and what fields need to be calculated.

Three reports are needed for this system:

3.1 Hours worked by each individual member of staff

This report may be requested at any time by any member of staff who wishes to know how many hours they worked during a given period. A query facility will be included so that the start and end dates can be entered at run time. Also, the user will be given the option to either print or display the information.

3.2 Report of course hours and taught hours for management

Include a reasoned discussion of why particular fields and totals are included, and why particular formats have been chosen for data items. It is the reasoning as much as the result, and the thoughtful consideration of user needs, that is required for high marks.

This report is designed to help management plan timetables and staff requirements for the next year. The user will be allowed to define the period covered by the report at run time, so that figures can be obtained for example for one term, or an academic year (starting September), or a financial year (starting in April). It will include totals at the bottom of the report, and a count of the number of courses run since this information could be of use in planning both rooming requirements and staffing levels.

3.3 Financial report

This report shows the receipts, costs and profit for each course, with totals at the end of the report. Again, the period covered by the report will be specified by the user at run time. Profit is a Calculated field, and totals at the end of the report are Summary fields. All numeric fields will be displayed to two decimal places (because they are currency fields), and dates as dd-mmm-yy (e.g. 31-Oct-92). This will remove any confusion as to whether the date is in the American format (mm.dd.yy) or the British format with the day preceding the month.

3.4 Staff details display

There will also be a facility to display all staff details on the screen. No special report format is required for this, as Paradox has a built in facility for displaying a table which is quite adequate for this purpose.

Two specimen report layout charts are shown on pages 3 - 13 and 3 - 14.

Report Layout

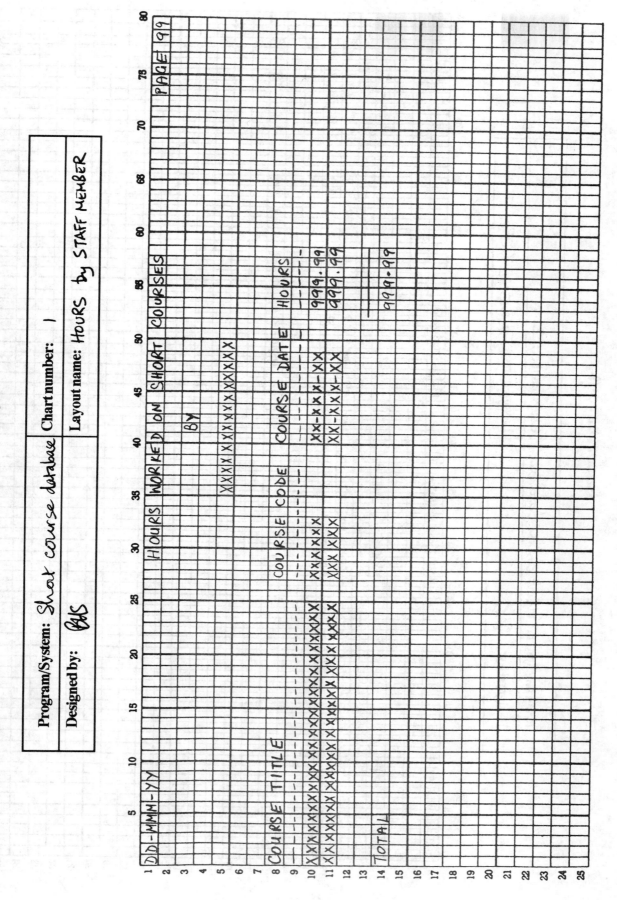

Program/System:	Short course database	Chart number: 1
Designed by:	BJS	Layout name: HOURS by STAFF MEMBER

```
         1         5        10        15        20        25        30        35        40        45        50        55        60        65        70        75        80
 1  DD-MMM-YY                              HOURS WORKED ON SHORT COURSES                                                              PAGE 99
 2
 3                                                              BY
 4
 5                                         XXXX XXXXXXXX XXXXXXX
 6
 7
 8  COURSE TITLE                           COURSE CODE         COURSE DATE        HOURS
 9  ----------------                       ----------          -----------        -----
10  XXXXXXXXXXXXXXXXXXXXXXX                 XXXXXXX             XX-XXX-XX          999.99
11  XXXXXXXXXXXXXXXXXX XXXXXX               XXX XXX             XX-XXX-XX          999.99
12
13
14  TOTAL                                                                         999.99
15
16
17
18
19
20
21
22
23
24
25
```

Report Layout

Program/System: Short course database	Chart number: 2
Designed by: BHS	Layout name: FINANCIAL REPORT

```
         5    10   15   20   25   30   35   40   45   50   55   60   65   70   75   80
1  DD-MMM-YY                SHORT COURSE FINANCIAL REPORT                   PAGE XX
2
3
4  COURSE TITLE               CODE   DATE      TOTAL FEES  TOTAL COSTS  PROFIT
5  -------------------------  ------ --------- ----------  -----------  ----------
6  XXXXXXXXXXXXXXXXXXXXXXXXX  XXXXXX XX-XXX-XX 99,999.99   99,999.99    99,999.99
7  XXXXXXXXXXXXXXXXXXXXXXXXX  XXXXXX XX-XXX-XX 99,999.99   99,999.99    99,999.99
8
9                                              _________   _________    _________
10 TOTAL                                       99,999.99   99,999.99    99,999.99
11
12
13
14
15
16
17
18
19
20
21
22
23
24
25
```

4. Analysis of data requirements

In order to produce the three reports, the following information will be needed

course code
course title
course date
duration of course in hours
names of each staff member teaching on a course
hours of teaching or preparation by each member of staff
fee charged per person
number of people on course
total receipts
total costs
profit

Profit can be calculated as Total receipts - Total costs, and so does not need to be input or held as a field on the database. All the other fields need to be input.

There is additional information on the current costing sheet which is currently used, and some of this needs to be collected in the new system as it may be needed on future reports. The following fields will therefore also be held in the new system:

Lecturer costs
Overheads
Advertising
Non-standard course costs

Justify the inclusion or exclusion of particular data items

The user has stated that some fields are not required:

Grade is not used for any short courses
Mode of attendance is always Part-Time day for short courses
Venue is written on the costing sheet so that the administration can verify that overhead costs have been correctly calculated but need not be held.

It would be useful in the new system to hold the telephone numbers and School (Department) of each staff member so that they can be easily contacted when required. Therefore this information will also be held in the new system.

Data formats also need to be decided. Dates will be held as dd.mmm.yy to avoid any confusion with the default American format mm/dd/yy.

Hours are occasionally calculated to the nearest quarter and will therefore be held as numeric fields to 2 decimal places. All currency amounts will be held to two decimal places.

Course code is always 6 digits, and 25 characters will be used for course title. Staff name will be 15 characters, surname followed by initial(s), and telephone numbers will be held as 12-character alphanumeric fields so that brackets, hyphens etc may be included. Department will be abbreviated to 6 characters.

5.   File design

There are two entities which can be identified in this database; courses and staff members. There is a many-to-many relationship between courses and staff, because one course may have many staff teaching on it and one staff member may teach on many courses.

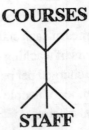

COURSES

STAFF

A many-to-many relationship between files causes problems (e.g. redundancy) on a database, and so the next step was to normalise the database.

First of all, repeating groups were identified; ie staff name and staff hours (since there may be many staff members teaching on a single course). All redundant data may be removed from the table of courses by removing these repeating groups, giving the following tables after normalisation:

COURSES table
<u>course code</u>, course title, course date, duration, taught hrs, lecturer costs, overheads, advertising, non-standard costs,fee, no students, total fees, total costs
      (key field is underlined)

STAFFHRS table
<u>course code</u>, <u>staff name</u>, hours

STAFF table

staff id, staff name,work tel, home tel, school

6.   Relationship between files

There is no longer any direct relationship between the COURSES table and the STAFF table in the normalised database. The table STAFFHRS acts as a link between the two tables, as shown in the EAR (Entity Attribute Relationship) model on the next page.

In a database project it is essential to normalise the database. This process is more fully explained in Chapter 4 of Part 1.

Diagram showing entity relationships

(<u>course code</u>, course title, course date, duration, taught hrs, lecturer costs, overheads, advertising, non-standard costs, fee, no students, total fees, total costs)

(<u>course code, staff name</u>, hours)

Diagrams such as these are useful for showing the relationship between files. Their inclusion is recommended.

(<u>staff id</u>, staff name, work tel, home tel, school)

The diagram shows, for example, that COURSES and STAFFHRS are related by a one-to-many relationship, and STAFF and STAFFHRS are similarly related.

File structures

File structures are shown on pages 3 -18 to 3 -20.

File Structure

File name	COURSES	External file ID	COURSES.DB
File Organisation		Key fields	COURSE CODE
Record length			

Used by:

Program name	Description	Program name	Description

General file description — Holds details for 'COURSE' entity

Record name	General record description

Field description	Field name	Format	Dec pl.	Validation check
Course Code	COURSE CODE	A6 *	← key field	
Course Title	COURSE TITLE	A25		
Start date of course	COURSE DATE	DATE		
Duration	DURATION	N	2	≥3, ≤20
Taught hrs incl. prep	TAUGHT HRS	N	2	
Lecturing costs	LEC COSTS	$	2	
Overhead costs	OVERHEADS	$	2	
Advertising Costs	ADVERTISING	$	2	
Non-standard costs	NON-STAN COSTS	$	2	
Fee per student	FEE	$	2	≥0, ≤600.00
Number of students	NO STUDENTS	N	0	≥2, ≤12
Total fees or block fee	TOTAL FEES	$	2	
Total costs	TOTAL COSTS	$	2	

File Structure

File name	STAFF		External file ID	STAFF.DB
File Organisation			Key fields	STAFF ID
Record length				

Used by:

Program name	Description	Program name	Description

General file description	Table giving details of 'STAFF' entity

Record name	General record description

Field description	Field name	Format	Dec pl.	Validation check
Staff ID	STAFF ID	A4 *		
Staff name	STAFF NAME	A15		
Work phone number	WORK TEL	A12		
Home phone number	HOME TEL	A12		
School / Unit	SCHOOL	A6		

File Structure

File name	STAFF HRS		External file ID	STAFFHRS.DB
File Organisation			Key fields	STAFF ID + COURSE CODE
Record length				

Used by:

Program name	Description		Program name	Description

General file description — Table of staff hours taught on each course

Record name	General record description

Field description	Field name	Format	Dec pl.	Validation check
Staff ID	STAFF ID	A4		Must be on 'staff' table
Course code	COURSE CODE	A6		Must be on 'courses' table
Hours	HOURS	N	2	

7.   Data validation

The following validation checks will be made when inputting new courses:

Thorough validation of input data, and a discussion of why and how particular fields are validated, will earn you marks.

1.   The course date is automatically validated by Paradox as being a valid date.

2.   Course duration will be range checked, and should be between 3 and 20 hours. No short courses are ever less than 3 hours, and 3 days is the maximum length, at 6 or 6 1/2 hours per day.

3.   The fee charged per person must be in the range 0.00 to 600.00. Occasionally a course may be given for other staff members for which no charge is made, and £600.00 is a figure agreed with Mr Morris as a reasonable maximum.

4.   Number of students on course must be between 2 and 12. Although normally a maximum of 10 people are accepted, there could be a rare occasion when up to 12 are taken.

Note: Total fees received could be calculated automatically as fee x number of students, but after some discussion this was ruled out because some students occasionally come free, or a block fee is charged for a whole group of students from one organisation.

When entering staff hours, the following validations are carried out:

1.   Course code is looked up on the course table to ensure that only valid courses are entered. The course title and date will then be automatically displayed to enable visual confirmation that the correct code has been entered. An error message will be displayed if the user attempts to add a non-existent course, and the entry will not be accepted.

2.   Staff ids are looked up on the staff table to ensure that only valid staff ids are entered. The user will be able to display staff ids and names and select one, if they wish, by the use of function keys.

8.   User interface design

8.1   Input data

Input data for the course details will be taken directly from the costing sheets, a sample of which is shown on page 3 - 10. Therefore the screen layout will be set out as far as possible in a similar format in order to make data entry as easy as possible.

Show that you have thought about your screen design in relation to input documents

Staff names and staff hours will be entered separately from a written note kept by Mr Morris, who jots down the names when he plans who is to teach on the course and who is to be credited with the preparation of the course manuals.

Paradox allows for automatic lookup and display of fields from other tables, so for example when entering staff hours for a given course, when 'course code' is entered and validated the title, duration, taught hours and start date will be automatically displayed. When staff id is entered, staff name will be displayed.

Screen layouts are shown on page 3 -23 and 3 -24.

8.2   Menu design

The Paradox Personal Programmer allows the creation of customised menus for an application, with a user-defined description of each menu option. The menu is in the form of a 'menu bar' at the top of the screen from which the user may select using the first letter or the cursor keys. A 'help' screen may be included with each menu, and for this application, a help option will be included in the main menu containing an explanation of each menu item. The opening menu will thus appear as

```
Staff  Courses  Hours  Help    Leave
Add, delete or view staff details
```

An outline chart showing movement between menus is shown below. The Escape key is used to return to the previous menu.

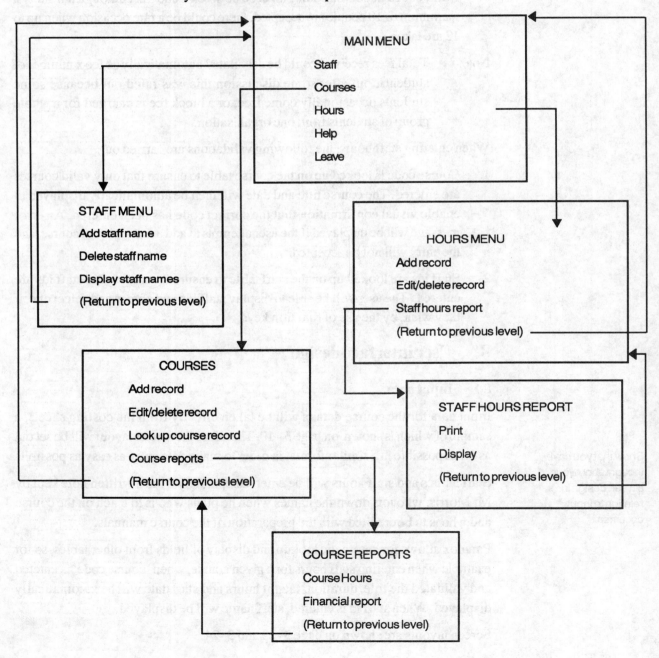

MAIN MENU

Staff

Courses

Hours

Help

Leave

STAFF MENU

Add staff name

Delete staff name

Display staff names

(Return to previous level)

HOURS MENU

Add record

Edit/delete record

Staff hours report

(Return to previous level)

COURSES

Add record

Edit/delete record

Look up course record

Course reports

(Return to previous level)

STAFF HOURS REPORT

Print

Display

(Return to previous level)

COURSE REPORTS

Course Hours

Financial report

(Return to previous level)

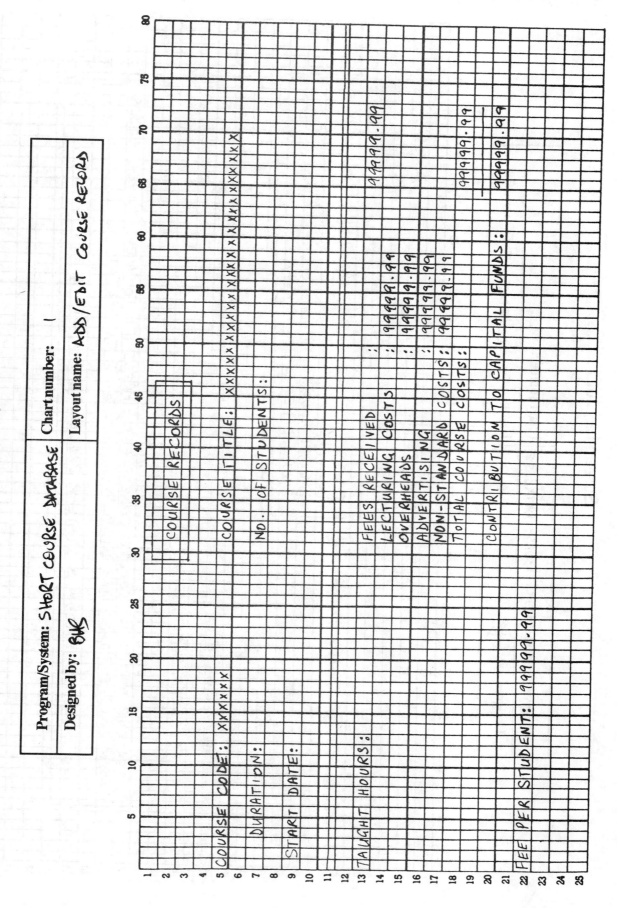

Screen Layout

Program/System: SHORT COURSE DATABASE	Chart number: 2
Designed by: *BHS*	Layout name: ADD/EDIT STAFF HOURS

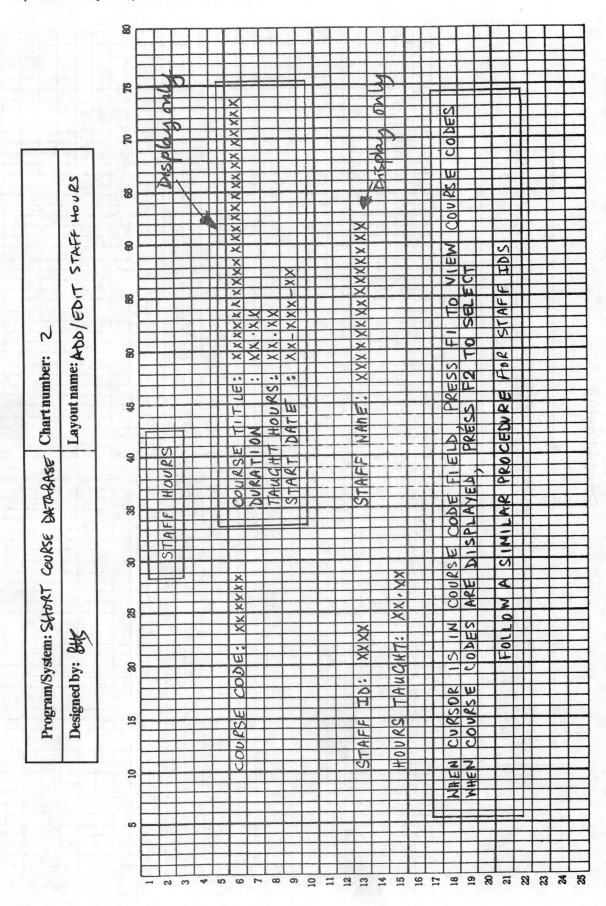

9. File and system security

This system will be operated by the organiser of the short course program, using a computer in a busy staff room. It may also be accessed by other members of staff who require instant information on, say, number of hours worked last month, or the code for a particular course they taught on.

Some security measures are therefore essential. Only the organiser should be allowed to change data on the files, in order to avoid staff members updating their own records, which could lead to errors or records being added twice by two different people. However, staff should be allowed to view any information on the files, and print out reports if they wish.

This will be implemented by allocating an 'owner password' to the organiser, giving him all access rights, and an auxiliary password to other users which will allow Read Only access to all parts of the system.

Paradox automatically saves new data from time to time to minimize data loss in the event of a power failure or other mishap. The AutoSave option is set to Yes by default, meaning that work is saved frequently, especially during lulls in typing.

Full backups of all files will be made weekly using DOS.

10. System outline chart

INPUT	PROCESSES
course code & title	add new courses
course date	edit/delete courses
duration of course (hours)	look up course record
taught hours	print course hours report
costs (broken down)	print course financial report
fee per student	add new staff name
number of students	delete staff name
total fees received	display staff names
total costs	add staff hours record
staff id, name, tel, school	edit/delete staff hours record
staff hours	print/display staff hours
FILES	
staff	
courses	**OUTPUT**
staffhrs	staff hours report/display
	course hours report
	course financial report
	staff names display

11.   Hierarchy chart showing main modules

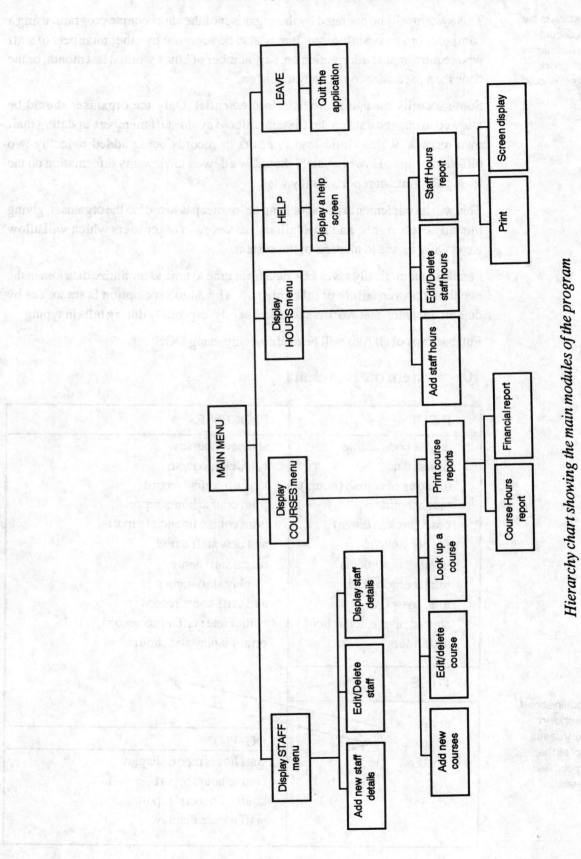

Hierarchy chart showing the main modules of the program

12. Test strategy

12.1 Test data

The following test data will be used to test the system.

Specify the test data, with reasons for its selection.

Thorough testing is a vitally important part of any project, but is often haphazardly done and inadequately documented!

Staff ID	Staff name	Work tel	Home tel	School
1	Turner J	424	487772	Comp
2	Biddle M	424	481244	Comp
3	Young E	424	481244	Comp
4	Horsfall A	424	Needham 651	Comp
5	Lawson B	279	Eldoret 698	Art
6	Glen E	424		Comp

(no validation is carried out on staff names)

Courses

code	course title	date	dur'n	taught hours	fee	no. stu	fees	costs
XED251	Wordperfect	19.08.91	12	20	100.00	8	1188.00	800.00
XED081	Intro to MSDOS	10.10.91	6	20	99.00	10	990.00	600.00
XED231	Ventura	19.10.91	12	14	198.00	4	792.00	800.00
XED171	Smart database	24.11.91	12	14	99	5	495	550.00
XED202	Intro to SuperCalc	31.10.91	12	12	120	12	720.00	700.00
XED101	PageMaker	16.11.91	12	14	198.00	5	990.00	700.00
XED181	Smart WP	28.11.91	6	6	99.00	3	297.00	250.00

Show that your test data is designed to test all validation checks, and includes valid, extreme and incorrect data

Attempts to add invalid data, which will test all the validation checks, are included in the test plan on the next page. Courses XED231 and XED171 will show a negative profit, to test the correctness of calculations.

Dates are entered out of sequence, and include some in October and some in other months so that reports for October may be tested.

Staff Hours

Course	Staff ID	Staff name	Hours
XED251	2	Biddle M	15
XED251	3	Yonge E	5
XED081	1	Turner J	8
XED081	5	Lawson B	6
XED231	2	Biddle M	14.25
XED231	1	Turner J	11.75
XED171	2	Biddle M	6.5
XED171	3	Yonge E	5.5
XED171	1	Turner J	2

12.2 Test plan

The detailed test plan for the module testing is given below. The tests are designed to test every option on each menu, using both valid and invalid input.

Staff names menu.

1. Add staff records (see test data)
2. Delete Glen E. (Test delete)
3. Edit staff record Young E; change to Yonge E. (Test editing of staff record)
4. Display all staff names (5 names should be displayed)

Course menu.

5. Add course records (see test data)
6. Edit XED101; change to XED999 (tests result of changing the key field; this should be impossible)
7. Attempt to enter 32 hours for duration on XED171 (range check message)
8. Attempt to enter 13 for no. of students on XED202 (range check message)
9. Attempt to enter 32.10.91 on XED202 (date validation error message)
10. Attempt to enter 1000.00 for fees on XED202 (range check message)
11. Add XED251; duplicate record for WordPerfect (Should be impossible)
12. Delete XED202. Test delete and Ctrl-U 'Undelete' facility
13. Look up XED251. Test 'Toggle' between form view and list view
14. Print course hours report for all courses in October 1991 (3 courses)
15. Print course financial report for all courses (7 courses, total profit 1072.00)

Staff Hours menu.

16. Add records (see test data)
17. Try to add XED222 (should be rejected, not on course file)
18. Try to add XED251, ID 99 (rejected, ID 99 not on staff file)
19. Edit XED251, staff ID 2. Try to change to ID 53 (rejected, does not exist).
20. Edit XED251, staff ID 2. Change to 20 hours (extreme of hours range)
21. Delete record for XED251, staff ID 3 (Test delete, & Ctrl-U 'undelete')
22. Print staff hours report for staff ID 1, October 1991 (1 record, 14.25 hours)
23. Print staff hours report for Turner J, taking in all dates. Enter Trner j (misspelt) when prompted for staff name. (3 records, total 21.75 hours)
24. Enter 50 staff hours records and print course hours report (tests addition of large volume of data)

Password checks

25. Test effect of entering wrong password (no access should be given)
26. Enter password 'staff' (auxiliary password) and attempt to edit data (should see error message displayed)

Margin notes:

You should write down each test, numbered for convenient cross-referencing to actual output, the test data used and the expected result.

An alternative format for the test plan is shown in the first specimen project on page 2-22.

Include a test for a larger volume of data.

Test the password routine

Section 3 - Testing

Testing analysis

Test runs and results cross-referenced to the test plan on pages 3 - 28 are given in Appendix H, pages 3 - 53 to 3 - 58. There follows an analysis of the results:

a.   Tests 1 - 4.   OK.

b.   Tests 5 - 10. All the validations on input worked exactly as specified. It is impossible to show, for example, that the user cannot perform Test 6 (change course code from XED101 to XED999; this should not be allowed as it is the key field). However, the cursor does not go to that field which therefore cannot be edited, which is the desired effect.

c.   Test 11. Paradox has a rather strange way of coping with attempts to add records with duplicate keys, which is discussed in the Systems Maintenance section (page 3-30)

d.   Tests 12 - 13. The 'Undelete' and 'Toggle' facilities are built-in to the Paradox software and are convenient extra features. On-screen help is provided for the user as to which function keys are used.

e.   Tests 14 - 15. Some errors did surface during testing, for example date formats on these two reports were displayed as mm/dd/yy, but this has now been corrected, as can be seen from the test runs.

f.   Tests 16 - 24. All worked satisfactorily as can be seen from screen dumps and printouts in Appendix H.

g.   Tests 25-26. If the wrong password is entered, whichever table the user attempts to use or view, a message ' table is password protected' appears. If the auxiliary password 'staff' is entered, the same message appears if the user tries to edit data, but data may be viewed or printed.

In your analysis of the test data you should attempt to show that it performs a complete check on all eventualities.

The test data and the tests to be performed were chosen carefully to test all the various paths in the program. For example:

* all menu options have been tested

* all validation checks have been tested

* the effect of attempting to add duplicate records has been tested

* data for courses has different dates and different named staff, to ensure that the reports which allow the user to input name and/or dates pick out the correct records (eg test 23)

* all calculations have been performed manually and compared with actual output. Data has been chosen to check that a negative profit, for example, is correctly displayed and the overall total correctly calculated.

* courses were entered in a random sequence to check that they would be sorted into key sequence.

Section 4 - System Maintenance

1. Summary of the software facilities

One way of beginning this section is to state what software you have used and give an overview of how you developed the system.

The Short Course Database system has been written in Borland's Paradox 3.5, a powerful database-management system. Using the Paradox Personal Programmer, it is possible to create a complete menu-driven system which enables the user to store, retrieve, sort, print, change and ask questions about the data by selecting options from menus and filling in custom designed data-entry forms.

This system has been entirely created using the Paradox Personal Programmer, to the design specified in the Design section of the report. (See Page 3 - 23 for hierarchy chart and pages 3 -18 to 3 - 20 for file structure charts).

The menu tree of the completed system can be printed out from within Paradox Personal Programmer by selecting Summarize, Menu from the Main menu. A printout is shown below.

Menu tree

Original printouts generated by the software package provide useful evidence of how you tailored the package to the user's requirements. You may prefer to put such printouts in an Appendix, and refer to them in the main text.

```
9/05/92                        Application Menu Tree:              Page  1.1
                               ======================

Main
     ├── Staff
     │        ├── Add [ DataEntry ]
     │        ├── Edit/delete [ Edit ]
     │        └── Display [ View ]
     ├── Courses
     │        ├── Add [ DataEntry ]
     │        ├── Edit/Delete [ Edit ]
     │        ├── Look up [ View ]
     │        └── Report
     │                  ├── Hours [ Report ]
     │                  └── Financial [ Report ]
     ├── Hours
     │        ├── Add [ DataEntry ]
     │        ├── Edit/Delete [ Edit ]
     │        └── Report
     │                  ├── Print [ Report ]
     │                  └── Display [ Report ]
     ├── Help [ Help ]
     └── Leave [ Leave ]
```

2.   Disk directory and space requirements

The complete application is named SH3 and is held in a directory called SHORT. A listing of this directory is given below.

```
Volume in drive C is DOS400
Volume Serial Number is 1767-9C86
Directory of C:\SHORT

[.]            [..]           SH31.LIB       SH3CPL.SC      SH3P.R
STAFFHRS.DB    STAFFHRS.PX    STAFF.DB       STAFF.PX       COURSES.DB
COURSES.PX     SH3.SC         SH31.SC        SH3P.SC        SH3UTL.SC
SH3UTL.LIB     SH3LIB.SC      SH3CP.LIB      SH3CP.SC       SH32.SC
SH3P.DB        STAFF.F1       STAFF.VAL      STAFF.F2       SC3.SC
SC4.SC         SC5.SC         SH33.SC        SH34.SC        SH32.LIB
COURSES.F1     SC1.SC         SC6.SC         COURSES.VAL    SH301.SC
COURSES.R1     SC7.SC         SH302.SC       COURSES.R2     SC8.SC
SH3M2.DB       SH3S2.DB       SH3S2.F1       SC9.SC         SH3S2.VAL
SC10.SC        SH35.SC        STAFFHRS.F1    SH36.SC        STAFFHRS.VAL
SC11.SC        SH303.SC       SH304.SC       SH3S1.R1       SH3M1.DB
SH3S1.DB       SC12.SC        SC13.SC        SCH1.SC        SH3G.SC
SH3H1.SC       SCH2.SC        SC2.SC         SH3.DB
         64 file(s)       252995 bytes
                        5617664 bytes free
```

The following points may be noted:

State how much disk space is required for the application.

- The application involves altogether over 60 files and occupies at present just over 250K of disk space. This will grow as the number of data records on the database increases.

Show that you understand the file extensions.

- Paradox Personal Programmer generates different types of files when creating an application. The data files or tables (courses, staff, staffhrs) have an extension .DB. Certain files are 'owned' by these tables, for example input forms (eg COURSES.F1) and report forms (eg COURSES.R1). On the next two pages an annotated list of the libraries, scripts and tables used in the application is given. The list is produced from the Personal Programmer by selecting Summarize, Menu from the opening menu.

In your own project you are advised to include all the scripts, annotated briefly to explain their purpose.

- 'Scripts' (ie program modules) generated by Paradox are given an extension .SC. There is a total of 33 scripts in this application. A specimen listing of SH31.SC is given in Appendix G on page 3-53.

Sh3 Menu Structure   Page   1

Menu Path:
/Main/

Script containing this menu: Sh31   *appears in directory as SH31.SC*
Library containing the procedures for this menu: Sh31   *in directory as SH31.LIB*

Selection Name	Selection Action	Source Table	Map Table	Tables Used	Query, Help, or User Script
Staff	Menu				
Courses	Menu				
Hours	Menu				
Help	Help				
Leave	Leave				

Sh3h1 contains the Help screen display

Menu Path:
/Main/Staff/

Script containing this menu: Sh32
Library containing the procedures for this menu: Sh31

Selection Name	Selection Action	Source Table	Map Table	Tables Used	Query, Help, or User Script
Add	DataEntry			Staff	
Edit/delete	Edit			Staff	
Display	View			Staff	

Menu Path:
/Main/Courses/

Script containing this menu: Sh33
Library containing the procedures for this menu: Sh31

Selection Name	Selection Action	Source Table	Map Table	Tables Used	Query, Help, or User Script
Add	DataEntry			Courses	
Edit/Delete	Edit			Courses	
Look up	View			Courses	
Report	Menu				

Menu Path:
/Main/Courses/Report/

Script containing this menu: Sh34
Library containing the procedures for this menu: Sh32

queries have extensions .SC in directory

Selection Name	Selection Action	Source Table	Map Table	Tables Used	Query, Help, or User Script
Hours	Report			Courses	Sh3q1
Financial	Report			Courses	Sh3q2

Menu Path:
/Main/Hours/

Script containing this menu: Sh35
Library containing the procedures for this menu: Sh32

Selection Name	Selection Action	Source Table	Map Table	Tables Used	Query, Help, or User Script
Add	DataEntry	Sh3s2	Sh3m2	Courses Staff Staffhrs	
Edit/Delete Report	Edit Menu			Staffhrs	

This data entry script uses all 3 tables

Menu Path:
/Main/Hours/Report/

Script containing this menu: Sh36
Library containing the procedures for this menu: Sh32

Selection Name	Selection Action	Source Table	Map Table	Tables Used	Query, Help, or User Script
Print	Report	Sh3s1	Sh3m1	Courses Staff Staffhrs	Sh3q3
Display	Report	Sh3s1	Sh3m1	Courses Staff Staffhrs	Sh3q4

These reports use all 3 tables

3.   Creating and modifying the application

Three steps are necessary to start the Personal Programmer:

1.   Create a directory in which the application will be stored (in this case C:\SHORT) and log on to this directory (CD\SHORT).

2.   If the AUTOEXEC.BAT file was not changed when Paradox was installed to include Paradox35 and Paradox35\PPROG in the PATH command, you should do so now, or type

PATH C:\PDOX35;C:\PDOX35\PPROG and press <Enter>

3.   Type PPROG and press <Enter> to start the Personal Programmer.

An introductory screen as shown below now appears.

```
Create Modify Summarize Review Play Tools Exit
Create a new application.
```

```
==============The Paradox Personal Programmer==============

  Select an action from the menu.

The information in these boxes will help you to create applications.  The
top box shows the current status of the application on which you are
working.  This bottom box contains additional information and help.

The Personal Programmer menu works just like the Paradox menu --
Use the - and - keys to move the highlight to the selection you want...
then press J to choose the highlighted selection.  Press [Esc] to return
to the previous menu.
```

Creating the system and making modifications to it entails basically the same steps. To make modifications, choose Modify from the menu shown above, enter SH3 as the name of the application to modify, and when asked for the password, enter **sysmgr**. The following menu appears:

```
Tables MenuAction NotDefined Splashscreen DO-IT! Cancel
Select one or more tables to add to or remove from the
application
```

4. Defining the structure of each table

The structure of each table in the system is first defined. Screen dumps of each of the three table structures in this system are shown below. (Screen displays are obtained from Paradox by selecting Tools, Info, Structure and then entering the required table name.)

Viewing Struct table: Record 1 of 13   Main

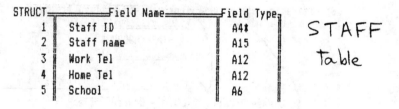

```
STRUCT         Field Name        Field Type
     1    Course Code            A6*
     2    Course Title           A25
     3    Course Date            D
     4    Duration               N
     5    Taught Hrs             N
     6    Lec Costs              $
     7    Overheads              $
     8    Advertising            $
     9    Non-stan Costs         $
    10    Fee                    $
    11    No Students            N
    12    Total Fees             $
    13    Total Costs            $
```

COURSES table

Viewing Struct table: Record 1 of 5   Main

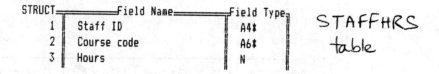

```
STRUCT         Field Name        Field Type
     1    Staff ID               A4*
     2    Staff name             A15
     3    Work Tel               A12
     4    Home Tel               A12
     5    School                 A6
```

STAFF Table

Viewing Struct table: Record 1 of 3   Main

```
STRUCT         Field Name        Field Type
     1    Staff ID               A4*
     2    Course code            A6*
     3    Hours                  N
```

STAFFHRS table

5.   Specifying menus and associated actions

The complete menu tree is then specified by selecting MenuAction from the menu. Paradox Personal Programmer then asks you to define an action for each menu item, for example, Submenu, DataEntry, Edit, View or Report.

6.   Customising the data entry forms

Custom data entry screens for all data entry are designed using screen layout forms (see page 3 - 23 and 3 - 24). This step includes the formatting of each data item and specification of validations required.

The screen below shows an example of a customised data entry form being created. Using the facilities within the Personal Programmer, a 'TableLookup' validation check has been added to both the Course Code field and the Staff Name field. Thus the course code is looked up on the courses table and only valid course codes are permitted. The fields in the box on the right (Course title etc) are then automatically displayed, but have been made 'Display-Only' so that they cannot be changed from this screen. (The cursor will skip over these fields.)

In order to display fields from three different tables on the same screen, a 'multi-table view' was set up specifying which fields were to be displayed and how the tables were linked. An example of a view definition is shown on the next page.

> You need to give clear descriptions of the features of the package that you have used, such as customised input screens and report forms.

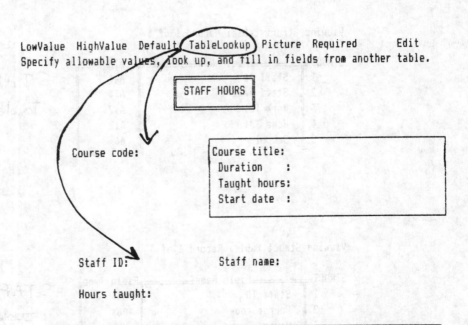

7. Customising the report forms

The software allows positioning and formatting of each field on a report, and these facilities have been used on all the report forms, together with the ability to display calculated and summary fields, as for example the 'Profit' field on the Short Course Financial Report (see page 3-13). The option to send the report to the screen instead of the printer has been used for the Staff Hours report (see page 3-14).

As an example, the creation of the course hours report is described below.

This does not aim to be a tutorial, since it is aimed at a programmer, but does show the steps you have gone through to customise the report.

The tables to be used in the report are first specified (in this case, all three tables). Next, a 'view' is defined specifying what fields are required on the report and how the fields in one table are linked to those in a second table. The screen dump below shows that staff id, course code and hours will be selected from the Staffhrs table, and the corresponding staff name looked up from the Staff table. The course title and course date will be looked up from the Courses table.

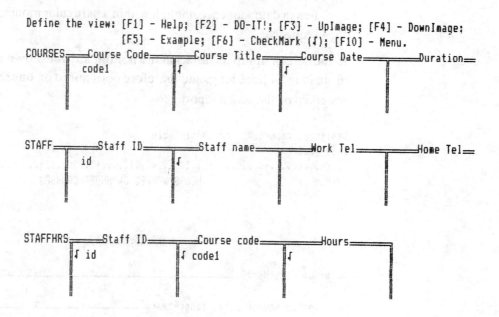

A query is next set up to enable the user to enter start and end dates, and **either** the used id **or,** if the user does not know the id, the user name. Using the keyword 'like' will enable Paradox to find the name even if it is misspelt. (See next page for the format of a query.)

Specifying selection criteria using a query form

```
Select records to display: [F1] - Help; [F2] - DO-IT!; [F10] - Menu.
Specify the selection criteria for the records you want to show to the user.
 ═══Course Title═══    ═══Course Date═══      ═══Staff name═══    ═══Staff ID═══
║                  ║ ║ >=*date1,<=*date2 ║  ║                 ║ ║ *id          ║
║                  ║ ║                   ║  ║                 ║ ║              ║
║                  ║ ║                   ║  ║   like *name    ║ ║              ║
║                  ║ ║                   ║  ║                 ║ ║              ║
```

The report format itself is then designed. Three groups were defined:

* a group of 5000 records. This is an arbitrarily large number of records, to enable a group total (which appears just under the records) rather than a final total (which appears at the bottom of the page) to be printed.

* a subgroup sequenced by year.

* a further subgroup sequenced by month. This causes the report to be more or less in date sequence, though within a particular month, records may be out of sequence.

In the screen dump the totals at the bottom are not shown as the report format is more than 24 lines long, and therefore does not fit on one screen, but they will be observed on the actual report.

```
Designing report R1 for Sh3s1 table                         Report Ins 1/2
Page Header
....+...10....+...20....+...30....+...40....+...50....+...60....+...70....+...8*
dd-Mon-yy                  HOURS WORKED ON SHORT COURSES             Page 999


                                    BY

                             AAAAAAAAAAAAAAA


───group records=5000──────────────────────────────────────────────────

──────group Course Date, range=Year─────────────────────────────────────

──────────group Course Date, range=Month────────────────────────────────

┌table────────────┬──────────┬──────────┬──────┬─────────────────────────
│
Course Title       Course code Course Date Hours
─────────────────── ─────────── ─────────── ──────
AAAAAAAAAAAAAAAAAAAAAAAAAAA  AAAAAA    dd-Mon-yy   999.99
Ltable────────────┴──────────┴──────────┴──────┴─────────────────────────

──────────group Course Date, range=Month────────────────────────────────

──────group Course Date, range=Year─────────────────────────────────────
```

8.   Security

An 'owner password' has been allocated which gives the user full access rights to all parts of the system. This has initially been set to '**sysmgr**' (lower case), but you are advised to change this as soon as possible. Do not lose or forget the password as without it you will not be allowed to enter or edit data or programs!

An 'auxiliary' password has been set to '**staff**'. This gives other users read-only access to the files. No access will be allowed except through the use of one or other of these passwords.

To change the password, from the main menu in Paradox select Tools, More, Protect, Password. Select whether to protect a table or a script, and enter the name of the table to protect. You will be asked for the current password, and then given the option of changing the master or the auxiliary password. If you choose to change the master password you will also be given the chance to change the auxiliary password, using a screen similar to the one shown below.

```
Defining auxiliary password 1 of Staffhrs table              Password
[F1] for help with setting password options.  [F7] for table view

 ┌────────────────────────────────────────────────────────────────────┐
 │ Auxiliary password:  staff                                 Page 1    │
 │                                                                      │
 │ ┌──────────────────────────────┬───────────────────────────────────┐│
 │ │ Table Rights  ReadOnly        │ Family Rights                     ││
 │ │                               │                                   ││
 │ │ Enter one │ Rights conferred  │ Enter all that apply, ⌐ for none  ││
 │ │           │                   │                                   ││
 │ │ All       │ all operations    │ (F)orm    │ change forms          ││
 │ │ InsDel    │ change contents   │ (V)alCheck│ change validity checks││
 │ │ Entry     │ data entry and updates│(R)eport│ change reports       ││
 │ │ Update    │ update nonkey fields│(S)ettings│ change image settings││
 │ │ ReadOnly  │ no modifications  │           │                       ││
 │ ├───────────────────────────────┴───────────────────────────────────┤│
 │ │ Field Rights Enter ReadOnly or None for each field or leave blank for All.││
 │ │                                                                    ││
 │ │ Staff ID     ReadOnly                                              ││
 │ │ Course code  ReadOnly                                              ││
 │ │ Hours        ReadOnly                                              ││
 │ └────────────────────────────────────────────────────────────────────┘│
 └────────────────────────────────────────────────────────────────────┘
```

9. Designing a help screen

A help screen has been added to the main menu so that when the user selects Help, a screenful of information about the application is displayed.

10. Designing a SplashScreen

This is an opening screen displayed when the user starts the application. It shows the title

```
                    SHORT COURSE DATABASE
                      COMPUTING SECTION
                         XXX COLLEGE
```

11. Discussion of test results

Test runs and results cross referenced to the test plan on pages 3 - 28 and 3 - 29 are given in Appendix H, pages 3-55 to 3-60. The following points were noted:

1. All the reports allow the user to specify which time period to include in the report. The correct records were printed out but I was unable to find a way of displaying on the report, the dates which the user had entered at run time. Also, the totals were initially printed right at the bottom of the page and in order to force them to print directly below the rest of the report, I defined a 'group' of 5000 records, and printed the overall total within the group boundary.

2. Paradox will allow duplicate records to be added; for example, two courses with the same code. The records with duplicate keys are not added to the file but are put on to a separate 'Key Violation' table, which is then displayed to the user. They can to be edited on this table from within Paradox itself, given another key (e.g. Course code) and added to the original table (e.g. Courses). This is somewhat inconvenient and the user is recommended to avoid entering records with duplicate keys.

3. Records are automatically sorted by Paradox into key sequence, and initially the reports were printed in that sequence. This was unsatisfactory, and to get round the problem two further groups were defined, on Year and Month, since the data is automatically sorted within groups. This causes the report to be printed more or less in date sequence, as required, although the records may be out of sequence within a particular month. However this was considered an acceptable limitation, given the relatively small number of courses run each month. The alternative was to define another group on 'day', but as each group is separated on the report by two blank lines, this has the effect of triple spacing the whole report.

Section 4 - Appraisal

1.   User feedback

*Actually, the user's comments are not included here but if you can get the user to comment in writing, on official headed paper, then do so!

The system has been shown to Mr Morris and his handwritten comments are shown on the next page.* As can be seen, he is very pleased with the system which has been recently installed and is now in use in the Computer Section.

2.   System performance and future enhancements

Make some suggestions for enhancements or future developments.

The system has achieved the objectives as originally stated by Mr Morris, with the exception of any type of analysis showing for example whether the number of courses is increasing or decreasing. This would be a useful module to add to the system at some future date, possibly including a graphical presentation, which is possible within Paradox.

Relate what you have achieved to the original objectives.

The system is extremely easy to use and all the functions originally specified work as they should.

- The three reports are suitably formatted and can be easily produced whenever required

- The database contains all the required data and is easily added to or edited

- security measures have been implemented to prohibit unauthorised access.

Suggest briefly how to implement any improvements.

A suggestion has been made by Mr Morris that separate fields should be held for Teaching hours and Preparation hours, since the College management now intends to cost these differently. However as this was not in the original spec, it has not been included in the project although it could be implemented without much difficulty by adjusting the structure of the Staffhrs table.

In conclusion, I have enjoyed developing this project and have found the Paradox Personal Programmer very easy to use. It was a far quicker way of implementing a system than writing a program from scratch, and if I had not been learning the software at the same time as implementing the design, it would have been even faster!

User Manual

Table of Contents

SHORT COURSE DATABASE

User Manual

Introduction

Always start with an introduction so the user knows immediately what the system is all about.

This guide is written to help you to use the Short Course Database - a management information system which ensures that you have at your fingertips all the facts and figures about short courses that colleagues in the Computer Section and management at XXX College might want to know!

Installation

The system has been written for a stand-alone PC running Borland's Paradox (Version 3.5) database. You are recommended to install the Short Course Database software on the C: drive in its own directory, e.g. SHORT.

To do this, follow the instructions below:

1. Enter **c:** to log on to the C drive and enter **cd** to go to the root directory. Then enter **md short** to Make the new Directory. Type **cd short** to Change to the Directory **short**.

2. Enter **copy a:*.*** to copy all the files to the new directory on the C drive.

You are now ready to start running the program.

Starting the program

To start the program running from the hard disk,

1. Enter **cd \short** to change to the directory on the hard disk. Press <Enter>.

2. Enter **paradox sh3.** You should then see the title screen:

```
Password:
Enter password for the application; [Esc] to cancel; [Enter] for no password.
```

```
┌─────────────────────────┐
│   SHORT COURSE DATABASE  │
│   THE COMPUTER SECTION   │
│        XXX COLLEGE       │
└─────────────────────────┘
```

```
Software by B.Student
XXX College
April 1992
```

Security and passwords

At the top of the title screen you will see:

```
Password:

Enter password for the application; [Esc] to cancel;

[Enter] for no password.
```

There are two levels of access for this system, and you need to enter a password to get beyond this screen.

The 'owner password' allows free access to all parts of the system and should be known only to the person in charge of the database. It has initially been set to **sysmgr** (lower case) but this should be changed as soon as possible from within Paradox.

(To do this, select the Tools, More, Protect, Password options from the Paradox main menu. You will be asked to select Table or Script, and be asked for your password which you may then change). Do not lose or forget this password because without it you will not be able to gain full access to the system!

An 'auxiliary password' (initially set to **staff**) allows the holder to look at any data on the system and print reports, but no data can be entered or edited. Again, this password should be changed using the same procedure as above.

The opening screen

Systematically describe each menu option

The opening menu now appears:

```
Staff  Courses  Hours  Help   Leave
Add, delete or view staff names
```

You may make a selection from the menu by using the arrow keys to highlight the required selection and pressing <Enter>.

Press <Esc> to return to the previous level of menu, from any of the submenus.

Each of these menus and their corresponding actions will now be explained.

STAFF menu (add, edit, delete or view staff names)

Choosing **Staff** from the opening menu will cause a submenu to appear:

```
Add  Edit/Delete  Display
Add a new member of staff
```

Add

You should select the **Add** option to add all members of staff teaching on short courses to the database. This list of staff IDs is checked when later you come to record staff hours, and only IDs of staff members who have been previously added to the database will be accepted.

Staff ID and staff name are required fields, and you cannot leave either of these fields blank. The data entry screen is shown on the next page.

```
[F2] - Data entry completed, Esc - Cancel data entry, Ctrl-U - Undo last change
```

```
┌─────────────────────────┐
│  ADD NEW STAFF DETAILS  │
└─────────────────────────┘
```

Show examples of input screens in your user manual; you can glue in actual screen dumps or include them on a separate page.

```
Staff ID: 15            Staff name: Reader B

Work Tel: 556           Home Tel:    747832

School/Unit: Hum
```

Delete

If you wish to change a staff member's details or delete a staff member's record, choose this option. A similar screen to the one above will appear. To delete a record, press the <Delete> key; if you delete a record by mistake, you can restore it by pressing Ctrl-U before making any other changes.

Give the user guidance on data entry where necessary.

When any data entry form is displayed, you can press F7 to 'toggle' between the 'form view' shown above and the 'table view' shown below.

Display

Choose this option to view all the staff names that have been entered on the database. They will be displayed in 'Table view' (see below).

```
Press [F2] when finished viewing the table
Total records: 5
STAFF══╤═Staff ID╤═════Staff name═════╤════Work Tel═══╤═════Home Tel═══╤═School══╕
     1 ║ 1       ║ Turner J           ║ 424           ║ 487772         ║ Comp    ║
     2 ║ 2       ║ Biddle M           ║ 424           ║ 481244         ║ Comp    ║
     3 ║ 3       ║ Yonge E            ║ 424           ║ 481244         ║ Comp    ║
     4 ║ 4       ║ Horsfall A         ║ 424           ║ Needham 651    ║ Comp    ║
     5 ║ 5       ║ Lawson B           ║ 279           ║ Eldoret 698    ║ Art     ║
```

COURSES menu (Add, change, delete or report on courses)

Choosing Courses will cause a submenu to appear:

```
Add   Edit/Delete   Look up   Report
Add a new course
```

Add

Use this option to add a new course record, using the costing sheet as the source of the data. A data entry 'form' will appear on the screen as shown below:

```
[F2] - Data entry completed, Esc - Cancel data entry, Ctrl-U - Undo last change


                        ┌─────────────────┐
                        │  COURSE RECORDS │
                        └─────────────────┘

Course Code: XED776          Course title: Paradox 4.0

   Duration:      12         No. of students:         8

 Start date: 29.09.92

----------------------------------------------------------------------

Taught hours:      30        Fees received     :          1.600.00
                             Lecturing costs   :   810.00
                             Overheads         :   202.50
                             Advertising       :   100.00
                             Non-standard costs:     0.00
                             Total course costs:        1,212.50
                                                        -----------
                             Contribution to Capital Funds:  387.50
                                                        -----------
Fee per student:    200.00
```

Notes on data entry:

1. The course duration must be a value between 3 and 20.

2. The number of students must be in the range 2 to 12.

3. The date must be entered either in the format **dd.mm.yy**, for example 31.10.92, or in the format **dd-mmm-yy** (e.g. 31-Oct-92).

4. The fee per student must be in the range 0 to 600.00.

5. Contribution to capital funds (ie Profit) will be automatically calculated and displayed.

Edit/Delete

Use this option to edit a record. A similar form will appear, but you will not be allowed to edit the course code. If you have made a mistake in the course code, delete the record and add a new one by pressing the <Delete> key.

Look up

Use this option to look up a course record, using F7 to toggle between form view and list view.

Report

Choosing this option will cause a further submenu to appear:

```
Hours  Financial
Print a report on course hours
```

Short Course Hours report

The **Short Course Hours** report is is a management report giving for each course in a specified time period, details of the hours duration (for timetabling purposes) and taught hours (for determining staff requirements). These quantities are usually different because taught hours includes preparation time and double-staffing time. Totals are given at the bottom of the report.

For both this report and the Financial report, you will be asked to enter the range of dates that the report is to cover. This is so that you can print, for example, a report on all courses in a particular academic or financial year.

A prompt will appear:

```
Enter the earliest date to be included in the report:
```

When you have entered the date (using the format **dd.mm.yy** or **dd-mmm-yy**), a second prompt will appear:

```
Enter the latest date to be included in the report:
```

The report will start to print after you have entered the date.

Financial Report

The **Financial Report** is another management report, this time giving information on fees, costs and profits on all courses within a specified time period. Once again, you will be asked to enter the earliest and latest dates to be included in the report.

Examples of both these reports are shown on the next page.

Example of Short Course Hours report

```
5-Sep-92                    Short Course Hours                    Page   1


Course Title              Code   Course Date Duration  Taught Hrs  No Students
----------------------    ------ ----------- --------  ----------  -----------


Intro to MSDOS            XED081 10-Oct-91      6.00      20.00        10
Intro to SuperCalc        XED202 31-Oct-91     12.00      12.00         6
Ventura                   XED231 19-Oct-91     12.00      14.00         4

                                              -------    -------      ----
      TOTAL                                     30.00      46.00        20
                                              -------    -------      ----

      TOTAL NUMBER OF COURSES         3

      End of Report
```

Example of Financial report

```
5-Sep-92                 Short Course Financial Report              Page   1


Course Title              Code   Date       Total Fees  Total Costs  Profit
----------------------    ------ --------   ----------  -----------  -----------


WordPerfect               XED251 19-Aug-91   1,188.00      800.00       388.00

Intro to MSDOS            XED081 10-Oct-91     990.00      600.00       390.00
Intro to SuperCalc        XED202 31-Oct-91     720.00      700.00        20.00
Ventura                   XED231 19-Oct-91     792.00      800.00        (8.00)

PageMaker                 XED101 16-Nov-91     990.00      700.00       290.00
Smart Database            XED171 24-Nov-91     495.00      550.00       (55.00)
Smart WP                  XED181 28-Nov-91     297.00      250.00        47.00

Paradox 4.0               XED776 29-Sep-92   1,600.00    1,212.50       387.50

                                            ----------  -----------  -----------
      TOTAL                                   7,072.00    5,612.50     1,459.50
```

HOURS menu (Add, edit, delete or report on staff hours)

Choosing this option will cause a submenu to appear:

```
Add   Edit/Delete   Report
Add new staff hours
```

Add

This option allows you to add records of the number of hours staff members have worked on different courses, using the data entry form shown below:

```
[F2] - Data entry completed. Esc - Cancel data entry, Ctrl-U - Undo last change

                          ┌─────────────────┐
                          │   STAFF HOURS   │
                          └─────────────────┘

        Course code: XED776        ┌──────────────────────────────┐
                                   │ Course title: Paradox 4.0    │
                                   │ Duration    :      12        │
                                   │ Taught hours:      30        │
                                   │ Start date  : 29.09.92       │
                                   └──────────────────────────────┘


        Staff ID: 2              Staff name: Biddle M

        Hours taught: 18

        ┌────────────────────────────────────────────────────────┐
        │ When cursor is in course code field, press F1 to view course codes. │
        │ When course codes are displayed, press F2 to select.    │
        │                                                         │
        │      Follow a similar procedure for staff IDs.          │
        └────────────────────────────────────────────────────────┘
```

Notes on data entry:

1. You will only be able to enter course codes which you have already added using the Course, Add option from the opening menu. To see a list of courses, press the function key F1. You may select from the list displayed on the screen by pressing F2.

2. The information in the box on the right of the screen (course title etc) will be automatically displayed when you enter the course code. You cannot change this information from this screen; if you need to, return to the Courses, Edit/Delete menu.

3. You will only be able to enter a staff ID previously added to the database using the Names, Add option from the opening menu. Use the F1 key to display a list of these names on screen, and F2 to select one.

Edit/delete

A similar screen will be displayed if you select the Edit/delete option. To delete a record, press the <Del> key. If you delete a record by mistake, you can undo the latest deletion by pressing Ctrl-U.

You can move backwards and forwards through the database by pressing PgUp and PgDn, or you can press F7 to 'toggle' between this view and Table view. In Table view you will see 20 or so records on the screen at the same time and you can use the arrow keys to move to a particular record before editing or pressing <Del> to delete.

Report

The report available here gives details of all the hours worked on each course by a named member of staff between two specified dates. Individual members of staff may access this report for information at any time.

You will be given the choice of either printing the report or displaying it on the screen. Once you have made your choice, you will see the following prompts:

```
Enter the staff name for this report:
```

Here, you may enter the staff name - it won't matter if it's slightly misspelt - or press <Enter> and at the next prompt enter the staff ID instead:

```
Optionally, enter the staff ID
Enter the earliest date to include in the report:
Enter the latest date to include in the report:
```

Once you have entered this information the report will start to print or be displayed on the screen, according to the option chosen. A sample report is shown below.

```
5-Sep-92                    HOURS WORKED ON SHORT COURSES                Page    1
                                         BY

                                      Turner J

Course Title            Course code  Course Date  Hours
----------------------  -----------  -----------  ------


Intro to MSDOS          XED081       10-Oct-91     8.00
Ventura                 XED231       19-Oct-91    11.75

Smart Database          XED171       24-Nov-91     2.00

TOTAL                                             21.75
```

HELP

If you choose this option a help screen will be displayed as shown below, explaining the menu options and giving brief advice on how to use the system.

```
Press any key to end the help


                             THE MAIN MENU


     STAFF   - Choose this option to add, change, delete or view staff details.
               Each staff member must be given a unique ID of up to 4 characters.
               You cannot enter staff hours taught on a course unless the
               staff member's details have first been entered using the Add option.

     COURSES - Choose this option to add, edit, delete or report courses.
               Add details of a new course directly from the costing sheet,
               edit or delete as necessary, and print either an 'Hours'
               report or a 'Financial' report whenever you like.

     HOURS   - Choose this option to record, edit, or delete the hours worked
               by individual members of staff on each course.
               Any authorised member of staff may print a report of the hours
               they have worked on all courses between specified dates.

     YOU CANNOT MAKE CHANGES TO THE DATABASE UNLESS YOU KNOW THE CORRECT PASSWORD!
```

LEAVE

Use this option to leave the application when you have finished work. You will see the main Paradox menu appear on the screen:

```
View Ask Report Create Modify Image Forms Tools Scripts Help Exit
View a table.
```

Choose Exit to return to the operating system prompt.

Error messages

1. When you initially start the program by typing

    paradox sh3

    if an error message 'bad command or file name' appears, it is because Paradox was not installed with the appropriate path command. In that case, type

    path c:\pdox35; \pdox35\pprog

    and then try again, by retyping **paradox sh3** .

2. If you attempt to add two records with the same key field, for example adding course number XED251 twice, the duplicate record will be put on a 'key violation' table named KV1, which will then be displayed on the screen. You are recommended to re-enter the offending record using a unique key field, and delete KV1 using the DOS command **del KV1.*** after exiting from Paradox, making sure that you are in the **SHORT** directory.

3. If you attempt to finish data entry of Staff or Courses with an empty form displayed on the screen (by pressing F2 or Esc), you will see an error message 'Entry required in this field'. Press Delete to delete the empty record and then press F2 or Esc.

4. Various self-explanatory error messages such as 'Value between 3 and 20 is expected' if you attempt to enter more than 20 hours for the duration of a course, for example, may appear during data entry. You are probably trying to enter an invalid value in the relevant field, and you should use the backspace key to delete it before re-entering it correctly.

5. If you enter the wrong password, or use a password which does not allow you to make changes to the database, you may see any of the following messages, depending on which action you are trying to perform.

    'Courses table is password protected'

    'Not currently in a display image'

    'Form toggle (F7) cannot be used here'

    'Not a possible menu choice'

    Choose Leave from the main menu and restart the application, typing in the correct password.

System support

In the event of any problems, please contact B.Student, 0978-57809.

Appendix G - Specimen annotated script generated by Paradox

```
; Sh31          ⟵  Script sh31.sc

AppLib = "Sh31"
if (not isfile(AppLib + ".lib")) then
   Createlib AppLib
endif


proc Sh31Menu()
private x, escape, zzzmexit, zzzzexit, pword

  zzzzexit = FALSE
  x = "Staff"
  while (TRUE)
    Clear                        ⟵  Main menu displayed

    ShowMenu  ⟵
      "Staff": "Add, edit, delete or view staff details",
      "Courses": "Add, edit, delete or report on courses",
      "Hours": "Add, change, delete or report on staff hours",
      "Help": "See a help screen explaining the menu choices",
      "Leave": "Leave the application"
    Default x
    To x        ⟵  First option on the menu is
                    highlighted by default.
    switch
      case x = "Staff":
        ReadLib "Sh31" Sh32Menu
        escape = Sh32Menu()
        escape = not escape
        Release Procs Sh32Menu  ⟵  Script for 'Staff'
                                    menu

      case x = "Courses":
        ReadLib "Sh31" Sh33Menu
        escape = Sh33Menu()
        escape = not escape
        Release Procs Sh33Menu  ⟵  Script for 'Courses'
                                    menu

      case x = "Hours":
        ReadLib "Sh32" Sh35Menu
        escape = Sh35Menu()
        escape = not escape
        Release Procs Sh35Menu  ⟵  Script for 'Hours'
                                    menu

      case x = "Help":
        ReadLib "Sh3utl" PlayHelp

PlayHelp("Sh3h1")      ⟵  Help screen is displayed
Release Procs PlayHelp
                           if 'Help' selected

        escape = FALSE

      case x = "Leave":
        ShowMenu
```

```
                        "No": "Do not leave the application.",
                        "Yes": "Leave the application."
                   To zzzmexit

              zzzzexit = (zzzmexit = "Yes")
              escape = (zzzmexit = "Esc")

          case x = "Esc":
             escape = FALSE
        endswitch

        Reset
        ; reset ErrorProc value
        ErrorProc = "ApplicErrorProc"
        ApplicErrorRetVal = FALSE

        if (zzzzexit) then
           return TRUE
        endif

        if (not escape) then
           x = "Staff"
        endif
     endwhile
endproc

Writelib AppLib Sh31Menu
Release Procs Sh31Menu
```

User is asked to confirm they wish to quit if 'Leave' is selected

(In your own project, include all the package-generated code, annotated by hand if possible)

Appendix H - Test runs

The full test output is not included here, for reasons of space. In your own project, you might reasonably have 20 or so pages of printouts and screen dumps for the 20 or so tests in the test plan.

Don't forget to use hand annotations wherever they are needed to cross reference results to the test plan, or highlight significant output.

Screen dump for TEST 1 (Add staff)

```
[F2] - Data entry completed, Esc - Cancel data entry, Ctrl-U - Undo last change
```

```
┌─────────────────────────┐
│ ADD NEW STAFF DETAILS   │
└─────────────────────────┘
```

```
        Staff ID: 1            Staff name: Turner J

        Work Tel: 424          Home Tel:   487772

        School/Unit: Comp
```

```
[F2] - Data entry completed, Esc - Cancel data entry, Ctrl-U - Undo last change
```

```
┌─────────────────────────┐
│ ADD NEW STAFF DETAILS   │          TEST 1.
└─────────────────────────┘
```

```
        Staff ID: ___          Staff name:

        Work Tel:              Home Tel:

        School/Unit:
```

If user attempts to skip this field, an error menage is displayed

```
( A value must be provided in this field; press [F1] for help )
```

Test 4 (Display all staff)

```
Press [F2] when finished viewing the table
Total records: 5
STAFF──Staff ID────Staff name────Work Tel───Home Tel───School─
  1    1      Turner J        424      487772     Comp
  2    2      Biddle M        424      481244     Comp
  3    3      Yonge E         424      481244     Comp
  4    4      Horsfall A      424      Needham 651 Comp
  5    5      Lawson B        279      Eldoret 698  Art
```

Test 6 — Attempt to change course code

```
[F2] - Complete edit, [Esc] - Cancel edit, Ctrl-U - Undo last change


                          ┌─────────────────┐
                          │ COURSE RECORDS  │
                          └─────────────────┘


   Course Code: XED081       Course title: Intro to MSDOS

      Duration:       6       No. of students:      10

   Start date: 10/10/91

   -----------------------------------------------------------

   Taught hours:    20      Fees received   :          990.00
                            Lecturing costs :
                            Overheads       :
                            Advertising     :
                            Non-standard costs:
                            Total course costs:         600.00
                                                     -----------
                            Contribution to Capital Funds:  390.00
                                                     -----------
   Fee per student:   99.00
                                         ┌─────────────────────────┐
                                         │ Field cannot be modified │
                                         └─────────────────────────┘
```

Error message is displayed.

Test 7. (Test range check on duration)

```
[F2] - Complete edit, [Esc] - Cancel edit, Ctrl-U - Undo last change
```

```
┌─────────────────┐
│ COURSE RECORDS  │
└─────────────────┘
```

Course Code: XED171   Course title: Smart Database

Duration: 32   No. of students: 5

Start date: 11/24/91

Taught hours: 14   Fees received   :   495.00
                             Lecturing costs :
                             Overheads   :
                             Advertising   :
                             Non-standard costs:
                             Total course costs: 550.00

                             Contribution to Capital Funds: (55.00)

Fee per student: 99.00

Value between 3 and 20 is expected

Error message is displayed.

Test 17 - Try to enter a staff hours
record for a non-existent course

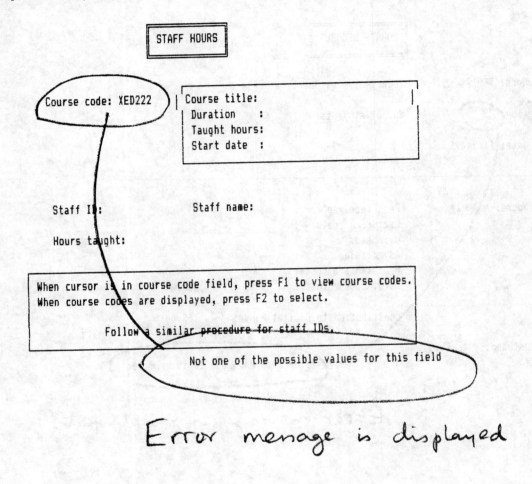

[F2] - Data entry completed, Esc - Cancel data entry, Ctrl-U - Undo last change

```
                    ┌─────────────────┐
                    │  STAFF HOURS    │
                    └─────────────────┘


      Course code: XED222    │ Course title:
                             │ Duration    :
                             │ Taught hours:
                             │ Start date  :



      Staff ID:                Staff name:

      Hours taught:


   ┌──────────────────────────────────────────────────────┐
   │ When cursor is in course code field, press F1 to view course codes. │
   │ When course codes are displayed, press F2 to select.  │
   │                                                        │
   │        Follow a similar procedure for staff IDs.       │
   └──────────────────────────────────────────────────────┘
              Not one of the possible values for this field
```

Error message is displayed

Test 18 - Try to add a staff hours record for a non-existent staff member

[F2] - Data entry completed, Esc - Cancel data entry, Ctrl-U - Undo last change

```
                    ┌─────────────────┐
                    │   STAFF HOURS   │
                    └─────────────────┘


    Course code: XED251      ┌──────────────────────────────┐
                             │ Course title: WordPerfect     │
                             │ Duration    :    12           │
                             │ Taught hours:    20           │
                             │ Start date  :  8/19/91        │
                             └──────────────────────────────┘


    Staff ID: 99            Staff name:

    Hours taught:

    ┌──────────────────────────────────────────────────────┐
    │ When cursor is in course code field, press F1 to view course codes. │
    │ When course codes are displayed, press F2 to select.   │
    │                                                        │
    │      Follow a similar procedure for staff IDs.         │
    │                                                        │
    │        Not one of the possible values for this field   │
    └──────────────────────────────────────────────────────┘
```

Error message is displayed

Test 23.   Enter TRNER J instead of TURNER J

Enter the staff name for the report, or press Enter <u>Trner J</u>

Paradox finds correct record

3 records printed, correct total of 21.75 hours

```
5-Sep-92              HOURS WORKED ON SHORT COURSES              Page  1

                                   BY

                               Turner J


Course Title          Course code Course Date Hours
----------------------  ----------  -----------  ------



Intro to MSDOS          XED081      10-Oct-91    8.00
Ventura                 XED231      19-Oct-91   11.75

Smart Database          XED171      24-Nov-91    2.00


TOTAL                                           21.75
```

Appendix I

Turbo Pascal Editing keys

and

Blank forms

Appendix I

Turbo Pascal 6.0 hot keys

The 'hot keys' shown below are shortcuts to various menu selections.

Hot key	Menu equivalent	Function
F1	Help	Displays a Help screen
F2	File/Save	Saves active editor file
F3	File/Open	Opens file
F4	Run/Go to cursor	Executes to cursor location
F5	Window/Zoom	Zooms the active window
F6	Window/Next	Cycles through open windows
F7	Run/Trace into	Traces into subroutines
F8	Run/Step over	Steps over subroutine calls
F10		Activates main menu bar
Alt-F1	Help/Previous topic	Displays previous Help screen
Alt-F3	Window/Close	Closes active window
Alt-F5	Window/User screen	Displays User screen
Alt-F9	Compile/Compile	Compiles active program
Alt-Space		Goes to system menu
Alt-C	Compile menu	Goes to **Compile** menu
Alt-D	Debug menu	Goes to **Debug** menu
Alt-E	Edit menu	Goes to **Edit** menu
Alt-F	File menu	Goes to **File** menu
Alt-H	Help menu	Goes to **Help** menu
Alt-O	Options menu	Goes to **Options** menu
Alt-R	Run menu	Goes to **Run** menu
Alt-S	Search menu	Goes to **Search** menu
Alt-W	Window menu	Goes to **Window** menu
Alt-X	File/Exit	Exits Turbo Pascal
Ctrl-F1	Help/Topic search	Gives language-specific help while in editor
Ctrl-F2	Run/Program reset	Resets running program
Ctrl-F7	Debug/Add watch	Adds a watch expression
Ctrl-F8	Debug/Toggle breakpoint	Clears or sets conditional breakpoint
Ctrl-F9	Run/Run	Executes active program

Turbo Pascal 6.0 Editor commands

This is a summary of the most useful editor commands. Notation such as Ctrl-KB means 'hold down the Ctrl key and press K. Then release both keys and press B'.

Function	Keystroke
(Movement commands)	
Page up	PgUp
Page down	PgDn
Beginning of line	Home
End of line	End
Top of window	Ctrl-Home
Bottom of window	Ctrl-End
Beginning of program	Ctrl-PgUp
End of program	Ctrl-PgDn
(Insert and delete commands)	
Delete line	Ctrl-Y
Delete block	Ctrl-KY
Delete to end of line	Ctrl-QY
(Block commands)	
Copy block to edit file	Ctrl-KC
Copy block to clipboard	Edit/Copy or Ctrl-Ins
Delete block (not saving to clipboard)	Edit/Clear or Ctrl-Del
Delete block (saving to clipboard)	Edit/Cut or Shift-Del
Hide/Display block	Ctrl-KH
Mark block begin	Ctrl-KB
Mark block end	Ctrl-KK
Move block from clipboard	Edit/Paste or Shift-Ins
Move block to edit file	Ctrl-KV

File Structure

File name		External file ID	
File Organisation		Key fields	
Record length			

Used by:

Program name	Description	Program name	Description

General file description

Record name	General record description

Field description	Field name	Format	Dec pl.	Validation check

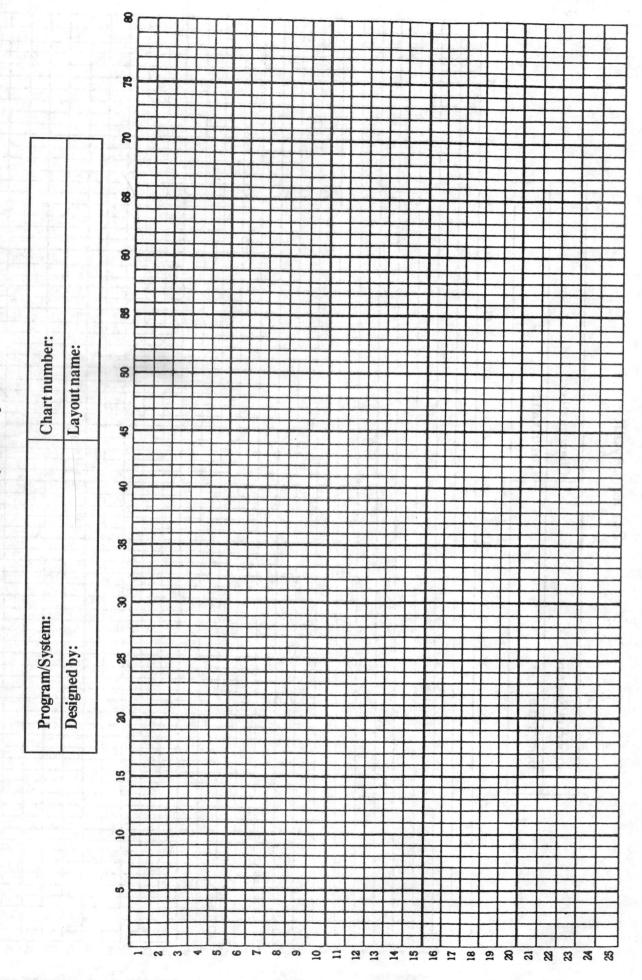

Report Layout

Program/System:

Designed by:

Chart number:

Layout name:

Screen Layout

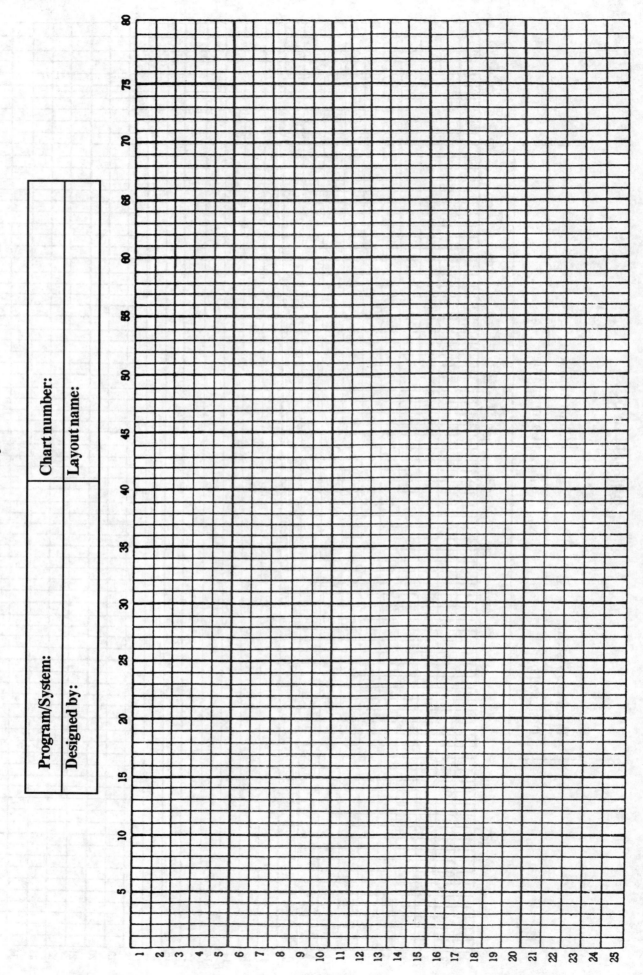

"The Complete Course Text"

Computer Science

CS French

ISBN: **1 873981 19 8** • Date: **June 1992** • Edition: **4th**
Extent: **656** • Size: **275 x 215 mm**
Lecturers' Supplement ISBN: 1 873981 41 4

Courses on which this book is known to be used
A Level Computing; BTEC National and HNC/D Computer Studies; City & Guilds; BCS; AS Level Computer Science; BSc Applied Science.

On reading lists of ICM, IDPM, BCS and ACP

This book provides a simplified approach to the understanding of Computer Science.

Notes on the Fourth Edition

This edition contains changes in content and layout which are aimed not just at covering the material on the latest syllabuses but at assisting the reader's study **for the latest examinations**. Parts targeted at contemporary computer applications and applications packages have been introduced. This reflects a significant shift in emphasis in examinations over recent years. Graphical User Interfaces (GUIs), development methodologies, desktop computers, applications packages and databases have been given more emphasis to reflect the examination requirements of developing and using computer systems. Obsolete material has been removed.

Contents:

Foundation Topics • Applications I: Document Processing • Storage • Input and Output • Applications II: GUIs and Multimedia • Computer Systems Organisation I • Programming I • File and File Processing • Applications III: Spreadsheets • Logic and Formal Notations • Computer Arithmetic • Computer Systems Organisation II • Software • Applications IV: Applications Areas • Programming II • Databases and 4GLs • Applications V: Information Storage and Retrieval • Systems Development • Applications VI: Business Industrial Computing • Computers in Contexts • Revision Test Questions.

Review Comments:

'I think the presentation is superb and content perfect for my course work.' 'Good basic book – recommended by all academic staff in the department.' – Lecturers

Free Lecturers' Supplement

Computing
An Active-Learning Approach

PM Heathcote

ISBN: **1 870941 86 1** • Date: **1991** • Edition: **1st**
Extent: **352 pp** • Size: **275 x 215 mm**
Lecturers' Supplement ISBN: **1 873981 37 6**

Courses on which this book is known to be used
A Level Computing; BTEC Nat and Higher; ACCA Info Systems; BSc Software Eng; C & G 419 (DP);
BTEC Cont Ed; BTEC First; Access to Computing; BTEC Nat Eng; AS;
C & G 726; BA Business Studies.

The aim of this book is to provide the classroom support material needed on Advanced Level Computing and BTEC courses.

There are many excellent textbooks on computing at this level (including *Computer Science* by CS French) which give valuable support and wider reading/reference for the student outside classroom time.

This book, however, has been designed as an interactive teaching and learning aid, eliminating the need for hand outs or copious note taking. It incorporates the following features:

- concise explanation of principles

- questions at appropriate points within the text (with space allowed for student to fill in answers) to enable the student to test and broaden knowledge and understanding, develop ideas, supply discussion points and test application of principles.

Teachers can explain each part of a topic in whatever way they like and use the concise explanations as the 'skeleton' of the classroom work. Students take an active part in the learning process via the questions interspersed throughout the text.

Apart from its value during the course, this is also an ideal book around which each student can build his/her revision programme.

The lecturers' supplement is in the form of a PC-compatible disk. It provides tips on implementation of the course and outline answers to all in-text questions and chapter-end exercises and examination questions.

Contents:
Introduction to Computers and Business Data Processing • Programming in Pascal • Data Structures • Databases • Systems Development • Programming Languages, Compilers and Interpreters • Internal Organisation of Computers • Operating Systems and Networks • Peripherals • Computer Applications and Social Implications.

Review Comments:
'Excellent for encouraging student participation.' 'Can be used as a course companion for all Computing modules (BTEC).' 'Excellent presentation – in line with both our syllabus and teaching methods.' 'Brilliant! A very comprehensive text – really welcome [BTEC HNC Computer Studies].' 'Excellent for open learning students.' 'Brilliant book – excellent learning approach.' 'Clear, explicit, novel approach.' – **Lecturers**

Free
Lecturers' Supplement

dBase for Business Students
Incorporating III and IV
An Active-Learning Approach

J Muir

ISBN: **1 873981 16 3** • Date: **June 1992** • Edition: **1st**
Extent: **192 pp** • Size: **245 x 190 mm**
Lecturers' Supplement ISBN: 1 873981 76 7

This book is aimed at students on computing and business courses of all types, who need to learn how to use dBASE III and dBASE IV and have access to an IBM personal computer or compatible. dBASE is the industry-standard database management system for the IBM personal computers and compatibles and this book includes references to the latest 1.5 version of dBASE IV.

The learning material in this book requires minimal (or no) input from a lecturer and can be used as a self-instructional guide.

Note: A copyright free $3\frac{1}{2}$" (750K) disk is provided free of charge to lecturers adopting the book as a course text. It includes all the programs, databases, etc used in the book.

Contents:

Preface: Who should use this book • Developments in dBASE • The scope of the book • The structure of the book • The active-learning approach • Hints on active learning • **Introduction:** Databases in Business • Database concepts and terminology • The need for computerised databases • The Quality Wines case study • **Section 1 – dBASE III – Using the assist:** Creating and searching a database • Producing reports, screens and views • **Section 2 – dBASE IV – Using the control center:** Creating and searching a database • Modifying and reorganising the database • Printed reports, screens and applications • **Section 3 – Commands and programming – dBASE III and dBASE IV:** Entering commands at the dot prompt • An introduction to dBASE programming • More advanced programming in dBASE.

MS Works
An Active-Learning Approach

D Weale

ISBN: **1 873981 30 9** • Date: **June 1992** • Edition: **1st**
Extent: **144 pp** • Size: **245 x 190 mm**

> *Courses on which this book is expected to be used*
> The many business courses requiring a basic knowledge of spreadsheets, databases and word processing via MS Works.

The aim of the book is to provide a 'user friendly' guide for students being introduced to spreadsheets, databases and word processing via MS Works.

It is very much a 'learning by doing' guide – requiring very little (if any) input from the lecturer, enabling students to learn and practice the commands and techniques using examples to which they can relate, ie business ones. A series of sessions, each self-contained, takes students step by step to a level at which they can happily use the program manual to master finer details.

Contents:

Preface • How to Use the Mouse with Works • The Works Tutorial • On-line Help • Word Processing • Revision • Spreadsheets • Graphs and Charts • Revision • Databases • Database Reports • Integrating Works Files • Mailmerging • Final Exercise • Suggestions on Layout • Summary of Commands • File Management • Configuring the System.

Spreadsheets for Business Students

An Active-Learning Approach

C West

ISBN: **1 870941 83 7** • Date: **1991** • Edition: **1st**
Extent: **176 pp** • Size: **245 x 190 mm**
Lecturers' Supplement ISBN: 1 873981 66 X

Courses on which this book is known to be used
CBA; CMS; BA (Hons) Acc. & Fin.; BEd Bus. Studies; CLAIT II; Dip. Voc. Ed. Bus. & Fin.; HNC/D; ACCA Level 1; BA Business Studies; BTEC Nat.; HNC Bus. & Fin.; BEng; HND Computing; HND Manufacturing Management; IPM; DMS.

The aim of this book is to provide a 'user friendly' guide for students on the innumerable courses where acquaintance with the basics of spreadsheets is required.

It is very much a 'learning by doing' guide – requiring very little (if any) input by the lecturer and can be used on any machine/system with Lotus 1-2-3 version 2.0 (or above) or compatible spreadsheets such as VP-Planner and As-Easy-As.

All examples have a business emphasis and students progressively gain confidence in the basics of:

- constructing spreadsheet models
- saving and retrieving files
- graphics
- printing spreadsheets and graphs
- using a spreadsheet as a data base
- creating and using simple macros.

The lecturers' supplement is a copyright-free $5\frac{1}{4}$" (360K)
PC-compatible disk, incorporating files in .WKS format for the models in the book, for checking students' activities.

Contents:

Models include:
VAT Calculations • Cash Flow Forecast • Integrated Cash Flow Forecast/ Profit & Loss Account/Balance Sheet • Accounting Ratios • Cost Behaviour • Cost Allocation and Apportionment • Cost-Volume-Profit Analysis.

Each session contains:
Objectives • Active Learning • Summary • Activities • Objective (Multi-choice) Test.

Review Comments:

'I like the worksheet approach enabling students to work at their own pace.' 'A wonderful time saver – congratulations.' 'Ideal for new modularised units – all activity based.' 'Tried it on 2 lecturers first – they found it easy, so able now to recommend it to students!' 'Good to use in open learning workshop.' 'Excellent in every way – a book like this, at its current price, has been wanted for years!' 'A very useful text – practical and easy to understand.' – Lecturers

Free
Lecturers' Supplement

Pascal Programming

BJ Holmes

ISBN: **1 870941 65 9** • Date: **June 1990** • Edition: **2nd**
Extent: **464 pp** • Size: **245 x 190 mm**
Lecturers' Supplement ISBN: 1 873981 62 7

Courses on which this book is known to be used
BTEC National and HNC/D Computer Studies; BCS Part 1; A Level Computing; BSc (Hons) Computer Studies; HNC Software Design; NDI; HEFC Info Tech; C & G 726/223.

On reading list of ICM

Pascal Programming can be regarded as a complete text on programming and the use of data structures. The aim of this book is to help the reader acquire and develop the skill of computer programming in a block-structured language and foster an understanding of the related topics of data structures and data processing.

Notes on the Second Edition

There are new chapters on recursion, sorting and searching, dynamic data structures, object-oriented programming and case studies. Chapters contain computer-generated illustrations to help explain the topics found in the text.

Greater emphasis has been placed on the use of Turbo Pascal. To demonstrate the use of the Pascal language statements, the text contains 75 documented programs. There are 120 questions, to which answers are supplied.

Note: With the lecturers' supplement is a free (and copyright free) PC-compatible disk incorporating all the programs in the text – saves keying in! Immediate use for illustrative and development purposes for lecturers and students.

(The programs on the disk need to be compiled using Borland Turbo Pascal compiler version 5.5 or later.)

Contents:

Computer Environment • Data • Instruction Sequence • Data Types • Selection • Repetition • Procedures • Program Development • Mathematics • Arrays • Sorting and Searching • Recursion • Text Files • Pointers • Dynamic Structures • Record Files • Common Extensions • Turbo Units • Object-oriented Programming (OOP) • Case Studies in OOP.

Review Comments:

'Excellent – no competition [BTEC ND Computing].' 'Affordable and Turbo Pascal and Syntax diagrams – great!' 'Far better than most books that are twice the price.' 'Good section on OOP. Good overall text for programming in Pascal.' 'Excellent value.' 'Good course text [HNC/D Computer Studies] at affordable price.' 'Excellent coverage of OOPs.' 'Comprehensive coverage of the topic and excellent value.' 'Ideally suited to our BTEC National course.' – Lecturers

Free
Lecturers' Supplement